MW01069533

# Cavalry of the
# American Revolution

The Battle of Hobkirk's Hill, April 25, 1781. The painting depicts the charge of the Continental dragoons. (*South Caroliniana Library of the University of South Carolina, Columbia*)

# Cavalry

*of the*

## American Revolution

*Edited by*

## Jim Piecuch

WESTHOLME
Yardley

© 2012 Westholme Publishing

All rights reserved under International and Pan-American Copyright Conventions. No part of this book may be reproduced in any form or by any electronic or mechanical means, including information storage and retrieval systems, without permission in writing from the publisher, except by a reviewer who may quote brief passages in a review.

Westholme Publishing, LLC
904 Edgewood Road
Yardley, Pennsylvania 19067
Visit our Web site at www.westholmepublishing.com

First Printing May 2012
10 9 8 7 6 5 4 3 2 1

ISBN: 978-1-59416-154-4

Also available as an eBook.

Printed in the United States of America.

# Contents

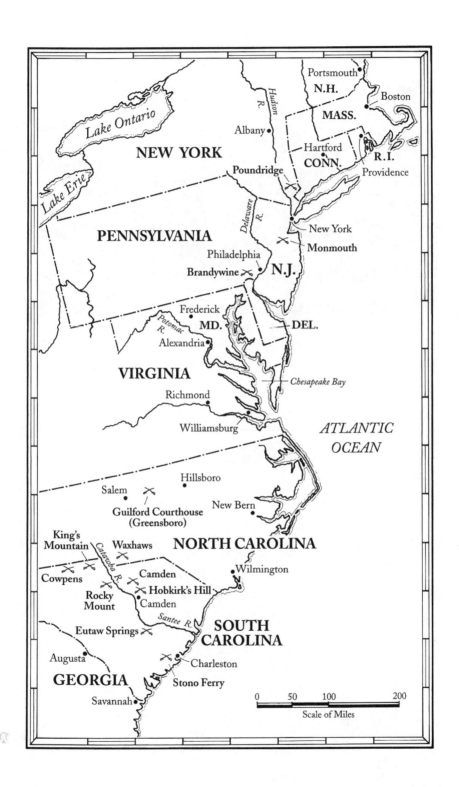

"The Assault," by Werner Willis, depicting Col. Banastre Tarleton leading a charge at Mecklenburg County Court House, North Carolina in 1780. (© *Werner Willis*)

# Foreword

*Jim Piecuch*

The role of cavalry in the American Revolution has received relatively little attention in histories of that conflict. A few cavalry commanders, most notably Henry "Light-Horse Harry" Lee and William Washington on the American side, and Banastre Tarleton of the British Army, have gained considerable renown, but other officers and cavalry actions have often been ignored or given only brief notice. The lack of attention accorded to cavalry operations is unfortunate, because the cavalry of both armies played an important part in the War for Independence.

This volume is an effort to fill some of the gaps in the story. It is not meant to be a comprehensive study of cavalry operations and commanders but rather is intended to highlight various aspects of cavalry's role in the struggle, with a focus on individuals, units, battles, and aspects of cavalry doctrine that have heretofore been overlooked. The essays cover the American and British perspectives as well as the broad geographic area in which the cavalry fought. Readers with an interest in military history in general, the cavalry arm in particular, or with a more specific interest in the American Revolution, along with researchers and academic historians, will find the essays useful as both a source of information and a starting point for further exploration of the topic.

When the American Revolution began in Massachusetts in 1775, neither the American commander-in-
chief, Gen. George Washington, nor his British counterparts expected cavalry to be of much use. Under the circumstances prevailing during the siege of Boston, the first
campaign of the war, neither side could employ cavalry
effectively. Washington believed that mounted troops
would be of little value in the hilly New England terrain,
pocked with woodlots and crisscrossed by seemingly endless stone walls and fences. Such features were hardly
conducive to the use of mounted troops. The British did
dispatch two cavalry regiments to America in 1776, the
16th and 17th Regiments of Light Dragoons, and these
troops proved useful in the New York campaign. As a
result, Washington and the Continental Congress decided
in late 1776 that the Continental Army needed its own
mounted arm, and eventually four regiments of
Continental Light Dragoons were formed, along with
additional units of Continental mounted troops assigned
to legions, a term designating a combined force of light
infantry and cavalry. The most famous Continental legion
was that of Virginian Henry Lee, and was commonly
known as "Lee's Legion." Two other legions, those of
Count Casimir Pulaski and Charles Armand Tuffin,
Marquis de la Rouerie, were also created; the remnants of
Pulaski's Legion, decimated at Savannah, Georgia, in
October 1779, were subsequently incorporated into
Armand's Legion.

The British created two legions of their own from
American loyalists recruited in the northern states. One,
the Queen's Rangers, was led by Lt. Col. John Graves
Simcoe, and the other, the British Legion, was commanded by Lt. Col. Banastre Tarleton. During the campaign in
the South later in the war, the British made efforts to
increase the strength of their cavalry by partially mount-
ing two other loyalist regiments, the New York Volunteers
and South Carolina Royalists, and creating a cavalry unit
of former slaves. Both sides augmented their regular cav-

alry forces with mounted militia, while several states organized their own cavalry units.

In the northern theater, cavalry's role consisted primarily of scouting, skirmishing, and raiding. These operations frequently resulted in fairly large clashes between the cavalry of the rival armies, and regular troops as well as militia often took part in such actions. In the southern theater, the open terrain and scattered nature of settlement increased the value of cavalry. Besides carrying out the same duties that mounted troops performed in the North, the cavalry in the South played a large and sometimes decisive part in major infantry battles. On August 16, 1780, at the Battle of Camden in South Carolina, American infantry forces under Maj. Gen. Horatio Gates and Lt. Gen. Charles, Earl Cornwallis's British foot soldiers were locked in combat, with neither side able to gain a decisive edge. Cornwallis broke the stalemate by ordering Tarleton's cavalry to charge through a gap in the American line, a deadly blow that routed the Continental troops. Five months later at the Battle of Cowpens, Lt. Col. William Washington's Continental Light Dragoons prevented Tarleton's cavalry from outflanking the American infantry, leading to an overwhelming Patriot victory. At Guilford Courthouse, North Carolina, on March 15, 1781, William Washington and Tarleton were again in action, engaged not against each other but against enemy infantry, and both performed successfully on different parts of the battlefield. Afterward, Washington marched south and participated in the American campaign in South Carolina, as did Henry Lee and his legion, while Tarleton headed northward with Cornwallis to Virginia. In early June 1781 Tarleton nearly captured Thomas Jefferson in a raid on Charlottesville, but in the end it was Tarleton who was captured, along with Cornwallis, at Yorktown when the British Army surrendered to George Washington's combined French and American force on October 19, 1781.

From reconnaissance to raids to charges on the field of battle, cavalry proved its worth throughout the Revolutionary War. Its value was emphasized by the American and British officers who regularly complained that they did not have enough mounted troops at their disposal.

The importance of cavalry is clear in the quotation from George Washington that provides the subtitle of the first essay, "The Continental Light Dragoons, 1776–1783: 'There Is No Carrying on the War Without Them'," by Gregory J. W. Urwin. The essay discusses the creation of the Continental Army's cavalry arm, and the steps that were taken to organize and provide officers for the mounted units. Urwin also provides an overview of the Continental cavalry's service during the war, from its first engagements in Pennsylvania during the 1777 Philadelphia campaign to the last battles in the South.

Lee F. McGee's "European Influences on Continental Cavalry," the second essay, examines how American cavalry operations were shaped by European military doctrine. McGee assesses the various contributions of British, French, Prussian, and other European officers to the development of cavalry tactics in the second half of the eighteenth century. By looking at the specific ideas of European cavalry officers who fought for the United States, he finds a strong Prussian influence evident in the practices employed by Lt. Col. William Washington.

Next, John M. Hutchins conducts a detailed examination of the "Cavalry Action at Poundridge, New York: Bloody Ban's Early Education." This battle, fought in Westchester County, New York, on July 2, 1779, was sparked when British Lt. Col. Banastre Tarleton led a British foray from the lines around New York City to strike the camp of the 2nd Continental Light Dragoons. Hutchins provides background on the military situation in the area at the time of the raid, as well as a thorough study of the battle and its ramifications.

Three other cavalry actions in the contested area between the British and American armies are described by Donald J. Gara in the fourth essay, "Cavalry Battles in New York and New Jersey." Gara tells the story of three cavalry operations: the British raid into Westchester County, New York, in August 1779; another British foray into Middlesex and Somerset Counties in New Jersey in October of that year; and a third British strike at Hoppertown in Bergen County, New Jersey, in April 1780. These raids demonstrate that, contrary to popular belief, the American and British forces in the northern theater were hardly idle during this time.

The fifth essay is entitled "Anthony Walton White: A Revolutionary Dragoon," by Scott A. Miskimon. White took an unusual path to cavalry command. He began his military service as an aide to George Washington, then became an infantry officer in a New Jersey regiment before being assigned to the 4th Continental Light Dragoons in 1777 as the unit's lieutenant colonel. White was later promoted to colonel commanding the 1st Continental Light Dragoons, and in May 1780 was defeated at Lenud's Ferry, South Carolina, by Banastre Tarleton. Miskimon traces White's career through all of its twists, including court martial trials and a post-Revolutionary return to the field during the 1794 Whiskey Rebellion.

Michael C. Scoggins is the author of the sixth essay, "South Carolina's Backcountry Rangers in the American Revolution." Scoggins reviews the history of the various backcountry mounted units in South Carolina, beginning with the formation of Col. William Thomson's Rangers in 1775. He goes on to discuss the organization of the backcountry militia and how the Patriots built on this system when Thomas Sumter, Francis Marion, and other leaders began forming bands of mounted partisans in 1780 to challenge the British forces occupying the state.

The next essay deals with an unusual aspect of the Revolution: American prisoners of war who enlisted in the

British Army after being captured. "Continentals in Tarleton's British Legion" by Lawrence E. Babits and Joshua B. Howard traces the history of the approximately one hundred Continental soldiers (out of several hundred Americans captured at the Battle of Camden in August 1780) who chose to volunteer for service in Tarleton's British Legion. Babits and Howard follow these men's careers as British soldiers, including the various troops and companies to which they were assigned, and how their presence may have affected the British Legion's performance at the Battle of Cowpens on January 17, 1781.

In "Cavalry Operations at Eutaw Springs: A Novelist's View," historical novelist Charles F. Price brings his own unique perspective to the Continental cavalry of the Revolution. Price sought to describe the events leading up the September 1781 Battle of Eutaw Springs, South Carolina, and the battle itself, with as much accuracy as possible in a novel. He therefore began researching the training, tactics, and details of day-to-day life for a Continental dragoon. In the process, he discovered much of historical relevance, including the influence of the Continental Army's inspector general, Baron Friedrich von Steuben. Price used this information to fill gaps in the historical record with plausible surmise, allowing him to present an account of the cavalry fighting at Eutaw Springs in his novel that is simultaneously fictionalized and authentic.

The final essay, by Jim Piecuch, focuses on "The 'Black Dragoons': Former Slaves as British Cavalry in Revolutionary South Carolina." The Black Dragoons were one of the most unusual units that fought in the War for Independence. Recruited from among the thousands of slaves who had fled to the British in hopes of obtaining freedom, the Black Dragoons were unique in that they had no white officers; every soldier, from commanding officer to private, was a former slave. Piecing together material from widely scattered sources, Piecuch presents the history of one of the most active units in the British Army in 1782, and the one most despised by its opponents.

A final word must be said about the various types of cavalry described in these essays and the terms used to designate them. Cavalry doctrine at the time of the American Revolution prescribed two roles for mounted troops: heavy and light. The former generally referred to the employment of cavalry alongside infantry and artillery on the battlefield, including the tactic of mounted charges against opposing infantry. In contrast, the light role comprised scouting, raiding, and pursuing disorganized, retreating enemy forces after a battle. Regardless of the type of cavalry unit, it could be employed in either the heavy or light role depending upon circumstances and the decisions of commanding officers.

European cavalry units bore a number of different designations according to their particular function, and not all of these varieties were present in North America. Dragoons were soldiers who, although mounted, were trained to fight as infantry as well as cavalry. They therefore carried carbines as well as sabers and pistols. The British and American dragoon units in the Revolution were designated light dragoons, as they were expected to fulfill the role of light rather than heavy cavalry. However, on some occasions both sides utilized light dragoons as heavy cavalry on the battlefield. Only rarely did dragoons act in their infantry role during the War for Independence. Hussars, a type of cavalry that originated in Serbia and was made famous by the Hungarians, were intended specifically for use as light cavalry, and unlike dragoons were not trained for service as infantry. Lancers could function as both heavy and light cavalry. They were distinguished by their primary weapon—a long lance that required great skill to use effectively. One troop of cavalry in Casimir Pulaski's legion consisted of lancers, but their service was brief and undistinguished. Other types of

European cavalry, such as cuirassiers, did not appear on American battlefields. It should also be noted that the term "troop" in a cavalry unit of the Revolutionary era was the equivalent of a "company" in the infantry.

## EDITOR'S NOTE

A brief explanation of some of the terms that appear in this book, and the way in which quotations are used, may be of help to readers. The terms "loyalist," "Tory," and "royalist," and their plural forms, are used interchangeably to refer to those Americans who supported the British during the American Revolution. Similarly, the terms "American," "Whig," "rebel," and "revolutionary" and their plurals are applied to Americans who supported independence from Great Britain. "Provincials" describes American loyalists who served in military units organized by the British to fight the revolutionaries. "Continental" or "Continentals" refers to the regular American Army, and were units and troops who enlisted for long-term service, received some degree of military training, wore uniforms (at least when they were available), and were the professional soldiers of the United States. Both the British and Americans also employed militia forces; "militia" and "militiamen" refer to citizen-soldiers who served for short terms, usually in times of emergency and close to their homes. Occasionally, however, militia could be dispatched to another state when a crisis loomed. Militiamen wore no uniforms, often provided their own arms and ammunition, and they might have little or no formal military training. "State troops" were, as their name indicates, recruited by state governments. They enlisted for longer terms of service and were generally better trained and more professional than the militia.

With regard to quotations, the spelling has not been changed, in order to retain as much as possible of their original sense and authenticity. Because spelling in the English language had not been standardized at the time of the American Revolution, different writers employed a variety of spellings for the same word or for the name of an individual. In some cases, the same writer may even have spelled the same word in different ways in the same sentence or paragraph. Readers should be aware that misspellings in quotations are not the result of editing or typographical errors, but instead originated with the eighteenth-century writer being quoted.

A Continental Light Dragoon. (*Barry Grant*)

# ONE

# The Continental Light Dragoons, 1776–83

## "There Is No Carrying on the War Without Them"

*Gregory J. W. Urwin*

WHEN THE THIRTEEN COLONIES STUMBLED INTO WAR with Great Britain in April 1775 and made the unprecedented decision to raise a regular army to fight it, they did not envision a place for cavalry in their new military establishment. The "New England Army" that Massachusetts, New Hampshire, Connecticut, and Rhode Island authorized to keep the British penned in Boston officially consisted of forty-one infantry battalions, plus one regiment and an independent company of artillery. When the Second Continental Congress subsequently adopted this force as "the American continental army" on June 14, 1775, it also voted to reinforce the New Englanders with a regiment of "expert riflemen" from Virginia and Maryland to act as light infantry—but Congress gave no thought to providing their army with a mounted component.

Europeans versed in military affairs may have found such a force structure curious. In the early 1700s, cavalry reigned as the decisive arm in the armies that shaped the destiny of the world's most powerful continent. John Churchill, the First Duke of Marlborough—Britain's greatest land commander of the eighteenth century, excelled in using the shock of massive mounted charges as a battle-winning tactic during the War of the Spanish Succession. Although the British generals who followed Marlborough in the century's subsequent conflicts never matched the brilliance of the duke's triumph at Blenheim, John Manners, Marquis of Granby, became a national hero for the series of cavalry victories that he won in the Seven Years' War. At the start of the War of Independence, the British Army, which most Americans today view mainly as an infantry organization, contained seventy line regiments of foot, but also twenty-five regiments of horse (and these figures exclude both the Foot and Horse Guards).

On June 15, 1775, Congress appointed George Washington, a Virginia planter renowned for his horsemanship, as commander-in-chief of "all the Continental forces." Despite Washington's equestrian background, he did not carp about his force's lack of cavalry. More than a year into the struggle, Washington disparaged the need for mounted troops in a general order to his army on October 27, 1776. He claimed that the woods and stone walls that broke up the country north of New York City made it impossible for cavalry to operate effectively. In a pointed reference to the two regiments of British light horse attached to Gen. William Howe's threatening host, Washington declared: "There is no Enemy more to be despised." He offered a reward of $100 to "any brave parties" of Continentals "for every Trooper, with his Horse and Accoutrements" that they captured.

Washington also regarded cavalry as a luxury that the Continental Army could not afford. A dry summer on Manhattan had left him with barely enough forage for the draft animals essential to hauling his supplies and artillery. He did not need to take on the burden of feeding hundreds of additional beasts by fielding a sizable mounted force. In fact, he had dismissed a regiment of militia light horse from Connecticut on July 16 because its four hundred to five hundred troopers represented a major drain on his resources—and because they refused to perform some of the more menial tasks associated with soldiering.

The nearly disastrous New York/New Jersey Campaign of 1776 eventually caused Washington to reverse his opinion on the place of cavalry in the Continental Army. The British 16th and 17th Regiments of Light Dragoons that rode for General Howe hardly compared to the mounted hordes that followed the Duke of Marlborough, but they had a daunting effect on Washington's Continentals and militia. In the Battle of White Plains on October 28, the 17th Light Dragoons turned a stubborn American defense into a hasty retreat by causing a panic among the militia stationed on Chatterton's Hill, the anchor for Washington's right flank. British troopers pulled off an even more sensational coup during Washington's humiliating retreat across New Jersey. On December 13, a patrol from the 16th Light Dragoons led by Lt. Col. William Harcourt and a young volunteer named Banastre Tarleton succeeded in capturing Washington's second-in-command, Maj. Gen. Charles Lee, at Basking Ridge, New Jersey. The loss of Lee, a former British officer whom many Patriots thought should replace the blundering Washington, constituted a severe psychological blow (although it ultimately turned out to benefit the Patriot cause).

Washington actually received some mounted reinforcements during the dark final months of 1776. Unfortunately, Maj. Elisha Sheldon's 125-man 5th Regiment of Connecticut Light Horse Militia and Maj. Theodorick Bland's three troops of Virginia Light Horse were not enough to save New York City or prevent

Howe's redcoats and Hessians from sweeping across New Jersey. Washington would have to rely on his infantry and artillery to shake the myth of British invincibility at Trenton and Princeton between December 26, 1776, and January 3, 1777.

The disasters of 1776 left Congress receptive to Washington's pleas for an army of long-service regulars. Congress also listened when Washington changed his tune regarding the value of cavalry. "From the Experience I have had in this Campaign, of the Utility of Horse," Washington wrote his political masters on December 11, 1776, "I am Convinced there is no carrying on the War without them, and I would therefore recommend the Establishment of one or more Corps . . . in Addition to those already raised in Virginia." Washington recommended that Major Sheldon be given "command of a Regiment of Horse on the Continental Establishment," and the accommodating legislators granted that wish the following day. Washington wasted no time in dispatching Sheldon back home to Connecticut to recruit six troops, each to consist of a captain, a lieutenant, a cornet, a quartermaster, two sergeants, two corporals, a trumpeter, a farrier, and thirty-four privates. A major, an adjutant, a surgeon, and a surgeon's mate would complete the staff of Sheldon's new regiment.

On December 24, Congress acted in a more comprehensive manner by permitting Washington to raise a total of 3,000 light horse. He authorized four new cavalry regiments over the next month. Bland's Virginia Light Horse became the 1st Regiment of Continental Light Dragoons, and Elisha Sheldon's command was designated as the second. Washington gave the two remaining regiments to members of his official family. Col. George Baylor, who took charge of the 3rd Regiment of Continental Light Dragoons, had served the army's commander-in-chief as an aide-de-camp during the first two years of the war. Stephen Moylan, the colonel of the 4th Continental Light

Dragoons, was an Irish Roman Catholic, normally a pariah class in colonial America. Moylan possessed such sterling personal qualities, however, that he managed to overcome the prevalent religious prejudices of the day and land such trusted positions as muster-master general and colonel-quartermaster-general in Washington's army.

On March 14, 1777, Congress approved a new table of organization for the Continental Light Dragoons that had been submitted earlier by Washington. Each regiment was to be commanded by a colonel, a lieutenant colonel, and a major, assisted by one adjutant, one quartermaster, one paymaster, one surgeon and his mate, one chaplain, one saddler, one riding master, one trumpet major, and four unpaid "supernumeraries." Following British Army practice, the regiments were divided into six troops, each containing one captain, one lieutenant, one cornet, one quartermaster sergeant, one drill or orderly sergeant, four corporals, one trumpeter, one farrier, one armorer, and thirty-two privates. While Washington appointed all light dragoon field officers, he permitted the regiments' four colonels to select their respective company officers. The commander-in-chief reserved the right to veto any of these choices, and he did not refrain from exerting his influence to secure commissions for relatives and friends.

Officer procurement did not pose as much of a problem to the Continental Light Dragoons as finding common soldiers to follow them. With enlistments in the Continental Army extended from one year to three years or the duration of the war, it became very difficult to recruit citizens with enough substance to own a horse. Horseflesh was also a rare commodity, which would prove to be a chronic problem for Washington's mounted arm throughout the conflict.

By June 16, 1777, Colonel Sheldon had succeeded in sending only sixteen equipped and mounted dragoons to Washington's headquarters at Peekskill, New York. Colonel Baylor managed to man and mount only a single troop in Virginia by this time, but his 3rd Continental Dragoons received a welcome bump in strength by absorbing Capt. George Lewis's troop of Virginia Light Horsemen, which had originally belonged to the commander-in-chief's bodyguard. Because of this connection, the 3rd Continental Dragoons became known as "Lady Washington's Own," but the regiment did not attain a respectable size until mid-August 1777, when it absorbed eighty mounted militia from North Carolina after they reached Philadelphia. Colonel Moylan enjoyed much better luck by sending recruiting parties ranging through Pennsylvania and Maryland. By early June, his 4th Continental Light Dragoons mustered 180 officers and men.

As Gen. Sir William Howe, lately knighted for his victories of the previous year, gave signs of resuming active operations, Washington fumed over his continuing deficit in cavalry. On June 17, he fired off an angry letter to Sheldon, ordering him to forward all his men to the main army without delay—whether they had horses or not. Four days later, Benjamin Tallmadge, the senior captain in Sheldon's 2nd Continental Light Dragoons, led four troops out of Wethersfield, Connecticut. Sheldon sent Lt. Thomas Young Seymour's troop north to participate in the Saratoga campaign and left some troopers on the east side of the Hudson River to monitor the British garrison in New York before hastening to join Washington with the rest of the regiment at the end of July.

Counting Captain Tallmadge's oversized squadron, Washington had only 260 light horse from the 1st, 2nd, and 4th Continental Light Dragoons at his disposal by June 24, 1777. Colonel Bland commanded this small composite corps. Its members wore a wide variety of uniforms. Some of the 1st Light Dragoons still sported the blue coats with red collars and cuffs that they had drawn from the Virginia public stores in 1776, but the entire regiment was converting to short brown coats with green facings, brass buttons, and yellow lace. Nearly every troop in the 2nd Light Dragoons seemed to have its own uniform. Eventually, Sheldon's troopers adopted the blue coats with buff facings that Seymour's troop wore at Saratoga. Baylor's 3rd Light Dragoons received white coats faced with blue. Stephen Moylan and his officers made an even more flamboyant choice by dressing themselves in scarlet. Washington accordingly directed his clothier general to issue the 4th Light Dragoons red coats with blue facings that had been captured from the enemy. That turned out to be a serious mistake. In the coming campaign, rebel infantry mistook Moylan's troopers for the British 16th Light Dragoons and fired at them. Washington peremptorily ordered Moylan to dye his men's coats a different color. The colonel selected green with red facings, although some members of the 4th were still seen in their old red coats through the fall of 1777. Washington tried to make the best of that situation for intelligence purposes. On September 30, he directed the formation of "a detachment of at least fifty Horse of which part are to be Colo. Moylans in their Red Uniforms, which will serve to deceive both the Enemy and Country people." The deceptive appearance of the 4th Continental Light Dragoons confounded Continentals as well as redcoats and loyalist civilians. On September 15, Lt. Col. Persifor Frazer of the 5th Pennsylvania Regiment and Maj. John Harper of the 2nd Pennsylvania Brigade mistook a party from the British 16th Light Dragoons for Moylan's troopers and became prisoners of war.

What the Continental Light Dragoons looked like did not matter half as much as how they performed. Although a consummate horseman, Washington did not exhibit much of an understanding of the potential of the mounted arm. At the start of the Philadelphia campaign, he refrained from concentrating his four new cavalry regiments into a mobile strike force, opting instead to disperse them to serve as escorts and messengers for himself and his major subordinates, and as scouts and pickets for his infantry. Washington temporarily parted with that practice when he deployed his forces behind Brandywine Creek on September 11, 1777, to check Howe's advance on Philadelphia. The Continental commander-in-chief reported "that all the Light Horse of the Army were Ordered on the right Wing to give Information." Unfortunately, Colonel Bland and his light dragoons proved slow in making their presence known to the officer most in need of their services. Maj. Gen. John Sullivan, the senior American commander in Washington's vulnerable right wing, complained: "I had but four Light Horsemen, two of which I kept at the upper Fords, to bring me Intelligence, the others I kept to send Intelligence to Head Quarters." Bland's troopers did not spot the large British column that Howe sent to turn Washington's right flank until 1:00 p.m., and it took another hour to warn General Sullivan. This serious lag in intelligence contributed significantly to Sir William Howe's victory that day.

Thanks to the impetuosity of a foreign adventurer, however, a handful of Continental horsemen tasted a little glory in the closing phases of the Battle of Brandywine. Count Casimir Pulaski, an exiled Polish revolutionary and seasoned soldier, had crossed the Atlantic to cast his lot with the rebel cause. Frustrated when Congress hesitated to grant him a commission, he attached himself to Washington as a volunteer aide. Conspicuous in hussar dress, Pulaski remained by Washington's side throughout the battle. As the rebel infantry began to disintegrate under heavy British hammering, Pulaski rallied the thirty light dragoons comprising Washington's personal escort and delivered a charge that briefly checked the advancing redcoats. This sortie gave the weary Continental infantry time to rally and conduct an orderly retreat.

Congress recognized Pulaski's quick thinking and courage two days later by naming him a brigadier general and commander of the Corps of Continental Light Dragoons. Although the dashing Pole had undoubtedly distinguished himself, this change of command in the midst of the Philadelphia campaign failed to alter the lackluster performance of the American cavalry. In many ways, Pulaski was an odd choice for such an important post. The count was brave enough and his devotion to the American cause genuine, but the elevation of a foreigner to the top cavalry command left the native-born American officers under him seething with jealousy and resentment. No one loathed Pulaski

Count Casimir Pulaski, from an engraving by Ant. Oleszczyynski. (*South Caroliniana Library, University of South Carolina, Columbia*)

more than Colonel Moylan, the senior field officer in Washington's cavalry. To make matters worse, the thirty-year-old Polish nobleman was abrupt, reserved, and prone to bouts of melancholy. He and his Polish aides despised their American colleagues as bumbling amateurs, which made friction inevitable. Pulaski later subjected Moylan to an unsuccessful court martial for disobedience and striking an arrogant member of the count's staff.

Much to the glee of Moylan and others, Pulaski fell flat on his face in his first opportunity to cross swords with the British. On October 2, Pulaski received orders to concentrate all the light dragoons he could spare from detached duty at Washington's headquarters. The count could barely muster two hundred troopers. The weakness of Pulaski's brigade may have robbed Washington of victory when he launched his surprise attack on Howe's camp outside of Philadelphia at Germantown on October 4, 1777. An officer in the British 2nd Battalion of Light Infantry, the first redcoat unit to feel the brunt of

Washington's onslaught, later wrote: "Had their Light Horse charged us . . . we must have been cut to Pieces." Later in the same engagement, the arrival of the British 16th Light Dragoons produced an intimidating effect that helped persuade Washington to withdraw from the field. Pulaski tried to deploy his troopers as a screen for Washington's retreat, but the 16th Light Dragoons charged and stampeded the American troopers back on their infantry. Apologists for Washington argue that a scarcity of forage prevented him from gathering all his horsemen in the same place at the same time, but that factor did not prevent Congress from authorizing more cavalry for the Continental Army a few months later.

With his army's logistics in disarray, Washington was forced to place the bulk of his troops in winter quarters at Valley Forge, Pennsylvania. Contrary to the popular myth, Washington's Continentals did not spend the entire winter of 1777–78 huddled around smoldering fires inside pitiful wooden huts. Washington spread his troops along a crescent from Trenton, New Jersey, to Wilmington, Delaware—with Valley Forge as the control center—to inhibit British efforts to draw food, forage, and loyalist recruits from the districts surrounding Philadelphia. Washington directed Pulaski to station most of his cavalry at Trenton, but many American horsemen found employment elsewhere along the arc-like perimeter. Washington especially relied on his most mobile units to harass the British and discourage local farmers from trading with the enemy.

This proved to be grueling work. As Benjamin Tallmadge, now a major commanding a squadron in the 2nd Light Dragoons, testified: "My duties were very arduous, not being able to tarry long in a place, by reason of the British light horse, which continually patrolled this intermediate ground. Indeed, it was unsafe to permit the dragoons to unsaddle their horses for an hour, and very rarely did I tarry in the same place in the night." Stationed west of the Schuylkill River, Capt. Henry Lee of Virginia, the commander of a troop from the 1st Continental Light Dragoons, endeavored to deny the British supplies and provide early warning for any enemy thrust at Valley Forge. Lee also gathered valuable intelligence on enemy activities.

In the meantime, lack of local support prevented Pulaski from converting Trenton into a viable base of operations. When four companies of American light horse arrived there on January 8, 1778, they discovered that there was "not a load of Hay in Town." In addition to hiding their forage, Trenton's inhabitants resisted Pulaski's request that they provide shelter for his troopers—and they absolutely refused to make room for his horses. In the end, the count sent two troops to Flemington and two to Pennington, while retaining only a small guard of dragoons at his Trenton headquarters. Pulaski's failure to maintain a mounted strike force within easy range of Philadelphia allowed the British garrison to draw supplies from New Jersey and parts of Pennsylvania.

As a result of these exertions, none of Washington's light dragoon regiments could muster more than 150 officers and men fit for duty by February 1778. Instead of adopting measures to bring these units up to strength, Congress decided to add more units to the cavalry corps. Count Pulaski had grown weary of his administrative tasks and jealous subordinates, and he lobbied for permission to raise his own unit. On March 28, 1778, Congress authorized him to raise an independent corps containing sixty-eight cavalrymen and two hundred light infantry. Ignoring Washington's guidelines, Pulaski filled his ranks with German and British deserters. By the fall, Pulaski's Legion consisted of three troops of cavalry, a rifle company, a grenadier company, two line infantry companies, and one "supernumerary" company, each containing twenty-five to thirty men. Pulaski did his best to dress his cavalrymen as Polish lancers, but their actual appearance fell far short of the sartorial splendor associated with the genuine article.

Congress pleased many of its constituents on April 7, 1778, when it promoted Capt. Henry Lee of Bland's 1st Dragoons to major and made his 5th Troop the nucleus of a two-troop formation known as Lee's Partisan Rangers. The twenty-two-year-old "Light-Horse Harry" had already distinguished himself as a champion raider and forager, siphoning a significant amount of the supplies that might have otherwise gone to the British in Philadelphia to the Continentals at Valley Forge. On May 28, Lee's Partisan Rangers received permission to raise a third troop of light horse. A little more than a year later, the unit became Lee's Legion, with the addition of a splendid company of light infantry from Delaware. The energetic Lee ensured that his two hundred officers and men were well dressed, well armed, and well equipped. He made them justify their appearance by performing a string of daring exploits.

The first four regiments of light dragoons underwent structural changes on May 27, 1778, when Congress reorganized the entire Continental Army. Each regimental staff lost its paymaster, chaplain, and four supernumeraries. The six-troop model remained intact, but now each of these units was supposed to contain a captain, two lieutenants, one cornet, one quartermaster sergeant, two sergeants, five corporals, one trumpeter, one farrier, and fifty-four privates. This new table of organization raised the recommended size of a Continental cavalry regiment from 280 to 416 effectives, but that total was only achieved on paper. As of June 1778, Moylan's 4th Dragoons mustered a mere 120 mounted rank and file. Baylor's 3rd Dragoons would attain a peak strength of just 159 enlisted men that year. For the remainder of the war, the Continental Light Dragoon regiments rarely counted more than 200 fit members on their rolls, and the average usually hovered between 120 and 150.

On the same day that Congress sanctioned this overly optimistic system of cavalry organization, it founded the Provost Company of Light Dragoons to serve as the Continental Army's military police. Commanded by Capt. Bartholomew von Heer, a German, this "Marchesie Corps" was supposed to number one captain, four lieutenants, one clerk, one quartermaster sergeant, two sergeants, five corporals, two trumpeters, forty-three provosts or privates, and four excarabineers or executioners drafted from the brigades under Washington.

In June 1778, Lt. Gen. Sir Henry Clinton, the new British commander who succeeded Sir William Howe on the latter's resignation, evacuated Philadelphia and withdrew overland toward New York. As Washington shadowed the redcoats and Hessians, his four Continental Light Dragoon regiments repeated the inglorious supporting roles they had played the previous summer and fall—reconnaissance, carrying messages, and protecting the high command. Once the British regained the safety of New York, however, American horsemen soon found themselves with as much action as they could handle.

Since Sheldon's 2nd Continental Light Dragoons drew its replacements and supplies from New England, it took position on the east side of the Hudson in Westchester County. This region, misnamed as the "neutral ground," comprised a no-man's-land between the lines, infested by roving bands of Whig and loyalist foragers known respectively as "skinners" and "cowboys," who terrorized local inhabitants and ambushed enemy patrols. For the next four years, the 2nd Continental Light Dragoons operated in this bleak and bloody area, keeping watch over British positions and movements, and countering enemy raids. "Our parties and those of the enemy had frequent interviews," Major Tallmadge recalled, "and sometimes not of the most friendly nature." He captured the essence of the regiment's duty during this period as "marching, and counter-marching, skirmishing with the enemy, catching cow-boys, etc., etc." Such life was as hazardous as it was fatiguing. On July 2, 1779, some two hundred British and loyalist cavalry surprised Sheldon's horse at dawn at Poundridge, New York, inflicting a dozen casualties and snatching the regimental colors in a savage mêlée of clanging sabers and broadswords. That banner fell into the hands of Lt. Col. Banastre Tarleton, now commander of the soon-to-be notorious British Legion, a loyalist unit. By this point in time, remounts had grown so scarce that Sheldon converted two of his battered regiment's troops into dismounted dragoons—a move made with Washington's full approval. Within two years, these troops would contain two-thirds of the regiment's two hundred personnel.

During these hectic years, Major Tallmadge earned a reputation as a raider that rivaled that of Light-Horse Harry Lee. He liked taking detachments of forty to fifty dismounted dragoons to harass British-occupied Long Island, where he had been born in 1754. Generally moving at night by longboat, he would slip across Long Island Sound, strike at dawn, and then depart as quickly as he had come. In one of his more memorable feats, Tallmadge used a swift American sloop to overhaul a British privateer. He then led forty-five of his seagoing dragoons in seizing this prize with a wild bayonet charge. Tallmadge rendered even greater service to the rebel cause by creating and managing an effective espionage network that functioned from 1778 until the war's end.

Life could be just as eventful and perilous for American dragoons west of the Hudson River. Early on September 27, 1778, four battalions of British infantry under Maj. Gen. Charles Grey (the same "No Flint" Grey who had conducted a successful night attack against Pennsylvania's Continental Line a year earlier at Paoli, Pennsylvania) crept up noiselessly on four troops from the 3rd Continental Light Dragoons encamped near Old Tappan, New Jersey. Relying solely on bayonets, the merciless redcoats hurled themselves on 104 sleeping Virginians and Carolinians, stabbing 36 and seizing 37 unhurt men as prisoners. Colonel Baylor took a musket ball through the lungs and fell into enemy hands, while his second-in-command died of his wounds. General Washington moved quickly to help the 3rd Dragoons recover from this devastating blow. He promoted his cousin, Maj. William Washington of the 4th Light Dragoons, to lieutenant colonel on November 20 and put him in charge of the 3rd Dragoons' ninety-two dazed survivors. Lt. Col. Washington found the regiment in such poor condition that it took him until the following September to rebuild its strength and make it ready for active duty.

With the British capture of Savannah, Georgia, in December 1778, the decisive theater of the Revolutionary War switched dramatically to the South. On February 2, 1779, Pulaski's Legion departed to assist Maj. Gen Benjamin Lincoln in an attempt to recover Georgia. The 1st Continental Light Dragoons followed in Pulaski's wake that July. Those two Continental units joined with mounted militia from South Carolina in supporting the poorly coordinated Franco-American assault on Savannah on October 9. Pulaski rashly tried to lead his cavalry brigade though the abatis screening the British redoubt on Spring Hill, but a canister shot knocked him out of the saddle and brisk enemy fire caused his lancers to veer off to the left. The valiant Pole died two days later. When Congress learned of this loss, it dissolved Pulaski's Legion, sending its surviving cavalry to the 1st Continental Light Dragoons and its infantry to the 1st South Carolina Continental Regiment.

Following the debacle at Savannah, General Lincoln retired to Charleston. A few months later, he found himself besieged by ten thousand redcoats, Hessians, and loyalists who had sailed down from New York under an unusually aggressive Sir Henry Clinton. The remnants of the 1st Continental Light Dragoons occupied a post about twenty-four miles outside of Charleston, where they were joined by Lt. Col. William Washington and his reconstituted 3rd Continental Light Dragoons. Washington's white-coated troopers arrived from the north just as Clinton started to disembark his army. Washington took command of the combined Continental cavalry force, which numbered 379 officers and men—a sizable mounted force by the standards of this conflict. A contingent of South Carolina militia dragoons brought the total number of rebel cavalry attached to the Charleston garrison up to 500 effectives.

Brig. Gen. Isaac Huger of South Carolina took charge of this American mounted corps. Lincoln assigned him the task of keeping open an avenue of communications and escape between Charleston and the interior. Huger also hoped to hinder the British as they attempted to encircle South Carolina's capital.

Sir Henry Clinton took the precaution of bringing along a sizable cavalry force of his own to help besiege Charleston. Lieutenant Colonel Tarleton commanded the light dragoons from his British Legion, plus an attached squadron of the 17th Light Dragoons. The loyalist and British troopers had endured a stormy voyage from New York. Many of their mounts had died en route and those that survived had been weakened by the ordeal. Consequently, Huger's Continental and militia horsemen faced feeble opposition—at first. The resourceful and relentless Tarleton requisitioned better horses for his men, and the rebels soon felt his sting. Once again, American cavalrymen would pay a stiff price for lack of vigilance. Tarleton surprised Huger's sleeping camp at Moncks Corner, about thirty miles above Charleston, at three o'clock on the morning of April 14, 1780. Fifteen American troopers died in the resulting fracas, seventeen suffered nonfatal wounds, and one hundred men and eighty-three horses were captured. The survivors fled through the swamps. William Washington and Col. Anthony Walton White of the 1st Continental Light Dragoons salvaged something out of the disaster by managing to rally nearly 250 troopers from their regiments.

Washington and White paused long enough to refit and recuperate, and then they moved back toward Charleston, intent on harassing British foraging parties and causing as much havoc as possible. Tarleton once again proved to be more than their match. He caught his foes at Lenud's Ferry with their backs to the swollen Santee River on the afternoon of May 6. The British Legion cut down forty-one Americans and captured sixty-seven. Most of the rest swam to safety without their horses, but no more than 125 regrouped to fight again. Colonel White and his officers returned to Virginia to recruit the 1st Continental Dragoons from scratch. Colonel Washington retired into North Carolina to procure new chargers for the troopers who remained with him. On May 12, 1780, Charleston and its five thousand defenders surrendered, and South Carolina now lay prostrate before the British invaders.

Congress quickly dispatched an army of Delaware and Maryland Continentals and militia from Virginia and North Carolina under Maj. Gen. Horatio Gates, the vaunted hero of Saratoga, to reclaim the Palmetto State. The only regular cavalry to accompany Gates's 4,100-man force belonged to a legion commanded by Col. Charles Armand Tuffin, Marquis de la Rouerie, a French adventurer and soldier of fortune. Officially composed of a dragoon troop, two fusilier or musket companies, and a rifle company, Armand's Legion mustered sixty horse and sixty foot for this campaign. A disproportionate amount of Armand's ranks consisted of untrustworthy German deserters, and the officers were all foreigners, including some inherited from Pulaski's Legion. Armand maintained lax discipline, and many of his men frightened their American comrades more than they did the British. Armand's independent corps earned no honors at the

Battle of Camden on August 16, 1780, where 2,200 red-coats and loyalists under Lt. Gen. Charles, Earl Cornwallis, trounced and scattered Gates's larger but poorly commanded force. Tarleton and his green-coated cavalrymen played a prominent role in Cornwallis's triumph, helping to rout the Maryland and Delaware Continentals after the rebel militia and Armand's Legion fled the field.

Tarleton was just getting warmed up. Two days after Camden, he surprised the camp of partisan leader Thomas Sumter at Fishing Creek. The British Legion killed 150 rebels and took 300 prisoners. Sumter and a mere fifty of his followers managed to get away. Tarleton also recaptured a company's worth of British and loyalist soldiers, plus precious supplies that Sumter had seized in some earlier raiding.

With Gates discredited, Congress finally heeded General Washington's advice and appointed Maj. Gen. Nathanael Greene to head the Southern Department. The only reinforcements the new commander brought along from the main army were the 250 personnel of Lt. Col. Henry Lee's Legion, which had been expanded by an act of Congress on November 1 to three mounted troops and three infantry companies. Greene found Gates's decimated remnants at Charlotte, North Carolina, on December 2, 1780. Of the one thousand Continentals present and fit for duty, eighty belonged to William Washington's combined 1st and 3rd Light Dragoons. Washington had divided his men into four puny troops led by ten officers.

Greene assigned Washington's horsemen to a flying column commanded by Brig. Gen. Daniel Morgan and sent the latter to challenge British authority in northwestern South Carolina. Washington and his troopers bluffed one hundred loyalists into surrendering a fort at Rugeley's Mill on December 4. At the end of the month, the 3rd Continental Light Dragoons and 200 mounted militia attacked 250 loyalists at Hammond's Store, killing or wounding 150 and taking 40 prisoners.

Stung by these forays, Lord Cornwallis, the British commander in the South, sent Banastre Tarleton and one thousand regulars to eliminate this nuisance on his western flank. Morgan met Tarleton at a place called the Cowpens on January 17, 1781, where Morgan deployed his militia as a lure to tempt the British into rushing pell-mell into the withering, measured volleys of his waiting Continentals. Commanding only eighty-two Continental light dragoons and one hundred or more mounted militia, Washington initially occupied a reserve position behind Morgan's Continental infantry. As the battle neared its climax, approximately fifty troopers belonging to the British 17th Light Dragoons skirted Morgan's left flank to attack rebel militia who were reforming to the rear of the Continental infantry. The watchful Washington reacted instantly to the threat, leading the American cavalry in a furious saber charge that scattered his British foes. Washington and his horsemen then raced to the opposite side of the battlefield to check a British Legion light dragoon troop that was attempting to turn Morgan's right flank. Then the stout Virginian unleashed his troopers in a third furious charge, which smashed through Tarleton's stymied infantry and caused the enemy's reserve cavalry to flee the field.

According to a frequently repeated story, Washington engaged in a melee with the green-coated troopers of the British Legion, breaking his saber in a duel with an enemy officer. Catching sight of Tarleton, Washington spurred his horse toward the enemy commander and managed to nick the latter's right hand with his ruined saber. The Englishman drew a pistol and fired a shot that grazed his antagonist's knee and wounded the Virginian's horse. As Washington struggled to control his stricken mount, Tarleton made good his escape. The Washington-Tarleton duel inspired several artistic renderings of the Battle of

Cowpens, but it actually belongs to the realm of legend. Tarleton was elsewhere on the battlefield at the time Washington and some of his dragoons engaged a trio of British cavalry officers. Some American observers mistakenly identified Washington's assailant, an officer of the 17th Light Dragoons, as Tarleton. There is no disputing, however, the totality of Tarleton's defeat. The humbled British cavalier managed to escape from the disaster, but he left behind 100 dead, 229 wounded, and 600 prisoners. Washington and his dragoons had amply avenged Moncks Corner and Lenud's Ferry.

Washington's 3rd Continental Light Dragoons stuck faithfully with Greene during his celebrated retreat across North Carolina into Virginia. They stayed with him when he turned south again to confront Lord Cornwallis at Guilford Courthouse, North Carolina. At the height of that bloody battle on March 15, 1781, Washington bowled into the 2nd Battalion of Foot Guards right after that crack unit routed the 2nd Maryland Regiment in Greene's last line of resistance. Ably assisted by the bayonets of the 1st Maryland Regiment, Washington's troopers broke the Guards and chased them back to the shelter of Cornwallis's artillery. According to an improbable legend, a single private in the 3rd Dragoons named Peter Francisco killed a dozen Guardsmen with his long broadsword.

The performance of William Washington and his Continental Light Dragoons during the first three months of 1781 imbued Nathanael Greene with a keen appreciation for the value of the mounted arm. As the Quaker general wrote Gov. Thomas Jefferson of Virginia on April 6: "Superior Cavalry is of the greatest importance to the salvation of this Country and without them you would soon hear of [our] detachments being cut to peces in every quarter. . . . The Militia can only be useful with a superior Cavalry and hundreds and hundreds of them would have fallen a sacrafice in the late operations had it not

Colonel William Washington dueling Lt. Col. Tarleton at the Battle of Cowpens, an engraving by S. H. Gimber. Although this encounter never took place, it became a popular subject of paintings of the battle. (*South Caroliniana Library of the University of South Carolina, Columbia*)

been for the goodness of our Cavalry and the great activity of the Officers commanding those Corps. Without a fleet Cavalry we can never reconnoiter the enemy[,] attempt a surprise, or indeed keep our selves from being surprised."

Cornwallis claimed victory by holding the battlefield at Guilford Courthouse, but he lost a quarter of his army in the process, which left him dangerously crippled. Greene captured his opponent's predicament with only minor exaggeration on March 30, when he informed Samuel Huntington, the president of the Continental Congress: "I have it from good authority that the Enemy suffered in the Battle of Guilford 633 [casualties] exclusive of Officers, and most of their principal Officers were killed and wounded. They have met with a defeat in victory." Cornwallis decided that he could best strike at Greene by wrecking the Quaker general's base of supply. Consequently, the dogged British general marched his 1,500 survivors to join approximately 5,000 British,

German, and loyalist soldiers that Sir Henry Clinton had sent to ravage Virginia, the arsenal and granary for the rebel war effort in the South. This fateful decision left the Carolinas open to Greene, who figured that he could do more damage there than by following the earl into the Old Dominion. Greene sent Lee's Legion behind enemy lines to cooperate with the partisan band commanded by Brig. Gen. Francis "Swamp Fox" Marion in attacking small posts. William Washington's Continental cavalrymen remained with Greene's army and helped tackle larger detachments. At Hobkirk's Hill, South Carolina, on April 25, the 3rd Continental Light Dragoons outflanked its foes once again and then carried off fifty prisoners while covering the American retreat. Colonel Washington's luck finally ran out, however, on September 8, 1781, at Eutaw Springs, where he charged the grenadier and light infantry companies from three British regiments that made a stand in a blackjack thicket on the right flank of the enemy line. The dragoons' horses became snarled in the dense and prickly brush, and they had to absorb a succession of rolling volleys. Washington's horse went down, and its rider, entangled in the stirrups, was bayoneted and captured. All but two of the unfortunate colonel's officers and half of his regiment were killed or wounded before the fight ended.

Ironically, Cornwallis's doomed invasion of Virginia set the stage for the most imaginative application of mounted force during the entirety of the Revolutionary War. The earl's move allowed him to reunite two of the British Army's finest loyalist units, the British Legion and the Queen's Rangers. Like the British Legion, the Queen's Rangers was a composite organization. Close to 40 percent of its men were horse soldiers—hussars and light dragoons—while the rest were superbly conditioned light infantry. Between these two commands, Cornwallis could now count on the services of roughly five hundred light dragoons and hussars. This represented the largest concentration of mounted might that the British achieved in the South. Cornwallis increased the potency and mobility of his loyalist troopers by having them seize every charger they could find on the horse-rich plantations of the Tidewater country. Taking a lesson from the enemy's use of mounted militia in South Carolina, Cornwallis exploited this same source of horseflesh to mount as many as seven hundred to eight hundred of his infantry. He also drew twelve thousand to thirty thousand black slaves to his banner by offering them freedom, and many who joined him brought along the steeds their naïve masters had commended to their care. Assured of an endless supply of thoroughbred remounts, Cornwallis's cavalry moved with unprecedented speed. For the first time in the war, a British army possessed the ability to outrun its opponents. This paralyzed the state militia, which feared swift reprisals if it resisted the invaders. Superior British mobility also prevented the few Continentals on the scene from engaging in the hit-and-run tactics that Greene had employed with such startling effect in the Carolinas. As the Marquis de Lafayette, the young French general commanding the Continental forces charged with Virginia's defense, complained in a letter to George Washington: "Was I to fight a battle I'll be cut to pieces, the militia dispersed, and the arms lost. Was I to decline fighting the country would think herself given up. I am therefore determined to scarmish, but not to engage too far, and particularly to take care against their immense and excellent body of horse whom the militia fears like they would so many beasts."

The only horsemen the rebels had to oppose Cornwallis's hard-riding soldiers were sixty raw recruits from the 1st Continental Light Dragoons, the remnants of Armand's Legion, and two hundred to three hundred citizen-soldiers from the Corps of Virginia Light Horse. The latter unit did not turn out in appreciable force until the campaign had practically run its course. Thus Cornwallis was free to subject Virginia to the same brand of hard war that Maj. Gens. William T. Sherman and Philip H. Sheridan meted out to the Southern Confederacy eighty years later. Then, just when much of Virginia seemed on the verge of submission, a peevish Sir Henry Clinton directed his aristocratic subordinate to take all of his troops and establish and fortify a naval base on Chesapeake Bay. Cornwallis chose Yorktown and began entrenching on August 2, 1781. That ill-advised move presented George Washington with a chance to change the course of the war.

Learning that a powerful French fleet was about to seal off the Chesapeake, the rebel commander-in-chief marched south on August 21 with half the Continentals from his main army and the French Expeditionary Force commanded by the Comte de Rochambeau, which had been sitting idle in the northern United States since the preceding year. Ninety-five of Moylan's 4th Continental Light Dragoons and a draft of eighteen men from Sheldon's Horse accompanied Washington's column. Moving quickly, the two allied leaders concentrated nearly sixteen thousand regulars and militia against Yorktown by September 30. The trapped Cornwallis and his eight thousand soldiers and sailors surrendered after an intensive siege on October 19, 1781.

Yorktown may have decided the outcome of the War of Independence, but it did not mark an end to the fighting. The 4th Continental Light Dragoons marched south to join Greene, who had succeeded in clearing the British from all of South Carolina except Charleston. The Quaker general had Moylan's Horse join Brig. Gen. Anthony Wayne in Georgia, where Pennsylvania Continentals and rebel militia were keeping the British hemmed in at Savannah. Wayne also operated against Indian bands that remained loyal to George III. When the British evacuated Savannah on July 11, 1782, Moylan's Horse returned to Charleston. There, Greene consolidated the 1st and 3rd

Continental Light Dragoons into a single battalion of five troops on November 9. Col. George Baylor, recently released from a British prison, briefly commanded this amalgamated battalion. When the last redcoats finally boarded their ships and sailed from Charleston on December 14, Greene stationed all his cavalry at Combahee to check any possible sorties from British East Florida. Unwilling to endure additional hardships with peace so close at hand, one hundred of these weary troopers deserted en masse in the spring of 1783.

By July 1783, all of the Continental Light Horse had been furloughed and sent home, with the exception of Armand's Legion, which did not cease to serve until October 29. A sergeant, a corporal, and eight privates of the Provost Company of Light Dragoons stayed at Washington's headquarters to carry messages as late as October 3, and they may have been the last American horsemen to personally serve the commander-in-chief. By November 25, 1783, the day the Continental Army underwent reduction to only one thousand infantry, every regular American mounted regiment had been officially discharged.

In conclusion, it seems fitting to evaluate the influence that the Continental Light Dragoons had on the outcome of the War of Independence. Was there really "no carrying on the War without them" as George Washington put it on December 11, 1776? Undoubtedly, the light horse filled a number of essential roles—particularly as couriers, scouts, and raiders. Nathanael Greene particularly credited his horsemen with the survival of the small, ragged army that he led in the Southern Department in 1781. "A good body of horse is every thing to an Army that is obliged to act upon the defensive," he counseled the Marquis de Lafayette on June 9, "and you will have little to fear either from a skirmish or even a defeat if you are well covered with horse, but without which you have every thing to apprehend, as the most triffling disorder may be improved into a route." Unfortunately, American light dragoons did not always perform as well as they did under Greene. Continental horsemen assigned to exposed positions repeatedly failed to remain properly vigilant, which led to shattering defeats at Old Tappan, Poundridge, Moncks Corner, and Lenud's Ferry. These blows, combined with a chronic shortage of horseflesh, restricted the size and diluted the effect of Washington's cavalry. As far as emulating the mounted shock tactics that elevated the Duke of Marlborough to the heights of military greatness, the Continental Light Dragoons enjoyed their finest hours under William Washington at Cowpens and Guilford Courthouse. These were small affairs by European standards, and Colonel Washington's impetuosity resulted in his becoming a British prisoner toward the end of 1781. All things considered, George Washington's mounted regiments were too few and too small to ever aspire to being the Continental Army's decisive arm. That honor went to the infantry, closely followed by Washington's well-served artillery.

TWO

# European Influences on Continental Cavalry

## *Lee F. McGee*

T HE RATIO OF AMERICAN CAVALRY TO INFANTRY DURING
the War for Independence was small compared with
that in European armies. European cavalry was traditionally divided into "light" and "heavy" units. Light cavalry
consisted of hussars and light dragoons and heavy cavalry
consisted of cuirassiers and dragoons. Each was expected
to perform a certain role, although this was not strictly
adhered to in practice. Even though limited in size,
American cavalry filled all of the roles expected of its
European counterparts. American cavalry can be divided
into three categories: militia, state, and Continental. The
majority of these units functioned as light cavalry.

The Continental cavalry, as originally conceived by
George Washington, was intended to fill the need for true
"light cavalry," hence the name Continental Light

This paper is dedicated to Ladislav Kortvelyesi, a Hungarian who had
unquestionable influence on the author.

Dragoons. In most European armies, light cavalry or light dragoons served as scouts and messengers, screened the main army, and performed reconnaissance. Most American colonies had prior experience with cavalry through the militia system. A militia cavalry tradition existed in the American colonies since at least 1646.[1]

George Washington's experience with formal cavalry operations prior to the Revolutionary War was limited. Although Washington did have exposure, primarily through reading, to some of the most influential works on warfare at the time, his military experience did not include heavy cavalry; the cavalry in the Virginia Regiment during the French and Indian War did not function as such.[2]

It was also widely believed that the use of cavalry in combat, specifically the traditional role of heavy cavalry, would be extremely limited in the northern theater of the war. This view was not shared by all American generals, but it limited the use of cavalry to those duties usually reserved for light cavalry or light dragoons. Also, some of the limitations placed on American cavalry were financial, as the resources to mount and equip a large cavalry force were not available.[3]

Aside from practical considerations, such as terrain, lack of manpower, and the mandate of cavalry's role from George Washington, other factors limited the success of American cavalry early in the war. In the first years of its existence, the Continental cavalry lacked any system of uniform training. There were also deficiencies in tactical knowledge and experience. It is important to note that the Continental infantry suffered similar deficiencies until Baron Friedrich von Steuben instituted an effective program of training and discipline in 1778.

Continental cavalry officers were judged severely deficient by Brig. Gen. Casimir Pulaski when he assumed command of the four regiments of light dragoons in December 1777. Pulaski found that the Continental cavalry as originally conceived was not up to performing its assigned tasks and was in desperate need of an infusion of professionalism. Therefore both the Continental Army command and the Continental Congress undertook an effort to professionalize the cavalry.[4]

Pulaski's appointment represented an effort in that direction, but it was neither the first nor the last attempt. However, after Pulaski failed to reform the cavalry, each of the four Continental cavalry regiments, as well as other cavalry units such as the cavalry of Henry Lee's Legion, was left to fend for itself. No further serious official efforts were made to turn the Continental cavalry into a force equal to its European counterparts.

In addition, regardless of the original intended use of the cavalry, there was no formalization of American cavalry tactical thought and no official drill manual adopted during the Revolutionary War. Several efforts were made, but by early 1783 there still was no uniform drill for the cavalry. There was simply no American adoption or adaptation of European cavalry drill or tactics on par with what von Steuben did with the Continental infantry.[5]

Did this matter? Many historians and researchers suggest that it did not. In the militia, where lack of formalized training might have been most manifest, mounted units usually performed admirably, not only in the light cavalry duties of reconnaissance and screening but also in some limited combat situations. However, there was a record of American cavalry in the war that stood in stark contrast to the light cavalry role. From late 1780 to late 1781, the Continental cavalry under Lt. Col. William Washington performed in a manner not consistently seen in any other years, theater, or form: militia, state, or Continental. This was not the role that was originally envisioned by George Washington, but on a small scale it was exactly what cavalry had been doing in combat in Europe for well over one hundred years. During four battles, and in several smaller encounters, William Washington's regiment functioned as heavy cavalry.

This is not to say that other Continental light dragoon regiments, militia, and state cavalry did not occasionally perform successfully in combat. However, Washington's Continental cavalry, over a substantial period of time, consistently achieved a level of success that suggests a move beyond its originally intended role. In his work on the history of the British Army, Sir John Fortescue argues that this was the case.[6]

The question then arises as to where this change of role came from and why it occurred. Many researchers who have studied William Washington emphasize his personality as having played a key part in his success, and this desire to succeed perhaps led him to expand the scope of his cavalry operations. A close examination of the record in the context of European practice, however, suggests that more than personality was responsible for Washington's success in leading mounted troops.

## The British Situation

By the 1780s, many historians would argue, the cavalry of most European armies functioned in much the same way. Despite the administrative legacy of the British cavalry, there is no evidence that the four Continental cavalry regiments received direct influence in terms of training or tactics from British sources. However, because the Continental Army was in a sense an offspring of the British Army, the state of British cavalry tactical doctrine at the time merits examination. If nothing else, this can serve as a guide to the true sources of unofficial Continental cavalry doctrine.[7]

Looking retrospectively at the British experience in the War for American Independence sheds light on the evolution of tactical thought in the British cavalry. After the war, at a time when the British cavalry was attempting to improve itself based on experience gained in the Revolution, David Dundas emerged as a leader in shaping British military thought. Dundas had trained as a cavalry officer and served in one of the most successful British mounted units, the 15th Light Dragoons, during the Seven Years' War. He feared that habits learned during the Revolutionary War would cause problems for the British Army when it inevitably had to face a European army on the battlefield. What would happen when the British, in the loose formation employed in America, came up against traditional European cavalry?[8]

British historian Sir John Fortescue discussed the effect that the American Revolutionary War had on the British Army in his *History of the British Army*. Many British officers returning from America advocated a move toward a more open order (that is, maintaining a greater space between soldiers in battle formation), and a reduction of an infantry line of battle from three to two ranks. Dundas, in reaction to this, published his *Principles of Military Movements, Chiefly Applied to Infantry*. Because of the lack of uniformity in drill from regiment to regiment, Dundas feared that some officers would adopt practices which were successful in America, and that in future conflicts these practices would leave the British army especially vulnerable to tactics employed by other contemporary European armies.[9]

The reforms and regulations initiated by Dundas were published in 1788, five years after the conclusion of the American Revolutionary War. Thus Dundas himself had no influence on the way American tactics developed. Yet in an army (the Continental Army) that was so influenced at its formation by that of the mother country, the tactics employed by the British would have had an effect on those of the Americans. In Virginia, for example, cavalry formation and administration nearly paralleled that of the British.[10]

Dundas had observed Prussian military maneuvers under Frederick the Great in 1785. According to Fortescue, "he saw three thousand cavalry advance at the trot in column of squadrons, and deploy for attack over a front of a mile in less than three minutes." British general Charles, Earl Cornwallis, was also present at these maneuvers, but was less impressed with the Prussians than was Dundas. The Prussian Army by the 1780s was no longer the same force that had fought the Seven Years' War (1756–1763). Even by the end of that conflict, the Prussian Army was showing signs of wear and decline, primarily because of hard service. Fortescue indicated that Cornwallis may have assessed the Prussian maneuvers more accurately than Dundas, as Fortescue praised the abilities of Cornwallis, specifically in leading large numbers of troops. According to Fortescue, Cornwallis learned this skill from Gen. Sir William Howe during the American War, and Fortescue went on to suggest that Cornwallis might have flourished leading cavalry.[11]

Cornwallis's experience with the use of cavalry during the American Revolution was not extensive, and, as Dundas suggested, part of the reason for the British move to two ranks and open order in that war was because of the limited use of cavalry by the Americans:

> The very small proportion of cavalry employed in the American wars, has much tended to introduce the present loose and irregular system of our infantry. Had they seen and been accustomed to the rapid movements of a good cavalry, they would have felt the necessity of more substantial order, of moving with concert and circumspection, and of being at every instant in a situation to form and repel a vigorous attack.[12]

Some scholars, such as Stephen Brumwell, suggest that the tactics learned by the British in the Seven Years' War (at least the North American theater of that war) and the American Revolution brought about positive changes in the British Army. But Brumwell does concede that Dundas's argument had some merit. "When the British Army encountered Napoleonic France its infantry fought elbow to elbow in Dundas fashion; they none the less employed a unique tactical device that can be traced back through the American War of Independence to the red-coats of Quebec—the 'thin red line' of two ranks," Brumwell observed. "In addition, the battalions composing the line were now screened by skilled light infantry who likewise drew upon techniques pioneered in America half a century before: this belated alliance between the best traditions of James Wolfe and Frederick the Great was destined to prove the nemesis of Napoleon's infantry from Alexandria to Waterloo." Clearly the British had applied the lessons of experience.[13]

Other authors believe that British success in America during the conflicts of the mid-eighteenth century only truly occurred when traditional European tactics were used. Guy Chet stated that:

> The success of American forces in the early battles of the American Revolution do not warrant a favorable assessment of "American tactics." Like earlier colonial wars, the American War of Independence consistently demonstrated the wisdom and tactical efficacy of European military conventions. Thus, despite the American victory in the war, the military leadership of the United States did not formulate a uniquely American military doctrine for the republic's armed forces. Rather, it looked to Europe for guidance in the science of warfare and the art of combat.[14]

The British Army had already been exposed to the rapid movements of professional cavalry, albeit on a limited scale, while serving in Europe during the Seven Years' War. However, British officers in North America seem to have disregarded the risk of cavalry attack during the Revolution, even though on several occasions the British were successfully attacked by American cavalry. Fortescue attributed British failures against American cavalry to the army's "looseness of formation," which "had been further encouraged by the very small part played by cavalry, as distinguished from mounted infantry, throughout the operations. It is true that Tarleton, and, still more conspicuously, the American Colonel Washington had occasionally wrought great results by the charge of a mere handful of sabers."[15]

The performance of Lt. Col. William Washington against British infantry demonstrated the vulnerability that was of concern to Dundas. Washington and the Continental cavalry in the southern theater in 1781 provided a case study for what well-trained cavalry (such as Dundas observed in Prussia) could accomplish against British infantry formations. Dundas's concern was based on the ability of the Prussian cavalry, yet American cavalry with no formal training in European cavalry tactics and maneuvers did precisely what Dundas feared.

Dundas's work illustrated, as did the views of his former commanding officer, Maj. Gen. George Eliott of the 15th Light Dragoons, that the leaders of British light cavalry believed there was something to be learned from the Prussian cavalry. Even on the heels of the successful performance of the British light dragoon regiments in the Seven Years' War, two of the authors of that success, Dundas and Eliott, were looking to the Prussians. They believed that the cavalry under Frederick the Great set the standard for mounted troops in the second half of the eighteenth century, and that the Prussians were to be emulated.[16]

Not all British commanders shared this opinion of the Prussians. Gen. John Burgoyne, for example, the former commander of the 16th Light Dragoons who had fought on the Iberian Peninsula during the Seven Years' War, did not think as highly of the Prussian cavalry. His assessment of its performance in the Seven Years' War was less favorable. Rather than simply studying other armies' practices, Burgoyne preferred a different method of learning the science of warfare, one that was an important element in the education of British officers in the late eighteenth century. Burgoyne believed that all British officers should spend part of their spare time reading military texts. In fact, he declared that in his opinion the best military texts of the time were not of British origin—they came instead from continental Europe, and were written in French.[17]

Historian Ira Gruber has explored this topic in the greatest depth, analyzing the libraries of eighteenth-century British officers in their entirety. Since there were no formal training academies for British infantry and cavalry officers in that era, British officers had to learn their craft through reading works on military subjects. The majority of military texts studied by British officers were produced by continental European writers. In regard to cavalry, there were many texts that touched on the subject, but only one was entirely dedicated to cavalry operations. This volume was *Regulations for the Prussian Cavalry*, published in 1757, and was found in the libraries of sixteen British officers. It was one of the forty most common texts in such collections.[18]

Gruber does not believe that British officers were primarily influenced by European, or even classical, military traditions. His work does demonstrate, however, that when British officers wanted to study the "art of war," they were more likely to turn to non-British sources. What implication did this have for the operations of the British cavalry, and whatever influence it might have had on the American cavalry? British cavalry units, heavy or light, may have been operating in a similar way to their Prussian counterparts. That method of operating, British cavalry tactics, likely originated in the Prussian Army.[19]

Among the few British cavalry texts produced in the late eighteenth and early nineteenth centuries, and perhaps the most influential, was Capt. Robert Hinde's *The Discipline of the Light Horse*, published in 1778. In this volume, Hinde asserted that the formation of the British light dragoons was influenced by the hussar regiments of continental Europe. This view has been shared by British historians ever since. In 1875 Edward Barrington de Fonblanque cited a French work, Jean Thomas Rocquancourt's *Cours d'Art et d'Histoire Militaires*, published in Paris more than three decades earlier, to support the claim that British light cavalry doctrine came from Prussia. Fonblanque expanded this assertion by correctly noting that Frederick the Great and his father borrowed the hussar tradition from the Austrians, who had in turn incorporated the original hussars of Hungary.[20]

Many subsequent British historians have agreed with this assessment. In his history of the 15th Light Dragoons, H. C. Wylly wrote that the light troops first assigned to the British heavy cavalry were based on the Austrian hussars. Maj. George Paget, the Marquess of Anglesey, wrote in his multivolume *History of the British Cavalry* that "the Prussian Cavalry, under Seydlitz and Ziethen, and especially Ziethen's incomparable 'Death's Head' Hussars, soon became the model for the world." Concerning the formation of the original light units of the British cavalry, Anglesey observed that "the men and horses thus raised were trained and equipped to perform the sort of duties which were later carried out by every regiment, but which till then, had been the preserve of irregular horse, modeled upon the Hungarian hussars."[21]

The British light dragoons were originally envisioned as performing the light cavalry role traditionally fulfilled by hussars. "These new regiments were known unofficially as 'hussars' because it was the original intention to employ them as irregulars," Anglesey wrote. The service of these original light dragoon units, specifically the 15th Light Dragoons, rapidly evolved beyond their originally intended function. At the Battle of Emsdorf (July 16, 1760) and beyond, the British light dragoons came into their own. Regarding Emsdorf, Anglesey noted that "this brilliant affair restored the cavalry's reputation, confirmed the value of light dragoons, and established the precedent, followed in so many subsequent engagements by

Britain's light horse, of charging through and through, without a moment's hesitation."[22]

Fortescue, in his *History of the 17th Lancers*, also commented on the origin of the British light dragoons. "A patriotic Englishman, the Duke of Kingston," observing the inadequacy of the cavalry, "raised a regiment of Light Horse (the first ever seen in England) at his own expense, in imitation of the Hussars of foreign countries." Allan Mallinson, in *Light Dragoons: The Making of a Regiment*, noted both the similarities and differences between the British light dragoons and hussars:

> There was really no difference, as far as the British army was concerned, between light dragoons and hussars although the Austrian army would not have expected to see hussars drilled in ranks as much as the British insisted, and the British notion of field discipline would certainly not have embraced the French definition of *hussar*. . . . they received no instruction in scouting and reconnaissance, the true work of the hussar. Some commentators have remarked adversely on the Fifteenth's casualties at Emsdorf, many gained in the twenty-mile pursuit which followed. Comparing them with the Prussian hussars who sustained no casualties at all, Fortescue suggests that the Fifteenth did not yet know their business as light cavalry, notwithstanding their undoubted courage."[23]

For the American cavalry, perhaps there was something more to its development than inheriting the British cavalry tradition. Even without the direct influence of British light cavalry doctrine on the Americans, the British concept of light cavalry was intimately tied to continental European light cavalry and the hussars. If there was no direct link between the American light dragoons and the British cavalry, American cavalry must have followed examples from elsewhere, specifically, the continental European armies. The complete story of European influences on the Continental cavalry includes several sources and individuals, many of which have been relegated to obscurity in the history of the American Revolution.

In attempting to professionalize the American cavalry, the Continental Congress turned to Europe for lessons. As a result, and despite repeated failures, the cavalry was exposed to professional European cavalry officers, many of whom had experience in the Seven Years' War fighting either with or against the Prussian cavalry, which was redefining the standard of mounted operations. When the Continental cavalry was successful against the British, it succeeded for the exact reason that Dundas later feared: the British were vulnerable to contemporary European armies. The British army in the South in 1781 was facing American troops employing the cavalry tactics and practices developed and refined by Frederick the Great.

FRENCH INFLUENCES

In October 1776, Silas Deane wrote to George Washington and the Continental Congress on behalf of Augustin Mottin de La Balme, who was also recommended by Benjamin Franklin. La Balme had served as a cavalry officer in the French heavy cavalry, and had written two treatises on cavalry, *Essais sur L'equitation, ou Principles Raisonnes sur L'art de Monter et de Dresser les Chevaux* in 1773, and *Elements de Tactique pour la Cavalerie* in 1776. He also served as the director of the riding school of the French Army's heavy cavalry.[24]

Washington initially suggested to Congress that the only spot available was in the 2nd Light Dragoons (according to Washington, La Balme would not accept less than a lieutenant colonel's commission). Congress appointed La Balme Inspector General of the Cavalry on July 8, 1777, and La Balme promptly informed General Washington that he considered his role as inspector general to include training the cavalry. However, no direct evidence of La Balme's activity or training of the Continental cavalry has been found.[25]

Whatever La Balme's role in the development of American cavalry may have been, it was overshadowed to the point of obscurity by the appointment of Polish volunteer Count Casimir Pulaski as general of the Continental cavalry on September 15, 1777. La Balme resigned on October 3, and expressed his dissatisfaction with Pulaski in his letter to Congress: "I saw I had orders to receive from a young man who (I dare say without any ostentation) is very far from the knowledge and experience I acquired about Cavalry." La Balme's opinion regarding Pulaski's lack of experience was shared by another Continental officer, Maj. Gen. Charles Lee. A man with extensive military experience in Europe, Lee believed that Pulaski was a good soldier, but perhaps not a good cavalry commander. Lee recommended that the strength of Pulaski's Legion be increased by assigning Maj. Henry Lee's cavalry to it. Charles Lee wrote:

> [B]ecause on Pulesky's principle of exercise (which I verily believe to be the best in the world) none but very young men are capable of being trained to the maneuvers—but it is not certain that either Count Pulesky or Major Lee understand the detail of Cavalry (on which so much depends) let some Quarter Masters or Serjeants who have served in the British Cavalry (and there are many on the continent) be found out, encourag'd with rank and emolument and employed—a Corps thus compos'd with brave and understanding Officers at their head, such as are Pulesky and Lee with a few subordinate officers knowing in the detail will render more effectual service than any ten Regiments on the Continent.[26]

Perhaps in response to La Balme's resignation, Congress appointed François-Louis Teissèdre, Marquis de Fleury, as brigade major under Pulaski. Within weeks, Fleury was transferred to Fort Mifflin to serve as an engineer. Since Fleury had been trained as an engineer, it was unlikely that he had much influence on the Continental Light Dragoons during his brief service with them. However, in a letter written on behalf of Fleury in 1779, George Washington noted that Fleury had "served as Brigade Major with the rank of Major first in the infantry and afterwards in the cavalry, in which stations he acquired reputation in the army and the approbation of his commanding officers, of which he has the most ample testimonies."[27]

Another French officer involved with the Continental cavalry was William Galvan. Before arriving in America in 1776, Galvan had been serving in a French regiment in the West Indies. Galvan stated that he had served as a captain in the French Army, but in which branch is unknown. He arrived in South Carolina, and initially could only secure a commission as a second lieutenant in that state's Continental infantry. Eventually he made his way north and worked for the remainder of the war with von Steuben, assisting the Prussian in his duties as the Continental Army's inspector general. Galvan also spent much of his time in 1779 and 1780 trying to secure a lieu-tenant colonel's commission.[28]

Galvan developed plans for both infantry drill and cav-alry maneuvers. He submitted them to George Washington, and Galvan claimed his ideas on cavalry were well received, writing to the commander-in-chief that he welcomed the news that "your Excellency has been pleased to approve my specimens for the manoeuvers of Cavalry." Galvan managed to train some troops in his maneuvers, and by December of 1780 felt that his work qualified him to serve as the inspector of the cavalry, which had then been formed into legionary corps. His request was denied by Washington, primarily because Galvan was not a major in the cavalry, and could not supersede an officer in that line. No copy of the cavalry maneuvers that Galvan submitted to Washington has been found. Galvan's prior service and the identity of the troops he trained could prove to be important, but without such information it is impossible to assess his influence on the Continental cavalry. His work and service prior to and during the Revolution deserve further study.[29]

The last French soldier who may have helped to shape American cavalry doctrine, Pierre-François Vernier, served as a French cavalry officer during the Seven Years' War. He was later assigned to a unit in the French West Indies before coming to America in 1776. Vernier was assigned to Pulaski's Legion; unfortunately, his service is not well documented. Records do show that Vernier took command of the remnants of Pulaski's Legion after that unit suffered heavy losses during the assault on Savannah, Georgia, in October 1779. In this capacity Vernier went on to work directly with William Washington in South Carolina in the spring of 1780. Vernier played a key role in one of the most coordinated American cavalry-only actions of the war at Rantowles Bridge but later died from wounds received at Moncks Corner.[30]

AUSTRIAN INFLUENCES

Mention must be made of Peter William Joseph Ludwig, the Baron de Glaubeck, since he served with William Washington during part of the southern campaign. Most primary sources describe Glaubeck as a fraud, while his military experience is rarely mentioned. For example, John Eager Howard, who had served in the South as a lieutenant colonel in the Maryland Line, wrote, "We had a German a volunteer who had been in the Hussars in Europe. He called himself the Baron Glauback, but turned out to be an imposter." Howard's commander, Maj. Gen. Nathanael Greene, apparently had more faith in Glaubeck's credibility. Writing to James Varnum in 1781, Greene said that Glaubeck "has been serving in the American Army as a volunteer upwards of two years. He is a Capt Lt in the Austrian service." Thorough research into Glaubeck finds no mention of Glaubeck's prior military service or experience as being fraudulent. Any references to him as a fraud deal specifically with money. Glaubeck acquitted himself well at the Battle of Hammond's Store in December 1780 and at the Battle of Cowpens, South Carolina, on January 17, 1781. He performed effectively, leading a North Carolina unit at Ramsey's Mill two months later. Until proof is found that refutes Glaubeck's service record in Europe, he ought to be given credit for knowing something about cavalry tactics.[31]

## POLISH INFLUENCES

Count Casimir Pulaski was appointed an officer in the Continental Army because of his experience fighting for the Confederation of Bar in Poland, where he commanded what was probably a mixed force of cavalry and light infantry from 1768 to 1771. Pulaski's suggestions for improving the American cavalry emphasized several themes, including augmentation of the cavalry and increased training. Pulaski also wanted to create a troop of lancers, since he had experience with such units in Poland. While Pulaski's suggestions to George Washington on improving the cavalry contained many ideas that seem to have been based on the former's experience, Pulaski was also willing to surround himself with knowledgeable and capable officers. His first recommendation was that Henry Bedkin be assigned to serve as his adjutant; at the time, Bedkin was assigned to the 4th Light Dragoons under Stephen Moylan, an officer with whom Pulaski frequently disagreed.[32]

Pulaski had a solid general understanding of the role of cavalry. Because of the limited size of the authorized Continental cavalry, he recommended that Washington employ mounted militia to carry out some of the light cavalry duties, and tried to restrict or at least control these duties in proposals he made to Washington. Pulaski was also very aware of what a strong cavalry could and could not do, particularly in the event the infantry suffered a defeat. In Pulaski's opinion, having a strong cavalry force available in reserve in the event of defeat could prevent a rout.[33]

Pulaski provided Washington with his assessment of the Continental mounted force in a letter of December 29, 1777:

> I make no doubt but your Excellency is acquaint-ed with the present ineffective State of the Cavalry. In this Situation it cannot be appropriated to any other Service then that of orderlys or recon-noitering the enemys Lines, which your Excellency must be persuaded is not the only Service expected from a Corps, when on a proper footing is so very formidable—Although it is the opinion of many that from the construction of the Country, the cavalry cannot act to advantage, Your Excellency must be too well acquainted with the many instances, wherein the Cavalry have been decisively Servicable, to be of this opinion, & not Acknowledge that this Corps has more then once completed Victorys."[34]

Pulaski suggested that Washington adopt regulations for the cavalry similar to those used in Prussia. Pulaski also requested that two hundred militia be mounted for light cavalry duties—he felt that two months would allow him enough time to complete the required training for these men. He went on to propose the appointment of a master of exercise to "inspect into the exercise and instruct the officers in their several duties." In terms of augmenting the strength of each troop in the cavalry, he stated that he had several men in mind who had served in the cavalry and addressed the lack of experience among the American officers: "We are deficient in officers Skilled in the Service of the Cavalry."[35]

It may have been around this time that Pulaski first suggested Michael Kovats for the master of exercise posi-tion. Pulaski believed that because he was in command, there might be a conflict if he had to fill the role of master of exercise himself in order to "correct the defects of the Superior officers." Pulaski insisted that the Continental cavalry "must be exercised & taught the Service from the Colo to the private." Washington recognized the value of what Pulaski was trying to accomplish. In his instructions of December 31, the commander-in-chief encouraged Pulaski to perfect the men in exercise, and even suggested forming a riding school. On January 14, 1778, Washington approved the appointment of Kovats as the exercise master, and over the next four weeks, Pulaski formulated his own regulations for the cavalry. Regrettably, a copy of these regulations has never been found.[36]

## Prussian Influences

The appointment of Michael Kovats is seldom mentioned in discussions of cavalry in the American Revolution. Kovats was discussed in a letter from quartermaster Henry Lutterloh to John Laurens, written on January 15, 1778, in which Lutterloh wrote that Pulaski "wishes also to have that famous col Covatch who served all last war with such a distinction with his own corps of 2000 men under the king of Prussia who gave him the Pour le Merite, here are officers and men who served under him, and he could get men enough. Pulasky wants him as his Excercising master, he will be better for that than the Frenchman we had Mosr Delabalme before who did never serve in Light Troops."

On February 4, Pulaski wrote that he hoped to begin the general exercise in fifteen days. Unfortunately, Pulaski never finished what he started. He submitted his resignation on February 28.[37]

The brief period of Michael Kovats's service as the Continental cavalry's master of exercise receives little attention compared with his subsequent appointment as colonel commandant of the cavalry of Pulaski's Legion.

Pulaski and Kovats made great efforts to turn their cavalry into an effective force, and the improvement of the Legion's mounted arm drew high praise from the British. After a clash outside Charleston, South Carolina, in 1779, during which Michael Kovats was killed, British brigade major Francis Skelly called Pulaski's horsemen "the Finest cavalry the rebels ever had."[38]

Michael Kovats. (*Barry Grant*)

Much of the credit for the development of the American cavalry belongs to Michael Kovats. Born in Hungary, he served as a hussar in the Austrian Army in the first Silesian War (1741–1742). Shortly afterward, for reasons that remain unclear, he joined or was forced to join the First Regiment of Hussars in the Prussian Army of Frederick the Great. He participated in several major battles while serving with the Prussians, and was universally praised by his superior officers. After leaving the Prussian Army, he returned to his native Hungary, where Empress Maria Theresa commissioned him a major in his former hussar regiment. When he met Benjamin Franklin in France to offer his services to the new United States, Kovats was eminently qualified to serve in and train cavalry.[39]

Given the nature of the role expected by George Washington for the American light dragoons, Kovats was the best officer to train the Continental cavalry. In Pulaski's opinion, Washington would need heavy cavalry as well, and Kovats's experience in Europe prepared him to train such a force. In the army of Frederick the Great, cavalry officers of all branches were required to train in a hussar regiment. In fact, hussars in the Prussian Army frequently functioned as heavy cavalry in battle.[40]

What was the extent of Michael Kovats's influence on the development of the Continental cavalry? This is a difficult question to answer. There is no direct proof that Kovats specifically instructed, trained, or influenced William Washington. If Kovats did influence the field officers of the Continental cavalry, why does Washington appear to be the primary example of that influence?

There were twelve cavalry field officers in the four Continental Light Dragoon regiments at the end of 1777:

*1st Regiment*
Col. Theodorick Bland—serving in Congress as of 1781.
Lt. Col. Benjamin Temple—transferred to the 4th Regiment on December 10, 1779.
Maj. John Jameson—promoted to lieutenant colonel of the 2nd Regiment on August 1, 1779.

*2nd Regiment*
Col. Elisha Sheldon—served until the end of the war.
Lt. Col. Samuel Blagden—resigned on August 1, 1779.
Maj. Benjamin Tallmadge—served until the end of the war.

*3rd Regiment*
Col. George Baylor—taken prisoner on September 28, 1778, effectively out of service.
Lt. Col. Francis Otway Byrd—resigned in July 1778.
Maj. Alexander Clough—killed on September 28, 1778.

*4th Regiment*
Col. Stephen Moylan—served until the end of the war.
Lt. Col. Anthony Walton White—promoted to command of the 1st Regiment on December 10, 1779.
Maj. William Washington—promoted to command the 3rd Regiment on November 20, 1778.[41]

At least five of the original twelve field officers were no longer actively serving when the year 1777 came to a close. Three (Sheldon, Tallmadge, and Jameson) continued to serve with the 2nd Light Dragoons. Moylan had his own personal conflicts with Pulaski, which may explain how little he was influenced by Pulaski's and Kovats's tactics. White never served with distinction as a cavalry field commander.[42]

What remains, and what is most important to the issue of Kovats's influence, is the role of William Washington in the South in the campaigns of 1780–1781. No Continental cavalry commander was more active in combat during that time span, and the fact that Washington served as a field officer during the period of Pulaski's leadership is hardly coincidental.

Given Washington's exposure to European cavalry officers, including La Balme, Pulaski, and Kovats, and Washington's subsequent performance in battle, it is reasonable to assume that officers trained in European cavalry tactics improved Washington's ability to lead cavalry. Despite the absence of direct evidence for such an assertion, Ira Gruber has suggested that it is reasonable to examine the accepted military thought of an era and draw conclusions based on its content and influence. Analyzing what William Washington did in combat, in light of Gruber's premise, points to the conclusion that the most important influence on Washington was Michael Kovats.[43]

As previously noted, there is only circumstantial evidence that Kovats actually trained American light dragoons, and it can likewise only be speculated that William Washington was the beneficiary of that training. However, adding to the probability that Washington had been exposed to the tactics of Michael Kovats is the known fact that Washington had worked closely with several of the officers who served under Pulaski and Kovats.

In addition to serving with Vernier in South Carolina, Washington also had a close relationship with Cornet James Simons. The South Carolinian served as Washington's adjutant for part of the war and had originally served under Pulaski. Simons may have been with Pulaski when the count was mortally wounded before Savannah in 1779. Simons was one of Washington's most trusted officers and continued to study cavalry operations after the Revolutionary War. Other officers of Pulaski's cavalry held a high opinion of William Washington. On March 24, 1780, three of them—Jerome La Brun de Bellecour, Baptiste Verdier, and Louis de Beaulieu— wrote to Maj. Gen. Benjamin Lincoln regarding the planned incorporation of the remainder of Pulaski's Legion into the Continental Army. The three officers specifically requested that they be assigned to Washington's command.[44]

It must be assumed that cavalry tactics were discussed at great length among the officers of the Continental cavalry serving in the South, especially given the lack of uniform training, drill, and any official tactical doctrine. During the time that William Washington was beginning to exercise his command of cavalry in battle and experimenting with the role that he would assume under Nathanael Greene, he was continuously exposed to men who had served under Pulaski and Kovats.

## THE END RESULT

Although it can be proven that William Washington was well acquainted with some of Pulaski's and Kovats's officers, there is no direct proof that he received any training or instruction in contemporary European tactics. However, another approach may provide insight. If the Prussian cavalry was considered the best cavalry in Europe, and Washington was exposed to both Prussian officers and European officers who had experience fighting the Prussian cavalry, can that influence be seen in his own tactics? The answer to this question can be found in Washington's employment of his mounted troops in the role of heavy cavalry, rather than in the light cavalry role that George Washington had envisioned for the Continental Light Dragoon regiments.

Further support for the theory that William Washington was influenced by Prussian cavalry doctrine can be found in the ideas and experience of his commanding officer during much of the southern campaign, Maj. Gen. Nathanael Greene. By the time Greene took command of Continental forces in the South in early December 1780, he had begun to show that he had been influenced by Frederick the Great. This was in large part due to the influence of Baron von Steuben, with whom Greene had spent a month. Greene even quoted from an as-yet-untranslated work of Frederick's *Military Instructions to His Generals*, published in 1768. While Greene never made direct references to the Prussian cavalry, he did compare his own army favorably to the Prussians. On September 17, 1781, he wrote to von Steuben regarding his soldiers' performance at the Battle of Eutaw Springs that "the gallantry of the officers and the bravery of the troops would do honor even to the arms of his Prussian Majesty."[45]

Greene also demonstrated an expanded view of the use of cavalry. On numerous occasions, he stated that if he had larger numbers of cavalry he could more effectively oppose the British. He told Alexander Hamilton on January 10, 1781, that he wished he had an additional "eight hundred to a thousand horse," predicting, "could we get a superiority of horse we could soon render it difficult for Lord Cornwallis to hold his position so far in the Country."[46]

Greene always kept Washington's cavalry close at hand, believing them to be indispensable in a general engagement. Greene was acutely aware of the role that a mounted force could play in a battle. Based on his experience with Washington's Light Dragoons, he felt that it was the best unit available to perform a role he considered important, that of heavy cavalry. There can be no doubt that Greene and William Washington discussed employing the cavalry in such a manner, although there is no surviving correspondence between them that mentions the topic. However, before the Battle of Cowpens, Greene instructed Daniel Morgan "to have Lt Col Washington's horse kept in as good order as possible and let the militia Light horse do all the fatigue duty. We may want a body of heavy cavalry, and if they are broken down on common duty we shall have nothing to depend upon."[47]

This statement reveals a great deal about Greene's tactical thinking. If the need arose for heavy cavalry in battle, he felt that Washington's regiment was the best prepared to fill that role. Greene also indicated that he believed militia cavalry were well suited for the light cavalry role. In scouting, reconnaissance, and screening, they may well have been the equal of the Continentals. Furthermore, Greene saw the potential for using William Washington's cavalry in battle in a way that had not yet been done during the war.

Other officers recognized this capability in Washington and his mounted troops. Lt. Col. Henry Lee, who had plenty of experience leading cavalry, described Washington as "bold, collected, and persevering, he preferred the heat of action to the collection and sifting of intelligence, to the calculations and combinations of means and measures, and was better fitted to the field of battle than for the drudgery of camp and the watchfulness of preparation." Referring to Washington's character as well as his military skills, Lt. Col. John Eager Howard observed that "Colo Washington with whom I was on the most intimate and cordial terms had not the activity of Lee and was not so well calculated for a partisan, but when he charged with his horse, he put himself in front of the column."[48]

In William Washington, Greene had the heavy cavalry commander he needed. In Greene, Washington had the commanding officer who could best utilize the abilities of his force. It can be argued that Greene's use of cavalry was not always the most judicious, but even Frederick the Great complained that his general officers did not always know how to use cavalry. In filling the role of heavy cavalry in 1781, Washington demonstrated that he had absorbed the lessons of the European cavalry commanders, and done so more thoroughly than other American-born Continental cavalry officers.

The Continental, state, and militia cavalry of the American army did not receive the formal training and discipline that the Continental infantry did. There were, however, efforts to professionalize the cavalry. Manuals, as yet undiscovered, were written. But clearly the Continental Light Dragoons were created to function as light cavalry. In that role, through the end of the war, they succeeded. But William Washington, in North and South Carolina, did something more.

The search for a Continental cavalry manual turned up an extremely valuable source on cavalry in the eighteenth century. Karl Emmanuel von Warnery, a Prussian general of hussars, wrote several books on the Prussian Army. His *Remarks on Cavalry*, published in 1781, was translated into French and English. As noted earlier, British cavalry officers praised the volume, and it was highly regarded well into the Napoleonic era. Warnery's work was truly original; no other text so thoroughly described cavalry tactics and how a cavalry officer should think on the battlefield.[49]

Perhaps most remarkable is that in many ways Warnery's work describes what the Continental cavalry was doing in the Carolinas in 1781. More specifically, Warnery provided justification for nearly everything that William Washington did, tactically, in the major battles of 1781 in the southern theater. An examination of four general principles illustrates the connection between what William Washington did and what Warnery recommended that an officer in his position should do.

First, much has been made of Washington's orders to his men not to use firearms during battle. Howard mentioned this in reference to the Battle of Cowpens. While such an order is not specifically mentioned in sources for other battles, a letter written by Maj. Richard Call reinforces the evidence that Washington gave such orders. Call described the sword as "the most destructive and only necessary weapon a dragoon carries." Washington's order to rely solely on the sword was standard operating procedure in European cavalry forces at the time.[50]

One of the controversies in cavalry tactical thought in the first half of the eighteenth century concerned the use of firearms. Until the middle of the century, cavalry forces would still fire either their pistols or carbines before, or instead of, charging. But as early as the turn of the century, King Charles XII of Sweden forbade the use of firearms by his cavalry. In Prussia, this tradition was first institutionalized by King Frederick Wilhelm, and continued by his son, Frederick the Great.[51] William Washington ordered his men not to use firearms because it was accepted cavalry practice in Europe.

The second example of how Prussian influence can be inferred from Washington's actions occurred at the Battle of Eutaw Springs, South Carolina, on September 8, 1781. Many historians have criticized Washington for his failure to obey Greene's order to attack British troops protected by thick brush in conjunction with Capt. Robert Kirkwood's Continental infantry. Instead, Washington attacked with his cavalry alone and was repulsed. Warnery would have supported Washington's decision. The Prussian very clearly explained that using infantry reserves in such a manner was unwise, since cavalry could reach any point on the battlefield much more quickly. In fact, waiting for infantry would have negated any advantage that the cavalry had in acting as a reserve. Speed and momentum were the advantages that cavalry had against enemy infantry. Slowed to the speed of its own advancing infantry, any attached cavalry would have been devastated by fire before they could be brought into action. They simply could not defend themselves except by acting offensively.[52]

The third conspicuous example of Washington employing European tactics was the flexibility of his force. It is clear that at the battles of Cowpens, Guilford Courthouse, Hobkirk's Hill, Eutaw Springs, and perhaps at Hammond's Store as well, Washington's cavalry was able to function effectively as heavy cavalry. But with the exception of these five engagements, Washington's force provided an effective light cavalry for Nathanael Greene's army.

Operating in this dual role, which in some measure had been forced on the Continental cavalry by circumstances, was standard in the Prussian Army. As noted, commanding officers of all cavalry branches of the Prussian cavalry were expected to spend some time training with the hussar regiments. One of the greatest Prussian cavalry generals, Friedrich Wilhelm von Seydlitz, was originally trained as a hussar. His regiment of cuirassiers was considered the standard for the Prussian cavalry. Prussian hussars, in addition to performing their traditional light cavalry role, were expected to act as heavy cavalry on the battlefield. The history of the Prussian army is full of examples of hussars, though nominally light cavalry, functioning as heavy cavalry in battle.[53]

Finally, two battles of 1781 stand out as occasions when the actions of the American cavalry conformed perfectly to Prussian cavalry tactics. New analysis of the Battle of Cowpens has changed current thinking regarding cavalry action there. The two most recent studies, Lawrence E. Babits's book *A Devil of a Whipping* and Daniel Murphy's article "Cavalry at Cowpens," both tackle confusing and often conflicting primary and secondary sources. At times it appears that William Washington and his cavalry were everywhere on the battlefield—and sometimes in two places at once. This was simply not the case. Washington's four charges during the battle, neatly spelled out by James Simons, were in line both with his appointed role as a reserve and his orders from Daniel Morgan to take advantage of any opportunities that arose. In pursuing the British 17th Light Dragoons around the American left flank, Washington found himself in a position to accomplish three simultaneous goals, all of which were consistent with Prussian cavalry tactical thought. First, part of Washington's regiment was sent in pursuit of the fleeing 17th Light Dragoons to prevent their returning to the battlefield. Second, Washington found himself on the British right, in a perfect position to strike the infantry in the flank. Third, Washington found himself in a position to disrupt the British rear and interfere with British command and control. While this last goal was never explicitly stated in Prussian writings, it is an objective that Washington nearly accomplished three times. The first was at Cowpens, and the second at Guilford Courthouse when he nearly captured Lord Cornwallis. The third was at Hobkirk's Hill, where some sources suggest that his dragoons may have temporarily captured the British commander, Lord Rawdon. The actions of Washington's cavalry at the Battle of Cowpens are a solid example of the Prussian concept of the correct way to employ cavalry in battle.[54]

Studies of the Battle of Hobkirk's Hill usually include criticism of Washington and his cavalry. He is accused of making too wide a circuit to get in the rear of the British force, of encumbering himself with prisoners, and of being unable to support Greene when necessary. This judgment is inconsistent with what Washington hoped to accomplish. Detaching cavalry in a wide circuit around the enemy flank to gain the rear was an accepted tactic in the Prussian cavalry. Closer analysis has revealed that Washington did in fact encounter combatants, and, as at Cowpens, disrupted the British rear.[55]

CONCLUSION

Cavalry in all forms played a decisive role in the southern campaigns of 1780 and 1781. Continental, state, and militia mounted soldiers filled a variety of roles. However, research on cavalry in the American Revolution has been limited, and thus the contributions of the American cavalry have too often been overlooked. Because of the admittedly small numbers of troops involved, cavalry actions do not receive as much attention as infantry battles. Even with the recent use of veterans' pension applications to shed additional light on the war, pension applications filed by men who served in the cavalry have so far provided little new information. Researchers cannot, however, be content with assuming that there are no sources that can be explored to aid in understanding the cavalry of the Revolution.

American cavalry did not develop its doctrines and practices in a bubble. It was a product of the eighteenth century, and was influenced by contemporary European ideas. Continental cavalry tactics had an intellectual pedigree, and it was European, and especially Prussian. The Continental cavalry also had a legacy.

In 1799, Maj. Gen. Charles Cotesworth Pinckney was charged with systematizing training and tactics for the American cavalry. He immediately turned to William Washington for guidance, telling Alexander Hamilton that he had "written to Brigadr. Genl. Washington to meet me here the middle of February to assist in forming a System for the Cavalry, by that time I hope you will be able to procure for me the British Exercise & maneuvers. I have not the plates of the French System. I have lately read with much pleasure Genl. Warnery's remarks on Cavalry, he was highly esteemed in the Prussian Service & deemed the next Horse Officer to Genl. Seydlitz."[56]

During the Revolution, William Washington transformed his Continental cavalry regiment into an effective professional force in the mold of the Prussian hussars. Nearly two decades after the war ended, his skills were sought in applying the same lessons to the cavalry of the independent United States.

# THREE

# Cavalry Action at Poundridge, New York

## Bloody Ban's Early Education

### *John Milton Hutchins*

ONE OF BRITISH LIEUTENANT COLONEL BANASTRE Tarleton's former officers, twenty years after the Siege of Yorktown, made a prediction that proved absolutely correct. "Should I live to a good old age," wrote George Hanger, "I am confident that I shall hear of the Northern and Southern powers in America waging war with each other." However, what Hanger could not have known was that, many years after the American Civil War, North and South still would be fighting, and the fighting would be about Tarleton and his contemporaries. This fighting would be among parochial historians, amateur

The author respectfully dedicates this paper to the memory of his friend John Bowman McLeod, Esq., a 1972 graduate of Wofford College (studying under Professor Lewis Pinckney Jones, among others) and a brother officer serving with the First Cavalry Division, 1976–1980. The late Captain McLeod was planning to attend this Revolutionary War Cavalry Conference at the time of his sudden death.

and professional, who would be debating which region suffered more in the War for American Independence and who contributed more to the ultimate victory.[1]

For example, the historian for the South Carolina Society Sons of the American Revolution, recently fired a shell in this war between kin. "The South largely won the War for the other colonies," wrote Joseph Goldsmith, indignant at the use of the word "skirmish" as it related to the war in the Carolinas. "We did it with non-glamorous guerilla and ambush tactics," he opined.[2]

Of course, South Carolina does have a stake in this heated battle without bullets. Professor Lewis Pinckney Jones of Wofford College more accurately wrote prior to the American Bicentennial Celebration that "the Palmetto State saw as much war as any state—one hundred thirty-seven battles, according to one respected authority. True, many of these battles were basically part of a civil war, and many 'battles' were hardly more than 'shooting scrapes,' but then there were others that truly and significantly affected the outcome of the war which gave America its independence."[3]

But as Professor Jones knew, one must not forget that this was the *American* Revolution. There were thirteen states that decided to hang together, desperately holding on to the Declaration of Independence. And while the theater of most active warfare might shift from Massachusetts to New York to New Jersey to Pennsylvania to Georgia and the Carolinas to Virginia, it was a war national in scope. Rhode Island and Connecticut felt the devastation. Maryland, Delaware, and New Hampshire contributed their regiments and their heroes.

Certainly, South Carolina in particular suffered during the last several years of fighting. Its principal city was occupied till the bitter end; it had a large and active loyalist minority, along with hostile Indians on the frontier. Could any other state compare with those travails?

New York not only compared, its situation was almost identical. "New York, more than any other colony," wrote a New Yorker a hundred years ago who was almost as strident as Mr. Goldsmith, "was the battle-ground of the war, as indeed, from its position, it always will be in any conflict with Great Britain. . . . New York [had a] trying position in the Revolutionary War . . . and was second to none of the thirteen colonies."[4]

This is something that Southerners, especially Southerners who glory in the mounted exploits of William Washington, Francis Marion, Harry Lee, Wade Hampton, Peter Horry, and William R. Davie, must remember. There was a war going on up north, and it was ever-present and often brutal. "Bloody Ban" Tarleton started his military career in the north, where John Graves Simcoe, who made it only as far south as Yorktown, was Bloody Ban's early tutor when it came to hating Americans and in the corrupting power of an independent command. Yes, there was continued fighting up north, and much of it was of the hit-and-run cavalry variety.

## NO-MAN'S-LAND IN WESTCHESTER COUNTY

With New York City occupied by the British since 1776, the area between this stronghold and the Whig territories of the Hudson Highlands around Peekskill became a no-man's-land. The loyalists who inhabited the highlands naturally were not popular. As Washington Irving was later to write: "A number of these took refuge within the British lines, joined the military bands of refugees, and became pioneers or leaders to foraging parties sent out from New York to scour the country and sweep off supplies for the British army." Because these loyalist refugees were usually mounted and often herded stolen cattle, they were called "Cow Boys."[5]

The situation in this area, Westchester County, soon approximated, in principle if not in degree and scope of ferocity, the situation in the backcountry of the Carolinas.

Again according to Irving: "In a little while the debatable ground became infested by roving bands, claiming from either side, and all pretending to redress wrongs and punish political offences; but all prone in the exercise of their high functions, to sack hen-roosts, drive off cattle, and lay farm houses under contribution."[6]

While Irving was a novelist, he actually sanitized the situation for a reading public. David Humphreys, an aide-de-camp to Gen. George Washington, recalled that he came across a desolate homestead in Westchester County once belonging to a prosperous family of eight or nine. The father, accused of being a loyalist, had fled to New York City. The mother was dead. This left a girl of fifteen to try to provide for her siblings. When Humphreys saw her, the careworn teenager said that their "last cow, which furnished milk for the children, had been taken away" and that she "knew not where to procure bread for the dear little ones." Later, Humphreys heard that marauders had again raided the house and the girl had fled, half-clothed, into a swamp, where she caught cold and soon died of the resulting pneumonia. Humphreys's tale mirrors many that could be told of the Carolinas.[7]

Thus the residents of the so-called "Neutral Ground" of Westchester County, like the citizens in the Carolinas, were trapped in a war zone and were victims of political forces that they could not control. Furthermore, since the countryside had scattered villages and numerous roads and wooded, dark byways situated between two armed camps, it was a region that invited, in addition to mere bushwhacking and murder, cavalry strikes and counterstrikes.

The British adherents were well represented for this type of low-intensity mounted warfare. DeLancey's Refugee Corps were regularly enlisted loyalists made up of four troops of light horse and seven companies of infantry. Also patrolling for the British were the mounted infantry of Lt. Col. Andreas Emmerich's Chasseurs and mounted Hessian Jaegers. In the spring of 1779, a Captain von Diemar organized a troop of hussars consisting of escaped Brunswickers who had been captured two years earlier at the Battle of Bennington. In addition, other British cavalry units were augmented for duty in Westchester County, including Lt. Col. Simcoe's Queen's Rangers, who recruited two companies of hussars, and Colonel Lord Cathcart's newly formed British Legion, whose infantry was augmented by the addition of several troops of dragoons.[8]

On the Whig side, there also were numerous mounted adherents. While the so-called Skinners were the Whig equivalent to the not-too-discriminating ruffians found among the Cow Boys, there also were some true patriots. According to a Westchester resident who interviewed many participants some fifty years later, "these bands, like those of their adversaries, consisted of both horse and foot, and held themselves ready at all times, for a march against their royal antagonists. In large operations, they never failed to accompany the regular troops. . . . Great pains had been taken in teaching them the military duties required of horsemen, by several officers who had belonged to the hussars or light dragoons of France or Germany." These mounted patriots, according to this account, found "fire-arms almost useless when in the saddle, [and] soon learned to place their entire reliance upon a powerful steed and a good broad-sword."[9]

Often augmenting these local defenders were two under-strength Continental regiments of dragoons, Elisha Sheldon's 2nd Light Horse and Stephen Moylan's 4th Light Horse. Prominent among Sheldon's officers was Maj. Benjamin Tallmadge. In addition to having some familiarity with this area of New York, Tallmadge was the ideal man to command cavalry in the rough-and-tumble conflict taking place there. "He was a large, strong, and powerful man and rode a large bay horse which he took from the British," wrote William Patchin of Connecticut. "He was a brave officer, and there was no flinch in him."

Additionally, since Tallmadge acted as the Continental Army's chief spymaster, the major often was in direct communication with General Washington.[10]

## THE 2ND CONTINENTAL DRAGOONS POSTED AT POUNDRIDGE

While the major field of operations began to shift south-ward, surprise attacks on exposed outposts remained one of the constants of the fighting in the North. These "enterprizes" were calculated to maintain morale and to keep the enemy off balance by "beating their quarters." Units of cavalry on both sides participated in such forays. Sometimes the mounted units were the predators and sometimes they were the prey.

The British, under Lt. Gen. Sir Henry Clinton, were especially active in these hit-and-run raids in the spring of 1779, striking into Connecticut and New Jersey as well as New York. While not all of the sorties were performed by British or loyalist cavalry, many were. Westchester County in particular was a target for these military attacks. But these British raids were mere diversions against isolated patrols and videttes. These actions would pale in compar-ison to the glory of bagging a whole regiment of Continental dragoons. At least, this was the idea that began to take form in the mind of General Clinton.

General Washington, meanwhile, had suggested to Major Tallmadge that the cavalry of the 2nd Continental Dragoons be posted in the vicinity of Bedford, with the commanding officer being allowed to pick the exact loca-tion, as long as it was "near enough the enemy to give assistance to the people" and still not "unnecessarily exposed or fatigued." Tallmadge, on June 27, wrote his commanding general that the neighborhood proposed by him was "very insecure," and that "Bedford is an open Country with many Roads leading to it, too many for the whole Detachmt. to occupy, much less defend."[11]

The village of Poundridge, however, was several miles east of Bedford, and therefore less exposed to the usual routes used by the British and loyalists. Consequently,

Colonel Sheldon and about ninety men of his 2nd
Dragoon regiment occupied this crossroads village. But
local residents could have provided a warning to the patriots who might have thought the place more secure than
Bedford. Poundridge had acquired its name as a location
where in former times Indians had been able, due to the
terrain, to catch game in a sort of natural pen or pound
along a ridge.[12]

However, Poundridge certainly seemed hospitable
enough for Sheldon and his officers, who were guests in
the home of prominent Whig captain Ezra Lockwood.
Sheldon's troopers were not that much worse off, apparently being quartered in the community's Presbyterian
Meeting House across the road from Lockwood's place.[13]

Adding to the sense of security shared by the blue-coat-
ed 2nd Dragoons was the knowledge that Moylan's green-
coated regiment was expected to move into the area soon.
Indeed, on June 27, Washington had written Tallmadge,
"Colonel Moylan's regiment is on its march to join you,
which will render the duty easier, and your troops there
more respectable."[14]

Unknown to the Americans, however, the British had
intercepted a letter from Washington to Tallmadge that
alerted them to the posting of the 2nd Dragoons at
Poundridge. The British apparently even had word that
Sheldon would be expecting Moylan and suspected that
Moylan might already have joined Sheldon. Therefore,
late on the thunderstormy evening of July 1, 1779,
Clinton sent from New York City a mounted force under
the command of young Lt. Col. Banastre Tarleton.
Clinton thought that Tarleton, who previously had served
under Simcoe in the green-coated British Legion, was
ready for his first independent command.[15]

Tarleton already was beginning to make a name for
himself as a partisan fighter. In late 1776, as a cornet, he
had accompanied the 16th Light Dragoons when they
captured American general Charles Lee, Washington's

second-in-command, at White's Tavern in New Jersey. In early 1778, as a captain, Tarleton had gone on the raid that almost caught Maj. Henry Lee napping at Spread Eagle Tavern near Philadelphia. Yet these were only a few of his exploits. Throughout the war, it would be hard to find another officer at the company and field-grade level who was involved in more significant battles and skirmishes than this ambitious officer.

Col. Stephen Moylan, commander of the 4th Continental Light Dragoons. (*Barry Grant*)

Tarleton later reported that he had with him only about two hundred men on this nighttime march, including cavalry and infantry from his legion, a detachment of seventy men from the 17th Light Dragoons, some Queen's Rangers, some hussars, and some jaegers. The hussars were some of Diemar's Black Hussars.[16]

Tarleton's estimate undoubtedly underreported his force. Especially since Tarleton knew that he might be facing both the 2nd and the 4th Continental Light Horse, the later American estimate that there were about 360 men in the British detachment is likely closer to the truth. This figure makes further sense, since the British knew that Captain Lockwood, Sheldon's host, was an officer in the local militia and also knew that there were about another hundred Continental infantrymen and militiamen under a Major Leavenworth watching the southern road between Bedford and Poundridge. Tarleton reported that his intelligence regarding the strength and position of Sheldon's regiment and the one hundred Continental infantry was confirmed at four o'clock on the morning of July 2, but that he could get "no tidings of Morlands [Moylan's] Regt: of Dragoons."[17]

If British spying had told Clinton and Tarleton much, American spies had likewise been doing their best to keep the patriots informed. One of Major Tallmadge's operatives in New York City actually sent a timely message, warning Tallmadge to be on his guard for an attack. However, the letter went astray and ultimately was delivered late. Fortunately, probably after Tarleton and his little army already had started on their way toward Poundridge, another patriot spy, Luther Kinnicutt, had succeed in alerting Captain Lockwood and Colonel Sheldon of the expedition. Since the foul weather significantly slowed the British march, the Continentals had time to take advantage of Kinnicutt's warning.[18]

Despite Kinnicutt's message, Sheldon personally believed that no attack would be made that wet night. Nonetheless, Sheldon took the precaution to have his men on alert and to have their mounts saddled. Captain Lockwood, wiser to the ways of Westchester County, was so sure that the report of an impending attack was accurate that his family sat up all night, fully dressed and ready to depart at first light.[19]

### THE BRIEF CAVALRY CLASH AT POUNDRIDGE

While Sheldon underestimated the effect of the weather on British initiative, the gloomy early morning of July 2 did have an adverse effect on the expedition, especially since Tarleton elected to take the less-traveled northern road out of Bedford toward his objective. Tarleton's Westchester guide missed the junction in the road leading south to Poundridge and the British column, having come within three hundred yards of its objective, failed to realize it, and continued to march eastward toward Ridgefield before the error was noticed.[20]

Sheldon's mounted sentinel near the north road saw the mysterious dragoons trotting past and he conscientiously and wisely galloped the half mile to Poundridge to report the movement to Colonel Sheldon. Sheldon not unnaturally assumed that these seemingly nonthreatening horsemen probably were Moylan's Continentals, merely looking for Sheldon's camp. Nonetheless, Sheldon sent Major Tallmadge northward with a few troopers to make contact with the unidentified unit. He also ordered his men, who had been in the process of unsaddling their mounts, to saddle back up. Meanwhile, having realized that they were on the wrong road, Tarleton's column turned south and apparently headed across the countryside toward the village.[21]

Tallmadge and his men rode up a slope toward the road to Ridgefield. As they mounted the top of the rise, they ran into the lead elements of Tarleton's force coming from the opposite direction. The British advance party was made up of the detachment from the 17th Light Dragoons. Its commander shouted for Tallmadge to surrender, but ordered his men to charge with his next breath.[22]

Tallmadge did not surrender. He wheeled his horse and galloped back to the village, shouting that the British were coming. This warning was timely enough to prevent his regiment from being taken completely by surprise, allowing the 2nd Dragoons to run to their horses and mount. By the time Tarleton's lead elements reached the crossroads village, they found the 2nd Dragoons mounted and waiting behind the Presbyterian Meeting House.[23]

Although it hardly is effective for a mounted force to receive charging enemy horsemen while standing still, Sheldon's men made a brave stand against the British vanguard. According to an early Westchester historian, "Sheldon's men withstood the charge, and then, in turn, became assailants. The hostile cavaliers thereupon became mixed up together, and a scene of wild disorder ensued, where individuals, for several minutes, fought hand to hand." However, while Major Leavenworth's militiamen initially had taken up positions to support Sheldon's Continentals, they quickly took to their heels.

This was because Tarleton was close behind his advance party with the rest of his strike force. Typically for him, he immediately ordered his men to attack. The rest of the 17th Light Dragoons were leading the way down the narrow road, which was bordered by stone walls, ditches, and trees.[24]

Sheldon and his men were overwhelmed by the violence of the main assault. The Continentals broke into a rush to the rear, heading toward Salem. Tarleton ignored the initial resistance in his report, stating simply that "the enemy did not stand the charge a general Route [rout] ensued." While the American trumpeters sounded withdrawal, their British counterparts simultaneously sounded the pursuit.[25]

Tarleton's men had a good time during this part of the engagement at Poundridge. Captain Lockwood's eleven-year-old niece, Prudence Lockwood, later recalled seeing the British dragoons "standing up in their stirrups and shouting and whirling their swords over their heads."[26]

## THE RUNNING FIGHT ON THE ROAD TO STAMFORD

For the American light horsemen, however, this second phase of the action was not a pretty sight. Robert Chambers, the historical novelist, accurately portrayed the chaos. "A mad anxiety to get away from this terrible and overwhelming force thundering on [their] heels under full charge possessed [them] all," he wrote, "and this paramount necessity held shame and fury in abeyance. There was nothing on earth for [them] to do but to ride and try to keep [their] horses from falling headlong on the rocky, slippery road."[27]

But the suppression of regimental esprit de corps was not universal. A few of Sheldon's dragoons refused to keep fleeing, and these troopers stopped, turned about, and engaged in hurried combat. Some carried on a running fight. Others jumped from their mounts and ran into the woods. Several simply gave up and surrendered. But the majority just rode their horses as fast as they could.[28]

Capt. John Buckhout was one of those just trying to get away. He heard a British pursuer shout at him: "Surrender, you damned rebel, or I'll blow your brains out." Buckhout ignored the order and trusted to speed. A bullet fired from the pistol of the pursuing dragoon from the 17th Regiment hit Buckhout's light horseman's helmet and grazed his scalp. Tarleton's rider, disappointed in his marksmanship, called out after Buckhout, "There, you damned rebel, a little more and I should have blown your brains out." Buckhout, as he successfully escaped his opponent, shouted back, "Yes, damn you, a little more and you wouldn't have touched me."[29]

Pvt. Jared Hoyt, another of Sheldon's dragoons, likewise was hard pressed in the speedy contest. One of Tarleton's men, cursing mightily, got within reach of Hoyt and was able to slice some skin and hair from the side of the patriot's head. Hoyt silenced the loudmouthed Briton with a backhanded swing of his saber, cutting the pursuer's cheeks from ear to ear. Hoyt also escaped the British that day. Ironically, Hoyt was from Stamford, Connecticut, the direction in which most of Sheldon's men were fleeing.[30]

While most of the 2nd Dragoons headed southward down the road to Stamford, others attempted to escape eastward on the New Canaan road. In pursuit of these were some of Tarleton's Legion under Sgt. Stephen Jarvis, one of Simcoe's Rangers. As Jarvis came around some bushes and up to a pond, he saw some of his men hacking at an apparently unarmed civilian while the man's wife pleaded for his life. Jarvis arrived in time to save the man, and he escorted the couple back to the house that they had fled.[31]

On the positive side for the Americans, the speed of their departure largely frustrated the plans of Tarleton to bag Sheldon's entire regiment. Tarleton told Clinton that "the difficulty of the country & there being no possibility" of cutting off the Continentals' escape prevented him from capturing the fleeing enemy despite a pursuit "for four Miles on the Stamford & Salem Roads." The New York City loyalist mouthpiece, James Rivington's *Royal Gazette*, in reporting the action, was obvious in its disappointment. "The Rebel officers and men," Rivington reported, "quitted their Jades and threw themselves over the fences to gain the swamp. By so sudden a flight, in so narrow a road, no great impression could be made, only on the rear."[32]

Colonel Sheldon's report of the running engagement was almost in agreement with Rivington's newspaper. Sheldon wrote to Maj. Gen. William Heath: "The enemy pursued hard on our rear for more than two miles, in the course of which a scattering fire was kept up between their advance and our rear and a Constant charge with the sword."[33]

### WHIG RALLY AND TARLETON'S SCORCHED-EARTH BEGINNINGS

Meanwhile, making the occasion one in which the amateurs rescued the professionals, the militia around Poundridge was turning out in force and firing on Tarleton's column. Encouraging the militia's active response was the fact that Tarleton's men were looting the neighborhood and abusing the noncombatants, including the wife of Judge William Fancher. One of the looters, apparently a noncommissioned officer, broke open a chest in the house and, over the protests of Mrs. Fancher, stole papers and put them in his blouse. Naturally, the home of Captain Lockwood did not escape such activity either. Unfortunately, because of Sheldon's skepticism about an attack, the Lockwood family had delayed too long in leaving and was at home when Tarleton's men arrived, although the captain had escaped. "Where is that damned rebel?" demanded a Briton of Mrs. Lockwood. She replied with a Presbyterian tongue-lashing. "Rebel?" she replied. "You are the Rebels, for you are rebelling against the King of Kings!" According to family tradition, Mrs. Lockwood, for her impudence, was struck with a sword, a blow from which she suffered the rest of her life.[34]

While these depredations were going on, Major Leavenworth had succeeded in rallying about four hundred of the local Whigs. Some of these men were shamed into doing their duty by neighborhood women, who jeered from their farmhouses. "Why don't you fight?" they demanded. "Why don't you face the enemy? Come! That's good boys! Do something for the good cause! Strike a blow for Congress!"[35]

The militia, once assembled, was soon pressing the British to leave the village. One militiaman, William Brown, fired his weapon toward the crowd of looters at the Fancher house. His scratch shot hit the noncommissioned officer there and knocked him from his horse, stunned. The wounded man's comrades, thinking him dead, took his spoils and abandoned him. As the wounded Briton started to regain consciousness, Brown, who had reloaded, got closer and shot him dead. Ironically, the victim, while a thief, had prevented his men from physically harming Mrs. Fancher.[36]

Tarleton claimed that he received gunfire from dwellings and outbuildings around Poundridge and along his route of withdrawal. He therefore enthusiastically burned a number of houses in and around Poundridge. "The *Inveteracy* of the inhabitants of Pound ridge & near Bedford in firing from Houses & out Houses obliged me to burn some of their meeting & some of their dwelling Houses with stores," Tarleton wrote. "I proposed to the Militia Terms; that if they wou'd not fire shots from buildings I would not burn. They interpreted my mild proposal wrong, imputing it to fear they persisted in firing till the Torch stopped their Progress." Included in the arson were Captain Lockwood's house and the Presbyterian Meeting House. Several of Tarleton's officers tried to dissuade the young lieutenant colonel from burning the Lockwood home, for it had been used as a hospital for both sides during the brief contest.[37]

The multiplying militia certainly caused Tarleton to withdraw hastily. As Prudence Lockwood was watching the British carry torches to burn her family's house, she saw militiamen firing from a wheat field to the west of Poundridge. She then saw the British, with a cry of "The rebels are upon us!" drop their firebrands, mount, and ride off. However, the speed and direction of their withdrawal also frustrated Major Leavenworth's attempt to cut the British horsemen off with his militia.[38]

This turn of events permitted some of the scattered 2nd Dragoons to make a respectable reappearance. It also allowed Colonel Sheldon to add a positive perspective to his report to General Heath. "The Militia being immediately collected," Sheldon concluded in his account, "we pursued the enemy following them down to [the town of] North Castle Church."[39]

Yet, when it came to Ban Tarleton, even such a withdrawal allowed him to participate in what was becoming a favorite hobby of his. His column, heading back along the less direct route whence they came, paused as they passed through Bedford in order to set fire to the Presbyterian Meeting House there. However, being pressed so closely by the militia, the British fled before the flames became uncontrollable, and the church was saved (only to be burned in another raid by Simcoe later that month).[40]

By the time Tarleton returned safely to his camp in the Bronx, he reported that the mounted infantrymen from his legion were "extremely fatigued by a march of sixty-four miles in twenty-three hours." Tarleton's little army also had with it more than a half dozen Westchester men, kidnapped during the retreat because they were prominent Whigs.[41]

## THE SKIRMISH AT POUNDRIDGE: A SCORECARD

The losses to both sides in the running skirmish at Poundridge were a reflection of the nature of the action, in which neither side was able to get a close-in advantage and come to grips with the enemy. Sheldon's Regiment, in addition to leaving one of its standards in a house at Poundridge to be found and taken by the British, had "one Corporal, one Trumpeter, and eight privates wounded; three Sergeants, one Corporal, and four privates missing; and twelve horses missing."[42]

Major Tallmadge, in his published memoirs, did not speak at length of this affair. He never even noted the losses suffered by his unit. He did, however, regret losing "a fine horse, most of my field baggage, and twenty guineas in cash, which were taken in my valise with my horse." Tallmadge also lost his personal servant, who was wounded and captured along with the equipage.[43]

Tallmadge lost more than just his personal property. In his valise were valuable papers relating to Whig spies in New York City. Washington was not happy with the loss of all of these papers, and he lectured Tallmadge for his neglect regarding them. "The loss of your papers was certainly a most unlucky accident, and shows how dangerous it is to keep papers of any consequence at an advanced post," the general wrote to his young subordinate. "I beg you will take care to guard against the like in future."[44]

As for Tarleton, he puffed up his exploit in his official report, saying that, "while the Greatest Part of the Regiment" escaped, his "estimate" of Sheldon's losses was 26 or 27 killed, wounded, and prisoners. He also claimed to have been "successful in killing wounding & taking 15" of the militia. Tarleton was more accurate elsewhere in his report when he opined that the greatest disgrace to the Continentals was "the Loss of the Standard of the Regiment, and of Helmets, Arms, and Accoutrements" including "Part of the Officers' and Regimental Baggage." The Americans believed British losses to be one dead, four captured, one horse killed, and four horses captured. This estimate was later partially corroborated by Tarleton when he offered to exchange American prisoners for six men he said that he had lost during his fight and withdrawal. However, in his official report, Tarleton described his losses as "trifling": one man killed, one wounded, and one horse killed.[45]

Thus ended what has been called a "little-known skirmish." George Washington, although not happy with the possible effect on his spy network, did not consider the running fight to be of much significance. In a report to the president of Congress, he merely noted that there was "a skirmish between a detachment of [Sheldon's] regiment and a body of the enemy's horse on the morning of the 2d, near Bedford" and that the British destroyed "a meetinghouse and two or three dwelling-houses."[46]

## Direct Results: Patriot Resurgence

As small as it was, the skirmish at Poundridge was one of the most exciting and colorful incidents in the career of the 2nd Continental Light Horse. It was, at least, in the words of historian Gregory Urwin, "a savage melee of clanging sabers and broadswords." And while it exhibited the risks involved when cavalry was posted to the front— where it belonged—compared to other such "enterprizes" by the British against the American cavalry, such as at Old Tappan and Little Egg Harbor, the 2nd Regiment got off quite cheaply. They even had chased Tarleton's vaunted cavalry, although mostly at a distance and with the necessary assistance of the despised militia.[47]

While there was no wanton butchery such as Tarleton was later accused of committing in the South, his arsonist's actions did not do much to win the hearts and minds of the civilian population. In the words of novelist-historian Robert Chambers, "the lightning blow of Tarleton at Poundridge" earned him "nothing and begot a hatred that can never die in American hearts." On the other hand, neither did the affair engender much local confidence in the American light horse. Locals in Westchester County long remembered the confrontation and chase along the Stamford Road as "Sheldon's Race Course."[48]

Not surprisingly, in military terms the American dragoons came out of this small engagement more ready than ever to take on the British and loyalists and to even the score. Indeed, the next month saw a number of aggressive patrols on the part of both the 2nd and the 4th Light Horse regiments. This activity culminated in a large-scale American cavalry raid throughout southern Westchester County in the first week of August. In this little-known combined operation,

Lt. Col. Banastre Tarleton, commander of light dragoons of his British Legion. (*South Caroliniana Library of the University of South Carolina, Columbia*)

hundreds of patriot horsemen and supporting infantry fought several skirmishes with hundreds of British and loyalist opponents. This thirty-hour period of intermittent, albeit coordinated, raiding and fighting probably constituted the largest cavalry battle in the war, excepting only the brief 1781 action at Gloucester Hook, Virginia.

As for Maj. Benjamin Tallmadge, he not only came away from Poundridge with the desire to get back at the British on horseback, he now was a much wiser man. The rebuke from his fatherly commander-in-chief had the desired effect. Tallmadge continued to be involved in espionage, but he was much more careful in protecting his agents. Indeed, prior to Gen. Benedict Arnold's defection,

Tallmadge successfully resisted giving the undercover traitor the names of patriot operatives in New York City.[49]

### DIRECT RESULTS: THE WRONG LESSONS FOR TARLETON

As for the British, Clinton, anxious to send good news to London, forwarded Tarleton's report, where it was published in the *London Gazette* and served to spread the fame of the so-called Green Dragoon. The affair immediately improved the career prospects of Banastre Tarleton, the young British cavalryman.[50]

But for Banastre Tarleton, the egocentric personality, the affair at Poundridge appeared to reinforce some dangerous character traits. Tactically speaking, Tarleton learned that it often was no disadvantage to fly to the attack even when the enemy was alerted. This was a risky lesson, one that would bring Tarleton both bloody victory and ignominious defeat in the South. In addition, Tarleton learned that it was no detriment, as least as far as his superiors and the British press were concerned, to destroy churches and to burn houses down over the heads of women and children. Thus, the somewhat comic-opera skirmish at Poundridge seemingly influenced later British cavalry actions—and related tactics—in the Carolinas.

### POUNDRIDGE'S TWENTY-FIRST-CENTURY EPILOGUE

There is no National Battlefield Park or major New York State Historic Site in the still beautiful and now somewhat exclusive horse country of Pound Ridge Township, although there is a historic marker outside the small Pound Ridge Historical Society building. While recognized in occasional special events by local citizens, the skirmish at Poundridge has been reduced almost to "mere" history. Unlike in the South, people in the Poundridge area are no longer capable of getting angry about such distant events.

But, and amazingly, this "little-known skirmish" has had a measurable effect even in the twenty-first century, especially on the United States' trade deficit, as the result of an incident that occurred just a few miles from Old Poundridge. The regimental color captured by Tarleton's force, and retained by Tarleton, was silk with thirteen alternating red and white stripes, with a lightning-emitting winged thundercloud in the center. On June 14, 2006, at Sotheby's in New York City, this trophy of war, along with three colors taken by Tarleton during the bloody Battle of Waxhaws, were put up for auction by a Tarleton descendant. The captured standard of Sheldon's regiment was sold to an anonymous bidder—reportedly an American—for a record $12,330,000.[51]

Since the flags taken by his legion at Waxhaws also sold for several millions at the same auction, Banastre Tarleton, if he is receiving news at his present location, likely could say: "Crime does pay." But these balance-sheet credits certainly relate only to financial matters, not eternal matters, in which Tarleton's debits would be overwhelming. Now, that is a moral conclusion upon which both parochial New York historians and parochial South Carolina scholars likely would be able to agree.

FOUR

# Cavalry Battles in
# New York and New Jersey

## *Donald J. Gara*

U NLIKE THE AMERICAN CIVIL WAR, WHEN CAVALRY RAIDS were conducted frequently by both sides, very few such raids were undertaken during the American Revolution, as the strength of cavalry forces in both the British and American armies was small. The regular British cavalry in America consisted merely of detachments of the 16th and 17th Light Dragoons. The former regiment returned to England in December 1778 with many of its rank and file drafted into the 17th Light Dragoons, which remained in America until the end of the war. The main cavalry forces available to the British Army were loyalist units to which the British dragoons were sometimes attached. The largest number of loyalist cavalry belonged to the British Legion (six troops), commanded by Lt. Col. Banastre Tarleton, and the Queen's Rangers (five troops), commanded by Lt. Col. John Graves Simcoe. Both units were composed of light infantry contingents as well as mounted soldiers.[1]

The Continental Army fielded more cavalry units than did the British. Four regiments of light dragoons were organized, two in 1776 and another two in 1777. These were augmented by three legions similar in organization to the British Legion and Queen's Rangers in that they included both cavalry and light infantry. The units were the 1st Partisan Corps, created in 1778 and placed under the command of a French officer, Col. Charles Armand Tuffin (Armand's Legion); the 2nd Partisan Corps, or Lee's Legion, formed in 1780 and led by Lt. Col. Henry "Light-Horse Harry" Lee; and Pulaski's Legion, commanded by Brig. Gen. Casimir Pulaski, a Polish officer, and organized in 1778. In addition, there were a few regular independent units of light cavalry, a North Carolina light dragoon corps in Continental service, and mounted state militia.[2]

A cavalry raid is a military operation involving hit-and-run tactics, using the elements of surprise and mobility to catch the enemy unaware and inflict moderate to severe damage prior to escaping before retaliation can be organized. Numerous actions during the War for Independence fall into this category, including three important cavalry engagements in the northern theater: the actions at Westchester, New York, in August 1779; in Middlesex and Somerset counties, New Jersey, in October 1779; and in Hoppertown, New Jersey, in April 1780.

### THE LAST CAVALRY RAID IN WESTCHESTER COUNTY: JOHN GRAVES SIMCOE VERSUS ANTHONY WALTON WHITE, 1779

After capturing it in 1776, the British Army occupied New York City for the remainder of the American Revolutionary War. To protect their most important territory, York (now Manhattan) Island, the British established outposts on Staten and Long islands as a precaution against surprise attacks. However, the biggest danger to the British position was at the northern tip of York Island, where only a small creek, named Spuyten Duyvil Creek by the earlier Dutch inhabitants, separated the island from the mainland (Westchester County). This creek connected the Hudson River on the west side of York Island with the Harlem River to the east. The first bridge across this creek, built in 1693, was named the King's Bridge to honor King William III of England. It was rebuilt in 1713 as a drawbridge. This bridge became an important link in colonial America, as it was part of the Boston Post Road, a major highway connecting Boston with New York City. The route was called a post road because the colonists first used it to deliver mail, but it was later developed into a wagon road.[3]

On January 18, 1779, the bridge suffered some damage from cannon fire during Maj. Gen. William Heath's ill-favored attempt to capture Fort Independence (also know as Redoubt Number 4). It was the largest of all the fortifications in the area and commanded both the Albany and Boston post roads. During the siege, Heath engaged in a cannonade with a Hessian battalion stationed at Hyatt's Tavern just across the bridge on nearby Marble Hill. The bridge was later rebuilt by the Hessians with an additional floating or pontoon bridge erected across the creek.[4] This location became the focal point for posting light troops and cavalry to give alarm and guard against any American troops that approached the area; it also saw use as a base from which to retaliate against raids by the Americans against loyalists in lower Westchester County.

The King's Bridge redoubt was equipped with barracks and brick and stone ovens and was protected by a semicircular earthwork. Its location in present-day Manhattan would be at about 230th Street and Broadway. It was not the only fortification near Spuyten Duyvil Creek. There were a total of sixteen redoubts and forts; some had been built in 1776 by American forces and subsequently taken over by the British, while others had been built by the British after they occupied New York City. The fortifications were located on either side of the creek from the Hudson River to the Harlem River. The seven redoubts on the north side of the creek were at that time in Westchester County, but in the latter part of the nineteenth century that land was absorbed into a newly created Bronx County. There were also five redoubts on the east side of the Harlem River, then part of Westchester County but now also in Bronx County.[5] All of these redoubts were manned by British, Hessian or provincial infantry who provided support to the light troops and cavalry posted at the King's Bridge redoubt.

Lt. Col. John Graves Simcoe. (*Barry Grant*)

Sometime after midnight of August 5, 1779, Lt. Col. John Graves Simcoe, commander of the Queen's Rangers, having completed his business in New York City, returned to his field headquarters at King's Bridge. While in the process of dismounting from his horse, he was informed that a local loyalist named Vincent had come into camp with news that a party of loyalist militia commanded by Maj. Mansfield Bearmore had been attacked a short time before, while they were sleeping in their quarters, by a large force of American rebels. Vincent reported that fifteen of his comrades had been taken prisoner. The loyalist encampment was located two miles below Delancey's Bridge and West Farms. Vincent managed to escape in the confusion.[6]

Later information indicated that the attacking force consisted of forty-five Continental dragoons, forty supporting Continental infantrymen, and about fifty mounted rebel militia from Lower Salem, all of them under the command of Lt. Col. Anthony Walton White of the 4th Continental Dragoons.[7]

Simcoe issued a "call to arms" and requested that Maj. Charles Cochrane of the British Legion attend him as soon as possible. Lt. Col. Banastre Tarleton, commander of the Legion, was not present, as he was in New York on business. As the senior officer present, Simcoe assumed command of the retaliatory expedition.

Simcoe left soon after dawn with the hussars of the Queen's Rangers, the available cavalry of the Legion, and a newly assigned independent troop of hussars under the command of Capt. Frederick Diemar. The infantry of the Queen's Rangers and the British Legion were directed to follow the cavalry as soon as possible. An invitation was also sent to Lt. Col. Ludwig von Wurmb, commander of the Hessian Jaeger Corps, to join the pursuit if he so desired.

Simcoe, with the Ranger hussars, caught up with White and his rear guard at New Rochelle. The pursuit was so close that many of the fifteen captured loyalist militiamen managed to make their escape. As the hussars were preparing to charge, the American dragoons fired their pistols and then retreated across a bridge, leaving their infantry under Capt. Frederick Pope to delay the British advance as best they could until reinforcements could come from Mamaroneck, less than a mile from the bridge, where White's main body was located. The aforementioned pistol fire caused no damage except for the killing of hussar sergeant Stephen Jarvis's horse. A bullet entered the animal's nostril and passed into its mouth. A stream of blood spouted and the horse sank upon his haunches, but Jarvis managed to spring clear before the animal's final collapse. The incident delayed the charge of the hussars, giving the American infantry enough time to take position behind a stone wall on the left side of the road.[8]

Simcoe intended the hussars to charge over the American infantry and then to concentrate their attack on the escaping rebel dragoons. He hoped that in the confusion of the attack the American fire would be inaccurate. Such was not the case. A heavy, galling fire was directed at the hussars under Capt. Alexander Wickham, and took serious effect. Hussar private William Thorton was killed and three other hussars wounded. Five horses were also killed or disabled. The hussars fell into confusion, including Wickham, who in wheeling his horse about only succeeded in adding to the disorder.[9]

White's infantry took advantage of the confusion and started to withdraw toward the nearby bridge. Simcoe, anxious not to let the Americans escape, ordered Diemar's hussars to pursue, followed by a Legion cavalry troop commanded by Capt. Jacob James. The rest of the Legion cavalry followed. As a precaution, Simcoe ordered the cavalry not to advance beyond the bridge without further orders, but some impetuous troopers crossed anyway and two or three of them were killed by American musket fire.[10]

Simcoe was determined to pursue farther; however, he wanted to find a way to circle around the retreating Americans, not only to get between them and possible reinforcements but also to avoid attacking them frontally on the road that they were following. If the Americans saw no one following immediately behind them, they would in all probability move more slowly than they would otherwise. He therefore sought a parallel road but could obtain no local guides to help him. Soon afterward, another of the loyalist prisoners escaped from White's force and informed Simcoe that additional reinforcements were not expected by the retreating Americans. The British commander determined to waste no more time. He ordered the cavalry across the bridge to continue the pursuit. The delay, however, enabled the Americans to put more distance between themselves and the pursuing British.[11]

During the chase, one of the Americans was killed by friendly fire; two or three others were killed by Diemar's hussars, and some drowned while passing through a creek bed. It was later reported in an American newspaper that "driven into a bad position, they [the Americans] were compelled to fight at a disadvantage and lost twelve men." The hussars and Legion cavalry continued the pursuit to Byram Bridge in Fairfield County, Connecticut, at which point it was discontinued as Simcoe considered it not prudent or useful to follow any farther.[12]

Hussar sergeant Stephen Jarvis recorded in his journal that upon reaching the Byram River, he noticed that "the enemy trumpeter had fallen into a deep hole in the river [while trying to cross with his horse] and was hanging onto the horse's mane" in order to stay afloat. Jarvis plunged into the river to try to take the man captive. The initial result was that Jarvis and his horse sank beneath the water, but he succeeded in getting back to the surface. He then reached out for the trumpeter, but the man escaped his grasp. When the Americans started firing several shots at him from the opposite bank, Jarvis decided that discretion was the better part of valor and abandoned any further attempts to capture the trumpeter.[13]

On the way back to King's Bridge, British cavalrymen searched the woods for American stragglers but found none. More of the loyalist militiamen, who successfully escaped the Americans' custody, joined the withdrawal. Toward six o'clock in the evening, the cavalry joined the supporting infantry, who had arrived too late to participate in the action. Soon thereafter, the entire force was back at its camp.[14]

The Queen's Rangers and the other light troops withdrew from the advance post at King's Bridge on August 8 and took post within the redoubt. The Rangers were permitted to rest. The cavalry strength of the Queen's Rangers had been increased two days earlier by the indefinite assignment of two former independent cavalry troops to Simcoe's command. These were Diemar's Hussars and the Bucks County Light Dragoons, a unit of Pennsylvania loyalists commanded by Capt. Thomas Sandford. The latter troop had formerly been attached to the light infantry of the Brigade of Guards. Sandford himself was a former quartermaster in the Guards brigade.[15]

In late September 1779, Lt. Gen. Sir Henry Clinton decided to shorten the British lines by moving them

A Queen's Rangers hussar. (*Barry Grant*)

southward, thus reducing the number of outlying posts. His motive was probably the need to increase the number of troops available for his forthcoming expedition to South Carolina. Five of the six redoubts north of Spuyten Duyvil Creek were demolished, including Fort Independence. The King's Bridge redoubt was retained to serve as an advance post for the four redoubts to be retained on the upper portion of York Island (Manhattan). Four of the five redoubts on the east side of the Harlem River were also demolished, the exception being Redoubt Number 8, which was retained as an advance outpost to resist or retaliate against any American incursions in that vicinity.[16]

Simcoe's August raid would be the last cavalry raid into Westchester County by British regular or provincial units. The British Legion, both cavalry and infantry, went south with Clinton at the end of December 1779, and subsequently served with Lt. Gen. Charles, Earl Cornwallis, in the South until their surrender at Yorktown, Virginia, in October 1781. The Queen's Rangers spent most of 1780 based on Staten Island, making occasional raids and forays into New Jersey, until their transfer to Virginia in late December 1780 under the command of Brig. Gen. Benedict Arnold. They, like the British Legion, surrendered at Yorktown.

Some cavalry raids by loyalist militia were made into Westchester County from Redoubt Number 8 in 1780–1781. This was a unit known alternately as the Westchester Light Horse or Westchester Refugees, commanded by Col. James DeLancey. They were commonly known to both sides as the "Cow Boys" because of their favorite activity of stealing cattle from rebel farms and selling them to the British Army. The Westchester area in which they operated was labeled the "Neutral Ground" by later historians.[17]

## MIDDLESEX AND SOMERSET COUNTY, NEW JERSEY, CAVALRY RAID—1779

Many historians believe that Lt. Col. Banastre Tarleton, commander of the British Legion, was a bold but impetuous commander and that his command functioned best when he was personally upon the field. John Graves Simcoe of the Queen's Rangers is considered a more methodical commander based on both his actions on the battlefield and his thoughts as expressed in his military journal. His men were better trained and disciplined than Tarleton's and functioned well even when Simcoe was not personally present. Both commanders possessed a great deal of charisma and their troops were willing to do whatever was required or asked of them.

Tarleton demonstrated his abilities as a cavalryman during a July 2, 1779, cavalry raid on Poundridge, New York. The raid was only a limited success, as the Americans were alerted to his approach. Nevertheless, the raid brought him favorable attention from the British high command given that he had covered a round-trip distance of sixty-four miles in twenty-three hours and dispersed

American units while suffering the reported loss of only one man killed and one wounded. Four months later, Simcoe received the opportunity to show his own skills as a cavalry leader.[18]

Simcoe received intelligence in late October 1779 that fifty flatboats, mounted upon carriages for easy transport and capable of carrying seventy men each, were at Van Veghten's Bridge on the upper Raritan River in New Jersey. The boats were said to be waiting to be moved to the American post at West Point, New York. Rumors were rampant that Gen. George Washington was planning an attack on New York City, and Simcoe feared that if these boats reached the American army they would greatly facilitate any such assault. He therefore proposed a plan to Lt. Gen. Sir Henry Clinton whereby he would make a bold dash with a force of cavalry and burn the boats and whatever other military property he could find.[19]

Simcoe discussed his plan with Brig. Gen. Cortlandt Skinner, the former attorney general of New Jersey and present commander of four provincial battalions known as Skinner's Brigade or the New Jersey Volunteers. Skinner believed the plan had fair prospects of success, and Simcoe accordingly submitted the proposal to Clinton, the commander-in-chief of the British Army in North America. Clinton gave his approval to the operation.[20]

While only cavalry would undertake the expedition, the infantry of the Queen's Rangers under Maj. Richard Armstrong would also cross into New Jersey. They would take position on the north end of the South River Bridge, which was located six miles from South Amboy in Middlesex County, to cover the withdrawal of the cavalry and attack any parties of the enemy that might be in pursuit. Intelligence revealed that the only possible opposition to Simcoe's expedition could come from New Jersey militia, as there were no Continental troops in the vicinity. Simcoe's return route would be via Hillsborough (present-day Millstone) and New Brunswick.[21]

The cavalry for the raid would consist of forty-six hussars from the Queen's Rangers under Capt. Alexander Wickham, twenty-two of the Bucks County Light Dragoons under Capt. Thomas Sandford, and ten Staten Island provincial dragoons under Lt. James Stuart, a native of New Jersey. The whole totaled seventy-eight men. At the time Simcoe proposed the expedition, Wickham's and Sandford's troopers were at Jericho on Long Island, acting under the command of Tarleton. Simcoe would launch the raid when these men were returned to him. Simcoe's request that General Skinner furnish guides for the operation was unsuccessful. However, Simcoe managed to recruit someone locally who knew the area through which the raiders would pass.[22]

Having assembled his units, Simcoe's infantry and cavalry departed Richmond on Staten Island at eight o'clock on the evening of October 25. They marched to Billop's Point, at the extreme southern end of the island opposite Perth Amboy, New Jersey, where they were to embark. Simcoe hoped to cross at midnight under cover of darkness, but the necessary boats did not arrive until three o'clock in the morning of October 26. The infantry crossed first and quickly secured every avenue into the town. The cavalry soon followed, and it was near dawn by the time the crossing was completed.[23]

The cavalry left Perth Amboy at daybreak with Sandford's dragoons in the lead, followed by Wickham's and Stuart's troopers. Soon afterward, Major Armstrong reembarked the three hundred infantry of the Queen's Rangers and landed on the opposite side of the Raritan River at South Amboy to take his designated position at the South River Bridge. In case of any unforeseen difficulties, Simcoe had arranged to send a messenger to Armstrong; the messenger would identify himself with the code phrase "Clinton and Montrose."[24]

The route taken by Simcoe's party went through Middlesex County from Perth Amboy to Bonhamtown (present-day Edison), then to Piscataway Township, where the cavalry turned north to Quibbletown (later named New Market, part of present-day Piscataway). Simcoe assumed the guise of American cavalry for his green-coated Rangers, while the red-coated dragoons of Sandford's troop passed themselves off as French. The deception worked all the way to their final destination, a distance of about twenty-three miles, with no alarms raised about the British presence in the area.[25]

One humorous incident that occurred during the journey was the capture of "Justice" Crow, a civilian. When Simcoe encountered him, he called Crow a "damned Tory" and despite Crow's protestations that he was a good patriot and only out courting a lady, he was sent to the rear as a prisoner. There the loyalist rank and file continued the pretense as a game to help pass the time. It probably made Crow very nervous about his eventual fate, for these armed men simply refused to believe that he was as good a patriot as they were pretending to be.[26]

Simcoe and his men passed several houses, where they were greeted with friendly salutations. At one point the troopers stopped at a forage depot of the American Army, and, claiming that his force was part of Maj. Henry Lee's Legion, a Continental unit that was also uniformed in green coats, Simcoe withdrew the customary allowance of forage and gave the usual vouchers without arousing any suspicion on the part of the American commissary officer.[27]

Approaching Quibbletown, Simcoe left his position with the vanguard of his column to speak with Lieutenant Stuart, who commanded the rear guard. Sandford's troop had just passed a tavern at a turn in the road when some men emerged with knapsacks on their backs. Thinking that they were a rebel patrol, the Ranger hussars, who had halted just opposite the tavern, quickly dismounted and with swords in hand took them into custody. The hussars then entered the tavern. Simcoe, passing the scene on his way to meet Stuart, worried that the capture of the men would make it impossible for him to continue passing his troops off as American and French cavalry, as he wished to do. Simcoe made a public statement that the individuals with knapsacks who had been seized were not the Tories that his men were looking for, and apologized for the error. He explained that his men had been deceived by seeing the knapsacks. He added that he was searching for a party of Tories, wearing knapsacks, who had escaped from Maj. Gen. John Sullivan's Continental troops and were believed to be trying to reach Staten Island. He and his command, he said, intended to intercept the fugitive loyalists.[28]

The ruse appeared successful and Simcoe and his cavalry moved on past the village. Unfortunately for them, however, one of the Americans recognized Simcoe and an express messenger quickly rode to New Brunswick, where some militia were posted, to give word of the British presence.

Outside the village, the British cavalry encountered a local boy with whom they continued the deception and from whom they sought additional information about the flatboats reported to be at Van Veghten's Bridge. The lad was eager to be of assistance and told Simcoe that there were at least eighteen boats left, the rest having been forwarded to Washington's army. The boy further stated that the horses for the carriages were at a farm about a mile from the bridge, and consented to lead the column westward to Washington's old encampment at Bound Brook, near the Raritan River in Somerset County.[29]

When Simcoe arrived at the campsite, he abandoned the deception and tried to burn the huts in order to alarm the New Jersey militia and lure them into the ambuscade set up by Major Armstrong at South River. The plan was thwarted because the huts were, Simcoe discovered, spaced too far apart and constructed mostly of noncombustible materials. The cavalry then continued to Bound Brook, and Simcoe stopped at the home of Judge Philip

Van Horne. Simcoe had learned that Col. Stephen Moylan of the 4th Continental Dragoons, a son-in-law of Van Horne, sometimes quartered at the judge's house, but Moylan could not be found. However, two American officers, both ill, were discovered on the premises. Their paroles were taken and they were instructed to mark the words "sick quarters" on the door of their room to prevent their being further molested by other elements of Simcoe's command. Simcoe told Judge Van Horne that he and his men were the advance party of the left column of the British Army, commanded by Brig. Gen. Samuel Birch, and that the commander of the column intended to quarter in the judge's house that evening. Adding to the misinformation, Simcoe stated that General Clinton and the rest of the British Army were en route to Morristown. Simcoe anticipated that this false news might become widespread and could cause great consternation among the Americans. It could possibly even induce the Continental Army to make some erroneous move, which Clinton could take advantage of to the benefit of the British.

Simcoe proceeded to Van Veghten's Bridge on the upper Raritan River, where he found the eighteen flatboats mounted on traveling carriages. The boats were full of water that required draining. The work of destruction began and was completed within forty minutes. The timbers of the boats were chopped through with hatchets that the troops had brought with them, and straw was placed in the gaps. Then grenades were fastened to the boats and set on fire. With the flames fueled by the straw, the boats were quickly consumed. The wheels of the carriages were hacked to pieces to render them useless.[30]

As the British soldiers finished their task, the countryside began to display the first signs of alarm. A rifle shot was fired at Simcoe from across the Raritan, but the shooter missed. Seeking to do additional damage to the rebels, Simcoe ordered the Dutch Meeting House, reportedly used as a forage magazine, to be burned. The commissary and his assistants were taken prisoner. In addition, a wagon full of ammunition was destroyed and some of the better-quality carriage horses were taken to replace the worn out cavalry mounts.[31]

Their work of destruction complete, Simcoe and his cavalry proceeded south to Hillsborough. Upon their arrival, they found three loyalists held captive inside the Somerset County Courthouse, one of whom was chained to the floor and close to starvation. Simcoe ordered the loyalist prisoners released and the courthouse burned. He also destroyed additional forage found in the area to prevent it from reaching Washington's army. The British paroled the Americans they had captured before leaving Hillsborough in the early hours of October 27. As the cavalry marched from the town, the troopers could hear the sound of alarm guns firing.

Simcoe concluded that the militia would shortly be gathering to cut off the retreat of his cavalry. The men soon came under fire from a few individuals to their rear who kept themselves concealed and repeatedly fired at targets of opportunity. Passing by a few houses, Simcoe told the female inhabitants to bring word to the snipers to cease firing or he would order his soldiers to burn every house along their route. One or two troopers had already been wounded by this fire, but none seriously.[32]

The three troops of cavalry proceeded east on the Amwell Road and passed through Middlebush. They were within two miles of New Brunswick when they first encountered serious opposition. Simcoe, riding in advance and accompanied by his hussar orderly Cpl. Edward Wright, heard a shout coming from somewhere to his front. Suspecting that perhaps an ambush lay ahead, Simcoe sent Wright to alert Captain Sandford, whose troop now formed the rear guard.

The road on which Simcoe's command was traveling was bounded on both sides by high rail fences, beyond which were deep woods. Simcoe realized that it was important to get off the road before an ambush could be sprung. He noticed a break in the fence on his right and ordered Captain Wickham and the Ranger hussars to follow him, but without informing them of his intentions. The troopers assumed that Simcoe was leading a charge upon a body of armed men and the hussars rode forward at a fast canter.[33]

The hussars had not gone far when a large party of men was seen concealed behind logs and bushes near the opening in the fence. This force consisted of thirty-five Middlesex County militiamen under Capt. Moses Guest, who had been dispatched from New Brunswick. Ironically, the ambush might have been avoided. Simcoe had intended to turn off the road onto higher ground before he arrived at the break in the fence, but his guide, Lieutenant Stuart, upon whom he depended to find the road, became confused because the landmark he sought no longer existed. It was a house that had been burned by the British on June 19, 1777, during Gen. Sir William Howe's fruitless June 1777 campaign to lure Washington's army out of its fortified camp behind the Watchung Mountains. Stuart did not know of the building's destruction.[34]

Simcoe heard someone shout "Now, now!" and before he could give any orders, a volley from the militia rang out and struck the ranks of charging hussars. Simcoe's horse was struck by five bullets; he was thrown to the ground and temporarily stunned by the fall. The hussars went through the broken fence in some confusion. Pvt. Matthew Coleman was killed and Pvt. John Stevens wounded and captured. When the cavalry reached high ground, the troopers halted and reorganized. The hussars, including Captain Wickham, were still too shaken to go back and try to rescue Simcoe if he was still alive, despite the urging of Sgt. Stephen Jarvis that an attempt be made.[35]

Meanwhile, Captain Sandford's and Lieutenant Stuart's dragoons followed the hussars, but the militia, after firing their volley, dispersed into the thick woods. This prevented the loyalist horsemen from coming to grips with them. The two troops joined the Ranger hussars on the high ground above New Brunswick.[36]

Sandford assumed command of the combined force and pondered his next move. The British force was in a precarious position because in addition to the militia at their rear, an estimated thirty additional American militiamen commanded by Capt. Peter V. Voorhees had arrived and taken positions on the front and flanks of the cavalry. Lieutenant Stuart, having received a slight wound in the hand, was in a disturbed mental state and could give Sandford neither assistance nor any information regarding possible escape routes. The troopers were likewise in a state of uncertainty. The Queen's Rangers' surgeon, Alexander Kellock, put a white handkerchief on the point of his sword and on his own initiative went to obtain information about Simcoe's condition. When Kellock found Simcoe still alive, he elected to stay and attend his wounded commander.[37]

Strong leadership was needed if the British forces were to escape. Sandford decided that the best course was for the troopers to fight their way through the militia, and he hesitated only briefly before ordering an attack. The cavalry first made a feint toward the mounted enemy at their rear, where Captain Voorhees had gone. In the charge, Voorhees was killed by one of the Ranger hussars with whom he was exchanging fire. Then the cavalry turned about and charged through the main body of militia, which had come out of the woods with the intention of pursuing the British horsemen. The militia fled back into the woods to escape the slashing sabers. Sandford then led the cavalry to the left as if he were heading toward New Brunswick. The American militia rallied and rushed to their right in an effort to cut off the escape route. Sandford promptly ordered another turn to his right, away from the militia, and bypassed them without receiving a single shot. It was a stratagem of which Simcoe himself could be proud. Captain Wickham, the Queen's Rangers' hussar commander, did not measure up quite so well under pressure, for Wickham apparently became rattled during the incident. Sergeant Jarvis sarcastically recalled in his postwar narrative that the "gallant Captain Wickham was riding about like a wild man, and lost his helmet and seemed to have lost his reason altogether."[38]

The cavalry proceeded to the rendezvous with Major Armstrong's infantry at South River Bridge. They occasionally encountered some small militia parties on the way, but these were quickly dispersed or taken prisoner. Cpl. James Molloy of the hussars was killed by one of a pair of militiamen. His assailant was immediately killed and the other captured and made to run alongside the mounted troopers. The prisoner was eventually allowed to ride behind one of Stuart's Staten Island dragoons who had been wounded in the thigh during the withdrawal. The dragoon received orders to shoot the prisoner if he tried to escape.[39]

At about four o'clock in the afternoon the cavalry rejoined the infantry after a dash of about seventy miles. The combined force departed for South Amboy, where the boats were found ready and the men and horses boarded. As the boats pulled away from the shore, parties of militia could be seen approaching. All the Americans found were several worn-out horses that had been left behind. The British troops landed on Staten Island on October 28 and returned to their encampment at Richmond. The cavalry had covered a distance of about eighty miles and the infantry thirty, without halting for food or rest. Their raid caused a commotion among the American forces; George Washington ordered Brig. Gen. Anthony Wayne to take some Continental light troops to aid the militia. Wayne marched fourteen miles on the evening of October 26 and thirty miles the next day, but he was too late. The raiding party was gone and the fear

that it was the vanguard of a serious British movement
into New Jersey proved unfounded.[40]

Casualties among the Ranger hussars were two killed
and one wounded. Stuart's troop had one man wounded,
and Pvt. Samuel Thomas of Capt. Robert McCrea's company of Ranger infantry was wounded at South River
Bridge. In addition, the raid's commander, Simcoe, along
with Surgeon Kellock, were prisoners. Sgt. John McGill
voluntarily joined Simcoe in captivity to act as his personal servant.[41]

When Simcoe recovered consciousness after being
thrown from his horse, he found himself surrounded by a
crowd of very unfriendly militiamen. They were angered
by the death of Captain Voorhees, a popular officer who
was to have been married on the following day. Jonathan
Ford Morris, a nineteen-year-old medical student,
stopped one militiaman from running a bayonet through
Simcoe while the British officer lay unconscious. Another
militiaman expressed regret that he had not shot Simcoe
through the head during the skirmish. Simcoe, whose
injuries were initially treated by Morris, was placed in
protective custody by senior officers. New Jersey governor William Livingston, upon learning of the capture of
Simcoe and the hostility expressed toward him, issued a
proclamation condemning the taking of revenge against
an injured enemy, and directed that the British officer be
treated properly according to the rules of war.[42]

Simcoe was taken to New Brunswick after his capture
and on October 28 he was moved to Bordentown, where
he and Kellock were permitted to move about freely within the confines of the village. On November 9, Simcoe
was moved to Burlington, several miles farther south,
where he was confined in the jail along with Sergeant
McGill. Kellock remained in Bordentown, and Simcoe
refused the surgeon's request to join him in his new and
inhospitable quarters in Burlington.[43]

At Burlington, Simcoe shared his captivity with Col.
Christopher Billop, a Staten Island loyalist. The

Americans kept Billop confined in irons and chained to the floor of the jail, not because of any offense that Billop had committed but in retaliation for similar treatment given some American prisoners held in New York. Simcoe, although closely confined, did not suffer the indignity of chains, probably due to the intercession of American major Henry "Light-Horse Harry" Lee, who considered Simcoe an honorable and worthy foe. Simcoe tried to obtain a parole to Staten Island pending exchange, but Governor Livingston denied his request. The governor believed that if British captives were kept in close confinement, it would serve as an incentive for the British to agree more quickly to a prisoner exchange.[44]

On November 28, Simcoe was removed from his comfortable room to another room normally reserved for felons. He sent letters of protest to Governor Livingston, and decided to initiate a plan of escape rather than wait for a possible future exchange that might be a long time coming. Sergeant McGill agreed to try to implement the scheme. During the jailer's absence, McGill used his charm to persuade the jailer's wife to permit him to roam about the town at night. McGill used this freedom to discover all the routes leading from the town and where the best horses were kept.

By continued attentions to the jailer's wife, on December 3, McGill managed to steal the key to the locked storeroom in the jail, which contained a supply of arms and ammunition belonging to Henry Lee's cavalry. McGill made a duplicate of the key using shoemaker's tools and returned the original to its former location. While McGill was engaged in this endeavor, Simcoe, who sometimes suffered headaches, possibly as a result of the fall from his horse on October 27, decided to exaggerate his discomfort to draw attention away from McGill's activities. Simcoe began acting like a man who was losing his reason; on one occasion he started "singing 'God Save the King' and playing to the air with [a] pin stuck in [a] window sash."

McGill attempted to gain access to the locked store-room on December 12. While he was trying to open the door, the duplicate key, made of pewter, broke in the lock. The broken portion of the key fell inside the lock, and McGill abandoned the effort. The mishap ironically proved to be fortunate for McGill, because about half an hour after he had made his attempt on the lock, a party of Lee's men arrived at the jail and retrieved their arms and ammunition from the storeroom [45]

Simcoe and McGill devised a new escape plan but never carried it out. An exchange was finally arranged on December 27, and Simcoe, Billop, Kellock, and McGill were released. Simcoe arrived at the Queen's Rangers' encampment on Staten Island on December 31. There he found that General Clinton and several thousand men had sailed southward to Charleston, South Carolina, only five days earlier. He also learned from Maj. John André, Clinton's adjutant general, that the Queen's Rangers would have been included in the expedition if his exchange had been obtained earlier.[46]

Simcoe did see action in the South, at Charleston and later as part of an expedition to Virginia, where he remained under the command of Lord Cornwallis until he was taken prisoner a second time at the surrender of Yorktown on October 19, 1781. After the war, Simcoe became the first lieutenant governor of Upper Canada (Ontario) in 1791. He did not forget the young man who had saved his life more than a decade earlier, and offered Morris, who was working as a physician and surgeon in New Jersey, generous compensation if he would relocate to Canada and become a British subject. Morris, however, declined the offer.[47]

HOPPERTOWN CAVALRY RAID, BERGEN COUNTY, NEW JERSEY, 1780

In April 1780, Lt. Gen. Sir Henry Clinton began his siege of Charleston. His invasion force, numbering about 8,700 men, arrived in the area of Savannah, Georgia, in early February, but did not entrench itself on Charleston Neck until the end of March. Clinton began closing the ring around the city but soon came to the realization that he did not have sufficient troops to completely cut off all escape routes. He therefore sent for reinforcements from New York. About 2,600 additional men departed from Sandy Hook on April 4, which included the infantry of the Queen's Rangers, commanded by Simcoe, plus a small detachment of fourteen Ranger hussars, commanded by Sgt. Stephen Jarvis, to be used for scouting duties. The remainder of the hussars was left behind on Staten Island under the command of Captain Wickham.[48]

The arrival of warmer weather in the north renewed British commanders' desire for offensive operations, and several raids were made into New Jersey and New York. One such raid took place on April 16 at Hoppertown (present-day Ho-Ho-Kus), New Jersey. The raiding party consisted of 120 cavalry from Staten Island and 312 infantry from the New York garrison. The cavalry were a detachment of 20 men from the 17th Light Dragoons under Cornet Thomas Tucker, 15 Staten Island dragoons under Lt. James Stuart, 45 hussars from the Queen's Rangers commanded by Wickham, and Capt. Frederick Diemar's 40 provincial hussars. The infantry force was comprised of 12 jaegers, 150 men of the Hessian Regiment Bose, 100 men of the Hessian Regiment Morbach, and 50 men of the Loyal American Regiment. The overall commander of the expedition was Maj. Christian DuBuy of the Regiment Bose.[49]

The cavalry crossed from Staten Island to New Jersey at Bergen Neck and Cole's Ferry on the evening of April 15 and proceeded north to English Neighborhood (present-day Leonia) near Fort Lee, where they joined the infantry under Major DuBuy at one o'clock on the morning of April 16. The expedition moved on to New Bridge on the Hackensack River, with six Ranger hussars under Sgt. William McLaughlin forming the advance guard. At about three o'clock in the morning they encountered an American outpost whose defenders fled after a brief resistance. An officer and three men were captured before they could escape. Fifty infantrymen, probably the Loyal Americans, were left at New Bridge as a rear guard and the rest of the British force continued the march to Hoppertown. They moved west from New Bridge, crossed the Saddle River Bridge, and passed the Dutch Reformed Church before reaching Ho-Ho-Kus Brook, where they turned northeast to Hoppertown.[50]

The expedition arrived at its destination about an hour after dawn. The objective of the raid was to kill or capture a party of about two hundred American soldiers stationed at Hoppertown and destroy whatever stores were found there. The American troops were Continentals of the 3rd Pennsylvania Regiment under Maj. Thomas Byles, who had been in command since April 3. By the time the British arrived, two American patrols had already been out and returned without detecting the enemy's presence in the area. Apparently those Americans who fled at New Bridge had not sent any warning to Byles. The Pennsylvanians were, shortly after the return of the scouting parties, paraded and dismissed.[51]

Major DuBuy had information that there was another bridge (present-day Glen Avenue Bridge) that crossed Ho-Ho-Kus Brook at the entrance to the town. A picket guard consisting of an officer and twenty men were reported as being posted in a nearby house. From there the American headquarters at the Hopper House was about a mile distant along the Hoppertown Road (present-day Sheridan Avenue), where it intersected with the road from Weehawken (present-day Franklin Turnpike). DuBuy decided on a surprise attack and ordered twenty-two-year-old Ranger cornet George Spencer to take twelve Queen's Ranger hussars, with an equal number of 17th Light Dragoons commanded by Cornet Tucker, and charge down the road until his force reached the American headquarters. They would be followed by the balance of the cavalry and infantry as soon as possible.[52]

A member of the 17th Light Dragoons. (*Barry Grant*)

Spencer and his advance guard rushed forward from their place of concealment and rode across the bridge without stopping. The surprised pickets managed to get off a few shots but did no damage. Other shots were fired from several houses alongside the road where the American troops were quartered, but these too had no effect, as the hussars, being moving targets, were difficult to hit. The remainder of the cavalry was directed to attend to these Americans while the advance guard continued to the end of the road.[53]

Upon his arrival near the house owned by John Hopper, Spencer found that he had only six men with him, the others not yet having caught up. He stopped when he saw about twenty-five Americans drawn up opposite him, no more than twenty yards distant on the other side of a ravine. Their senior officer, Major Byles, quickly consulted with two of his officers, Lieutenants James Glenworth and Henry Sherman, as to whether they should make their stand there or from the protection of the house. They decided to defend the house, where they all quickly took refuge.[54]

The Hopper House had three windows on the ground floor and two on the second story. American troops were posted at each of the windows. At the moment that the Americans withdrew into the house, Spencer, joined by four more Ranger hussars plus two troopers of the 17th Dragoons, crossed the ravine (over the present-day Maple Avenue Bridge) and reached the walls of the Hopper House. They were immediately fired upon from a smaller house about twenty yards away on the opposite side of the road. Spencer ordered six men to dismount, take cover, and fire at random into the windows of the Hopper House. He also posted two other men at the doors to prevent any escape. Three more soldiers, under Ranger corporal John Burt, ran to the second house, where they broke in and quickly captured its nine occupants.[55]

Spencer demanded the surrender of Major Byles and those of his men who were in the Hopper House, but without success. To rush the house would likely cost many casualties given that the defenders were well posted at the windows. Since the house was made of stone, they would need a cannon, which they did not have, to break down the walls. An attempt to break down the doors failed; they were too well constructed. One hussar was wounded in the effort.[56]

Spencer then conceived that if his men could not get into the house, they would have to force the defenders out. A corner of the wood-shingled roof was set on fire and soon the entire roof was in flames. By this point Spencer's men had suffered five casualties. Two Ranger hussars (Pvt. Robert Hughes and Pvt. John James) and one trooper of the 17th Light Dragoons were dead, and two other Ranger hussars (Pvt. Samuel Lindsay and Pvt. Thomas Shannon) were wounded. Spencer made another demand for surrender, which was again refused. The flames from the fire started spreading, and soon firing from the house stopped. By that time the rest of the cavalry, under Wickham and Tucker, had arrived on the scene, followed some minutes later by Diemar's hussars and DuBuy with the supporting infantry. The cavalry had been delayed on the narrow road because the mounted troopers had to wait for the infantry marching ahead of them to move out of the way. In addition, some of the horsemen had made a wrong turn at a fork on the Hoppertown Road and had to retrace their course. Nevertheless, they still managed to capture a significant number of prisoners. Spencer expressed the opinion that "had all the cavalry been in front, it would have been better . . . not one man could have escaped."[57]

Byles, with the house in flames and seeing that it was impossible to escape, decided to surrender. Unfortunately, as he opened the door he was shot in his left breast by one of Diemar's hussars. Due to his serious wound, Byles was given parole by Captain Diemar; however, he died of his wound three days later. After the surrender, a shot was fired from the top of the house. If not for the intercession of Diemar, many of the prisoners might have been shot in retaliation. American stores that could not be taken away were burned, and the expedition then headed back to New York with their captives. They were pursued by part of Byles's command that had escaped capture. These Americans succeeded in retaking four loaded wagons and about nineteen horses, but did not seriously impede the British march. At four o'clock on the afternoon of April 16, the infantry reached Fort Lee and crossed to New York. The cavalry returned to Staten Island by eight o'clock after a march of more than eighty miles without even stopping to feed their horses.[58]

British casualties were 3 killed and 9 wounded among the cavalry and 4 dead and 23 wounded among the infantry. Two of the cavalry wounded were from the Queen's Rangers, two from Diemar's Hussars, three from the 17th Light Dragoons, and two from the Staten Island Dragoons. The infantry dead were one from the Morbach Regiment, two from the Bose Regiment, and one of the Loyal Americans. The infantry wounded were one Jaeger, eleven of the Morbach Regiment, six of the Bose Regiment, and five from the Loyal Americans.[59]

American losses were much higher. Major Byles was the only American officer killed. Among the rank and file, about fifty were killed or wounded. Twelve officers and 182 men were taken prisoner. Since Byles was reported to have had only about two hundred men, the latter figure may be a mistake or an exaggeration. However, it may have included local civilians picked up by overeager soldiers or militiamen who turned out to support the Continentals. Of the Americans reported captured, five officers and twenty-one rank and file were taken at the Hopper House.[60]

The Ranger hussars resumed their garrison duties on Staten Island, with their thoughts probably directed toward their fellow Rangers who by now had probably joined the British Army besieging Charleston. That effort was now the only major military action currently in progress.

Cornet George Spencer, who had formerly been a quartermaster in the 16th Light Dragoons, was subsequently promoted to lieutenant on August 25, 1780, and assigned to a newly raised Ranger cavalry troop commanded by Capt. David Shank. Spencer served with the Rangers until the surrender at Yorktown. Spencer had artistic talents as well; all eleven maps used to illustrate Lt. Col. Simcoe's *Military Journal*, published after the war, were either prepared by Spencer or with his input. After the peace treaty was signed in 1783, Spencer and his family settled in Shelburne, Nova Scotia.[61]

Because there were no major clashes between the main British and American armies in the North after the Battle of Monmouth, New Jersey, on June 28, 1778, historians have tended to neglect later military operations in that theater. However, as the accounts of these three actions demonstrate, fighting continued in the North until the end of the War for Independence, albeit on a smaller scale. In these raids, skirmishes, and battles, the cavalry on both sides played a major role. While such fighting did not directly determine the outcome of the war, it influenced the plans and operations of American commander-in-chief George Washington as well as his British counterpart, Sir Henry Clinton. Both men hoped that this sparring would create an opportunity to strike a major blow at the opposing army, and the American and British cavalry strove valiantly in their efforts to give their commanders an opening to achieve a decisive victory.[62]

FIVE

# Anthony Walton White, a Revolutionary Dragoon

## *Scott A. Miskimon*

L
T. COL. ANTHONY WALTON WHITE STOOD ON THE BANKS
of the Santee River dripping wet and panting for
breath. Next to him was an equally soaked and exhausted
William Washington. A surprise attack minutes before by
Lt. Col. Banastre Tarleton's British Legion at Lenud's
Ferry had shattered their cavalry regiments, and they
barely escaped by jumping into the river and swimming to
the north shore. It was not the first time American officers
fled for their lives in this war, and it would not be the last.
White and Washington now gazed across the water,
humiliated in defeat and horrified at the carnage the
British Legion had wreaked upon their men. The Battle
of Lenud's Ferry was the worst moment of White's controversial career, and it would have repercussions he could
not imagine.

I would like to thank Sam Fore for generously sharing his knowledge of
Anthony Walton White with me and in particular for introducing me to
a number of unpublished documents that I had not previously discovered. These have added greatly to my understanding of White's career
and character.

Except for his defeat at Lenud's Ferry, South Carolina, in May 1780, White's role as a cavalry officer during and after the American Revolution has gone largely unstudied by historians, and no comprehensive biography of White has been written. This is unfortunate, because White's background, connections, personality, and actions mark him as one of the more colorful characters who served in the early American army. Frequently arrested and court-martialed, often denigrated, and always controversial, White nevertheless managed to remain in the thick of action, both during the Revolution and the Whiskey Rebellion of 1794.

FAMILY CONNECTIONS

Although White is best known as a leader of Virginia dragoons who fought in the South, he was a northern blue-blood, born and raised in New Jersey, a son of privilege and wealth who bore the names of his forefathers. His paternal great-great-grandfather was Col. Anthony White, a distressed cavalier who fled Britain in the wake of the English Civil War and settled in Bermuda. This Anthony White was an officer in the island militia, served in the colonial assembly, and eventually became Bermuda's chief justice. His son Leonard White fathered Anthony White II, who left Bermuda and settled in New York around 1715. Anthony White II married in the Dutch Reformed Church, and died at sea soon after the birth of his son Anthony White III.[1]

The third Anthony White was the father of Anthony Walton White, and he rose in prominence following his marriage to Elizabeth Morris, a daughter of Lewis Morris, the Chief Justice of New York who later became governor of New Jersey. Anthony White built a house for his new bride, Elizabeth, on the Raritan River near New Brunswick. The house was then called White House Farm, and later Buccleuch by a subsequent owner. Under that name the house stands today, and it is there that

Anthony Walton White was born on July 7, 1750. Little is known of his early days, except that he grew up on his father's estate, was privately educated, had three older sisters, and was the only son in the family. His father lived the comfortable life of a gentleman farmer. By the time Anthony Walton White was a teenager, his father was appointed to a succession of judicial positions, and no doubt his offices and wealth were deployed to young Anthony's advantage.[2]

## George Washington's Aide

It is difficult to determine the source of White's attraction to the patriot cause. There is no record of his father being active in opposing royal authority. It is likely that Anthony Walton White was attracted to the Revolution out of a young man's desire for adventure, position, or to establish his own reputation. It is also possible, however, that White's cousins played a role in shaping his outlook on the times. White's maternal grandfather, Lewis Morris, had a number of descendants, and two of the most prominent were his grandsons Lewis Morris III and Gouverneur Morris. These cousins of White were half brothers, and both played central roles in Revolutionary politics. Lewis Morris III was a member of the Continental Congress who later became a signer of the Declaration of Independence. Although warned about the dangers of memorializing his approval of independence, Morris allegedly proclaimed: "Damn the consequences. Give me the pen." Morris's younger stepbrother, Gouverneur Morris, also a member of the Continental Congress, would later play a crucial role in drafting the U.S. Constitution.[3]

In July 1775, Anthony Walton White turned twenty-five years old. War with Britain had started only three months earlier, and he was ready to leave home and join the Continental Army. During the siege of Boston, he traveled to Washington's camp at Cambridge,

Massachusetts, to present himself to the general and seek appointment as an officer. He carried with him a letter from George Clinton, the governor of New York, who wrote that White was "inspired with Love for our much injured Country" and that White was visiting Washington's camp "to offer his Services as a Volunteer in the Army under your Command." He also carried a letter from his father to General Washington. A few weeks after leaving home, White made it to Washington's camp. Endowed with his family connections and letters of introduction, he had an inside track to a prestigious appointment. Washington wrote to Governor Clinton and to White's father about his proposal "to take Mr. White into my Family as an Ade de Camp." But there was a hitch. Washington had already invited a Virginian named Robert Hanson Harrison to join him as an aide-de-camp. Washington knew the Virginian might not come; if he did not, the job was White's. In the meantime, Washington promised, "I shall be happy in making his time as agreeable as possible to him whilst he remains in the Camp."[4]

As it turned out, Harrison eventually arrived to take the position first offered to him—a position he would keep for six years. But White's time in camp was not agreeable, at least as far as Washington was concerned. As an aide-de-camp, even a temporary one, White fell short of the mark. And now that the position was filled, White needed to leave Washington's "family." Washington tried to smooth things over with White's father, and wrote that he had learned that two battalions were being raised in New Jersey and that he had urged White to return there immediately. Washington added that he was "firmly persuaded that [White's] merit would entitle him to an honorable appointment in one or the other of those Corps."[5]

The real truth was that White was not cut out to be an aide-de-camp. His abilities failed to measure up to the duties Washington required, either as a scribe or an assistant. Compounding his shortcomings was the fact that he would not leave. For months after his dismissal, White continued to believe that he would be made an aide-de-camp as soon as another position opened up. Washington confided to Joseph Reed about his dilemma over White: "I find it is absolutely necessary that the aids to the Commander-in-chief should be ready at their pen, (which I believe he is not,) to give that ready assistance, that is expected of them." The extent of Washington's responsibilities meant that he had "to have persons that can think for me, as well as execute orders. This it is that pains me when I think of Mr. White's expectation of coming into my family if an opening happens. I can derive no earthly assistance from such a man."[6]

## 1776: COURT-MARTIALED INFANTRY OFFICER

Despite his frustrating experience at headquarters, White remained an ardent supporter of the cause, joined a New Jersey infantry regiment, and obtained a commission as a lieutenant colonel.[7] His unit was the Third New Jersey Battalion, commanded by Col. Elias Dayton. For the first half of 1776, White served in the infantry without incident. His career in the infantry would soon end, and a new one in the cavalry would begin, from an affair of honor that erupted following allegations that White plundered a Tory's house. In the summer of 1776, White was serving in the Northern Army under Gen. Philip Schuyler and Colonel Dayton, and was stationed at Fort Stanwix. White and captains John Ross and Thomas Paterson were accused of ransacking Johnson Hall, the home of Sir John Johnson, a Tory leader in upstate New York. A Lieutenant McDonald had already been tried and convicted of the crime, but it was a scandal that kept growing and implicated more senior officers.

General Schuyler investigated the charges and was concerned that a public conviction of several officers would disgrace the army. He pondered whether to accept the offer that White and the other officers proposed, in which they would make a confession in front of their regiment. This would allow Schuyler to "Bury the Affair." Schuyler asked General Washington whether he should sweep the mess under the rug or have the officers court-martialed. Washington, with his typical strong dose of common sense and personal desire to be perceived as above reproach, replied to Schuyler that White and the others should be tried. White also wanted a trial. He wrote to General Schuyler and beseeched him to name the man who whispered accusations against him so that White could be publicly vindicated in court. He received his trial, and in mid-November, White and the others were found not guilty of having plundered Johnson Hall. It was the unanimous opinion of the court "that the charge against the prisoners was malicious and groundless, and therefore acquit them with honor."[8]

Just six days after his acquittal, however, White was back in trouble, this time for attacking another officer, Col. Richard Varick, secretary to General Schuyler. White believed Varick was one of his secret accusers, and seeking satisfaction, burst into Varick's quarters, drew his sword, demanded a duel, and then lunged at Varick. Unarmed, Varick dodged the attack and fled. White was arrested but escaped, and when a search party found him he was sitting on a tree stump, armed with two loaded pistols and three swords, and said he was waiting for his duel with Varick. White avoided a second court-martial when his friends intervened and arranged for him to be transferred to the cavalry.[9]

### 1777: A DRAGOON IS BORN

The Continental Army had four cavalry regiments, and during the course of the war White served in or commanded three of them. In February 1777, White became a lieutenant colonel in the newly formed 4th Continental Light Dragoons, commanded by Col. Stephen Moylan. William Washington, the commander-in-chief's distant cousin, served as major. White was immediately unhappy. Just a few weeks after joining the 4th Dragoons, he wrote to General Washington about his situation and complained that he had been overlooked in the appointments made of officers from New Jersey.

Washington replied in a fatherly letter in which he expressed his continuing desire to be supportive of White but also pointedly chastised him for the manner in which he left the Northern Army. Washington reprimanded him for having indulged "in a loose, unguarded way of talking, which has often brought your own veracity in question, and trouble upon others." By now, White had a reputation for loose talk that was considered disruptive among his fellow officers, and this had prevented Washington from appointing him to a different regiment. Washington was very direct in telling him that he would have to be convinced that White had changed his ways before he would give him a different appointment.[10]

In September 1777, the British launched their campaign to take Philadelphia, the capital of the young republic. White saw action at the Battle of Brandywine and was wounded in the leg. Within ten days of the battle, he was assuring General Washington "that my Wound is so much better that I am able to hop about again, and as I am not yet well enough to join my Regiment I should be happy to render any Service to my Country while I remain here [at Philadelphia]."[11]

White did not remain long in Philadelphia, however. Soon after the American defeat at Brandywine, Congress fled to York, Pennsylvania, and Philadelphia was about to fall to the British. With Congress gone—along with the Board of War, the state's governor, and all high-ranking army officers—White was the most senior officer left in the city. Despite his wound, he actively prepared for the American evacuation of the capital. To avoid ships on the Delaware River falling into the hands of the enemy, he ordered their owners to move the vessels upriver as far as their drafts would allow, and if they refused, he would burn the ships on the enemy's approach. He also recommended to General Washington that all the horses be removed from Philadelphia and the surrounding area, but was hesitant to carry this out without further instructions from Washington.[12]

Anthony Walton White. (*Barry Grant*)

The next day, Washington ordered Lt. Col. Alexander Hamilton to collect all the blankets he could coax the Philadelphians to donate to the army, and to take care of the matter of the horses. Hamilton in turn instructed White to commandeer all of the horses in Philadelphia and nearby areas and to take them to a secure location. The only horses that were off limits to White were those belonging to the poor whose livelihoods depended upon them, horses belonging to transient persons, and horses belonging to persons who were about to leave Philadelphia on their own.[13]

Washington soon granted his men the right to impress horses from Tories to provide mounts for those dragoons who were without horses. Washington's well-intentioned policy quickly deteriorated into a practice of theft and plunder. Four weeks after White began impressing civilian horses in Philadelphia, Washington read the riot act to his dragoon commanders because their men were stealing horses from the local inhabitants and pretending that they were doing so under Washington's orders. Washington's plan had envisioned that horses would be taken only from Tories living close to the British lines; records were to be kept and the owners reimbursed. Instead, the American dragoons "horribly abused and perverted" his plan into a "plundering scheme" in which they indiscriminately labeled people Tories and took what they wanted for private profit. Washington was livid and responded with directives to remedy this intolerable conduct. He revoked the right of impressments. The dragoons were ordered not to "meddle with the horses or other property of any inhabitant whatever, on pain of the severest punishment"—execution. To ensure compliance with his order, Washington demanded that all horses be branded with the Continental brand, and any man found with an unbranded horse would be court-martialed for marauding.[14]

## 1778–1779: A Slowly Rising Star

The campaign of 1777 came to an end, and the 4th Dragoons went into winter quarters, first at Valley Forge, Pennsylvania. By early 1778, the 4th was moved to Trenton, New Jersey, to train, reequip, and find more recruits. After the winter ended, White was on detached service, first with Gen. Philemon Dickinson and then with Gen. Charles Scott. The British evacuated Philadelphia on June 18 and began their march through New Jersey to New York City, where they were consolidating their forces. General Scott's mission was to shadow and harass the British left flank and rear and to collect intelligence. On June 28, during one of the hottest days on record, the 4th Dragoons joined Washington at the Battle of Monmouth. Badly mauled at Monmouth, the British continued their retreat through New Jersey. Soon after the battle, the issue of White's impressment of horses arose once again. While still on detached service, White impressed a horse belonging to a civilian, Robert Bowen. Although White issued him a receipt, Bowen complained about his horse being taken. White received a stern letter from Alexander Hamilton on behalf of Washington, telling him that "the General takes it for granted that the

Horse must have been pressed by proper Authority for the Public Service, as he cannot suppose you would have taken him on the principles represented by the Complainant, the supposition would be too injurious to be admitted."[15]

The British Army eventually completed its retreat to New York City, and in the fall of 1778, the 4th Dragoons were stationed in Middlebrook, New Jersey. By this time, William Washington had served under White and Moylan in the 4th for nearly two years. Disaster soon struck the American cavalry. In September, the British led a surprise night bayonet assault against the 3rd Dragoons at Tappan, New York, and left the unit in tatters, with men killed while begging for quarter. For the Americans it was nothing less than a massacre. In November, William Washington transferred from the 4th to the 3rd Dragoons and was charged with rebuilding and reequipping the regiment. White remained in the 4th, whose duties principally involved obtaining forage for his own regiment while cutting off the British supply lines leading into New York. The 4th Dragoons drove off British foraging parties in search of hay for their cavalry and confiscated milk cows from local Tories to prevent milk from reaching the city.[16]

By July 1779, the 4th was transferred to Westchester County, New York.[17] This area was the "Neutral Ground," a no-man's-land wracked by a vicious struggle between Whigs and Tories. Westchester County became an active front in the war, a place where an ambitious and daring dragoon officer could make a name for himself and advance his career. Certainly that was the goal of Lt. Col. Banastre Tarleton, a gifted, hard-charging young cavalry officer who had been given command of the British Legion, a provincial unit of dragoons that had just come out of winter quarters on Long Island and was now operating in Westchester County. White would soon skirmish with the British Legion in Westchester, and later more dramatically at Lenud's Ferry in South Carolina.

White's principal battle during this period involved a cavalry action in early August 1779 with the British Legion and the Queen's Rangers at New Rochelle, New York. The action grew out of a successful raid against local loyalists. With a hundred dragoons and fifty infantrymen from Gen. John Glover's Brigade, White led an assault against the loyalists at Westchester and rode away with a large group of prisoners in tow. One loyalist escaped the surprise assault and made it to where the British Legion and the Queen's Rangers were encamped. Lt. Col. John Graves Simcoe of the Rangers immediately gave the alarm and joined his dragoons to the cavalry of the Legion, which Maj. Charles Cochrane led while Tarleton was in New York. In this joint operation, the British had three hundred dragoons and two hundred infantry, giving them a three-to-one advantage over White. The Rangers and the Legion marched through the night, racing to catch up with White and cut him off before he could reach the American stronghold at Mamaroneck. As White's forces headed back to their lines, they made little effort to keep the prisoners they had taken, and many of them escaped during the march.[18]

The Rangers and the Legion finally caught White's exhausted cavalry and infantry at a creek near New Rochelle. White raced his cavalry across the bridge that spanned the creek, leaving the infantry behind to block the enemy from crossing. The foot soldiers threw themselves over a nearby stone wall, giving them temporary control of any passage across the bridge. Simcoe ordered his dragoons to rush the bridge, hoping his men would make it past the American infantry. It was a futile effort. The American musket fire was deadly effective. Fifteen British dragoons died in the charge and many were wounded. The American infantry escaped safely across the bridge, paused and turned around to fire at the enemy, and shot the Legionnaires off their horses. The American infantry ultimately frustrated the British effort to catch and destroy White's dragoons. General Washington appreciated White's initiative and success in striking at the enemy, and wrote that "White and the infantry appear to have acquitted themselves with much reputation."[19]

White soon got another chance to tangle with the British Legion in Westchester County, this time with Banastre Tarleton leading his dragoons. At dawn on the morning of September 6, Tarleton set a trap for White at Sherwood's Bridge, which crossed the Byram River. Tarleton left a small unit of loyalist militia at the southern end of the bridge, ostensibly as a guard but really as bait to lure the Americans into an ambush. Tarleton counted on White being unaware that the Legion was in the woods with three hundred cavalry and fifty infantrymen waiting to pounce and attack from behind. Patriot spies tipped off White and foiled Tarleton's plan, however. The rebel newspapers crowed over Tarleton's failure, gleefully mocking "the British hero [who] was . . . obliged to return much chagrined, and disappointed in his Don Quixotte expedition." The planned trap was a disaster for Tarleton, "which began with killing one, and wounding five of his own men, in a charge at the bridge; and ended in taking off all the geese, ducks and chickens in the neighbourhood of Kingstreet and the White-Plains." The rebel press concluded their account with one final jibe at the British, dryly remarking: "It is hoped a charitable construction will be put on the latter part of this glorious expedition, as we are credibly informed the British hospitals are much in want of poultry, the number of sick increasing daily."[20]

White's successes against the Legion and the Queen's Rangers likely contributed to his obtaining his own command. A few months later, near the end of 1779, White received orders to transfer to the 1st Continental Light Dragoons, now serving in South Carolina. For the first time in his career, White would be in command of a regiment.

## 1780: War in the South

Upon his transfer to the 1st Dragoons, White left New York and by January 1780 was in Philadelphia. Now that he had his own command, he wanted a promotion to full colonel. The Continental Congress and the Board of War sat in Philadelphia, so the city offered White the best opportunity to lobby for a promotion. Despite his recent successes in New York and his family connections, White was stymied in his efforts, and in late January, Washington ordered him to march without delay to South Carolina. The commander-in-chief was perfectly clear that although White would be in command of the 1st Dragoons, he would continue to serve as a lieutenant colonel. White appears to have gone over Washington's head, pressing for a promotion because of the vacant colonelcy in the 1st Dragoons. At the end of February, Congress considered his request but rejected it.[21]

Before heading south, White again turned his attention to matters of military justice. Courts-martial seem to have been a constant during White's career—either as presiding officer or defendant. In 1776 he had been tried and acquitted. The next year, he presided over the court-martial of his fellow dragoon officer Henry "Light-Horse Harry" Lee. He found Lee not guilty and fully exonerated him from groundless charges. White himself would be a defendant in three more trials, in May 1780, January 1781, and October 1781. Now, in January 1780, while in Philadelphia, he presided over the court-martial of Capt. Theophilus Parke. White found him guilty of forgery and defrauding his men of their pay, and sentenced him to be cashiered from the service "with infamy" by having his sword broken over his head on the public parade ground in front of his regiment and barred from ever holding a civilian or military position in the United States. General Washington approved the sentence.[22] After White completed his duties at Parke's court-martial, he finally marched to South Carolina and took command of the 1st Dragoons.

MONCKS CORNER—BIGGIN BRIDGE

In early 1780 the British invaded South Carolina for the third time. Their goal this time was to capture Charleston and, once taken, use its strategic position to fan out across the province, subdue it, and reassert royal authority before sweeping north to retake North Carolina. By the spring of 1780, the British laid siege to Charleston, trapping Maj. Gen. Benjamin Lincoln's Army within the city. The Royal Navy blocked the harbor and the infantry and artillery took up positions on Charleston Neck, just outside the walls of the city. The cavalry, particularly the British Legion under Banastre Tarleton, ranged across the surrounding countryside, capturing provisions for the army and skirmishing with the rebel horse. The British cavalry, however, was under a distinct disadvantage. During January the Legion sailed from New York to Charleston and was hammered by violent storms that put its transport ships at risk of sinking. To lighten the ships and save themselves, the Legionnaires threw all of their horses overboard. When the Legion finally arrived in the South, Tarleton's first order of business was replacing his lost mounts by buying or stealing every horse he could find. With zeal, gold, and guns, the Legion was soon remounted. The horses were small, slow marsh tackies— far inferior to what the Legion had lost and not as strong or as fast as rebel dragoon horses—but this was soon to change.

Brig. Gen. Isaac Huger was the highest-ranking Continental officer in South Carolina not trapped inside Charleston. Near Moncks Corner, about thirty miles north of Charleston, Huger collected a considerable number of American cavalry and militia units at Biggin Bridge, which crossed Biggin Creek near the headwaters of the Cooper River. Lt. Col. William Washington commanded the 3rd Continental Light Dragoons at Biggin Bridge. Remnants of Casimir Pulaski's Legion, who were survivors of the ill-fated American effort to recapture Savannah after it fell to the British, were also there, as were the 1st Continental Light Dragoons, temporarily led by Maj. John Jameson and waiting for Lt. Col. White, their new commander, to arrive.

As the choke point on the Americans' last remaining supply route into besieged Charleston, the Moncks Corner/Biggin Bridge position held immense strategic value. Maj. Gen. Benjamin Lincoln counted on his cavalry controlling the upper forks and passes of the Cooper River to allow reinforcements to arrive from the North or to be his escape hatch if he decided to abandon Charleston and decamp to the countryside.[23] The British were determined to break the American cavalry, seize control of Biggin Bridge and the upper Cooper River, and completely cut off Charleston from the South Carolina backcountry.

Because the American cavalry outnumbered the British Legion, Tarleton's best chance for success was a nighttime surprise assault. On the night of April 13, his Legionnaires rode silently in the darkness ahead of Lt. Col. James Webster's crack infantry regiments. Around three a.m. the British Legion arrived at Biggin Bridge and confirmed the Americans had deployed their troops like amateurs. The cavalry was posted on the west side of Biggin Creek in front of the bridge, but the militia were on the opposite shore, quartered in a church that overlooked the bridge. Because Huger put his infantry in the rear, there were no foot patrols scouting ahead of the cavalry's mounted sentinels. This meant that the American cavalry was unprotected from a surprise attack, and once an assault began, their freedom of movement would be restricted. They had Biggin Creek to their rear and swamp on either side of them. If they retreated, the rebel horsemen would have to run back through their own camp.[24]

The British Legion launched its attack against the American dragoons; some tried to defend themselves but were killed or wounded, and others, including officers, bolted to save themselves. Huger and Washington fled on horseback into the swamp and disappeared in the darkness while most of their men and officers retreated on foot because they were unable to mount their horses.[25]

The rebel infantry fared no better. Maj. Charles Cochrane, a Scot who commanded the mounted infantry of the British Legion, had his infantrymen dismount, fix bayonets, and charge across the bridge. The American militia crumbled under the onslaught and the British seized the bridge and took control of Biggin Creek. It was a decisive victory that gave the British the strategically crucial north Cooper River crossing and allowed them to freely move troops and supplies by land to the east of Charleston. The victory completed the job of cutting off communications between Charleston and the rest of South Carolina. The British also reaped important tactical advantages. Tarleton took one hundred dragoons and their officers prisoner, and seized fifty wagons filled with weapons, ammunition, and clothes. Thanks to the advantage of surprise, British losses were extremely light, with only three wounded troopers and five horses killed or wounded. Most important to the Legion were the hundreds of horses taken from the enemy that replaced the horses lost during its winter voyage south. As one British soldier described it, "Colonel Tarleton took so great a Number of exceeding fine Horses, as enabled him to produce 400 as well mounted and well appointed Cavalry as would do him Credit *en revue* at Wimbleton."[26]

The news of Huger's rout at Moncks Corner showed that neither Huger nor his cavalry officers were well prepared to fight against a fast-moving enemy like the British Legion. But Anthony Walton White was about to arrive in South Carolina. He had fought and beat the British Legion in the North. Could White repair the damage done to the American cavalry? And what of Charleston—what could be done to regain access to it?

## WHITE TAKES COMMAND

After their defeat at Moncks Corner, the 1st Continental Light Dragoons were headquartered at Cantey's Plantation on the north side of the Santee River near Nelson's Ferry. On April 23, White at last joined the regiment and took command.[27] He also asserted his authority over all cavalrymen in South Carolina, including his old comrade William Washington. As a result, William Washington's dragoons, the remnants of Pulaski's Legion, and Col. Daniel Horry's regiment all answered to White, even as they operated separately in the field. White was now twenty-nine years old and Washington a year younger. Although both men were lieutenant colonels, White had seniority. In the weeks after Moncks Corner, William Washington was called upon once again to rebuild a shattered regiment, but this time he would do it under White's command.

## PLAN OF ACTION

In the aftermath of Moncks Corner, and as the British tightened the noose around Charleston, White's dragoons rode from plantation to plantation in the lowcountry, covering fifteen to twenty miles a day. They roamed north and south of the Santee, ranging over a triangular region formed by Nelson's Ferry to the west, Georgetown to the east, and Moncks Corner to the south. The horsemen crisscrossed pine barrens, swamps, and savannahs, often traveling at night to avoid the heat of the South Carolina spring, then ate and rested during the day. Although constantly in motion, White's troopers rode without any discernible strategy for opposing the enemy or assisting General Lincoln's army trapped inside Charleston.

White was soon joined by another recent arrival to South Carolina, Col. Abraham Buford, whose regiment of Continental troops was one of the last waves of Virginians that left Petersburg for the long march south in order to relieve Charleston. Buford's detachment was an assortment of men from various regiments. Some were hardened combat veterans, while others were recent draftees who had not yet seen any action. By the time Buford reached Camden, South Carolina, in late April, news arrived that Charleston was surrounded. There was no chance now of slipping a large force past the British in order to reinforce the garrison trapped inside the city. Along with Buford's Continentals, hundreds of North Carolina militiamen were in the area, also awaiting orders for what to do next.

John Rutledge, the rebel governor of South Carolina who had recently fled Charleston, began amassing all available infantry regiments and cavalry units. Rutledge believed it was absolutely essential that the Americans immediately restore communications with the troops and citizens of the besieged city. To achieve his goal, he ordered militia troops to march as quickly as possible to Lenud's Ferry on the north side of the Santee River, about forty miles north of Charleston. Rutledge sent letters to Buford and White requesting that their respective units meet at Lenud's Ferry, and ordered arms and ammunition be gathered and brought to supply the troops he was collecting there.[28]

As the Americans massed their troops, each side gathered intelligence on the other's strengths and intentions. British lieutenant general Charles, Earl Cornwallis, needed to supply his forces besieging Charleston, and White learned that Cornwallis had extended his foraging parties so that they were now on the south bank of the Santee. White formed a plan in which his horsemen, Washington's dragoons, Horry's regiment, and what was left of Pulaski's Legion would separately cross to the south side of the Santee, meet at Lenud's Ferry, and from there mount a surprise attack in order to disrupt the enemy's collection of supplies.[29]

SOUTHWARD MARCH

On May 3, White ordered his men to be ready to march at a moment's notice. After dark they rode to Georgetown and united with all of the American cavalry who were fit for duty. White worked out his plan with Buford, who was supposed to march three hundred of his infantrymen in support of the operation. White's junior officers were kept in the dark about their mission, probably to ensure that the element of surprise would not be lost in case of spies, or if any of his men were captured before they reached their destination. Getting to Lenud's Ferry proved difficult. After only an hour's ride, White's troopers missed the correct path and became "much entangled" in the woods. They finally found the right road and halted for the night in a savannah. They stayed there for the better part of the next day, pounded by a nonstop rain.[30]

Finally, late in the day on May 4, White's dragoons crossed to the south side of the Santee and kept riding through the night. The next day they met up with Washington's unit at Lenud's Ferry, ate dinner, and then bivouacked that night in the nearby woods. It was a cold, blustery night, unusual for early May. The next morning, on May 6, a slave approached their encampment, armed with a sword at his side. He apparently believed that White's dragoons were either British or Tories and offered them his services. The slave told White that he was "a man of consequence among those of his Colour" and if White thought him worthy of a captain's commission he would raise a company of men to oppose the rebels. His own master was a rebel who was hiding in the swamp, and the slave boasted to his would-be comrades that he was well acquainted with the terrain and would track down his master and kill him.[31]

White listened to the slave's proposal, never letting on that he had blundered into the wrong camp. After the slave laid out his plan, White ordered his dragoons to whip the man and hang him. They gave him fifty lashes, then tied a noose around him and half hanged him, letting him dangle at the end of the rope for a while before cutting him down. White's dragoons then rode off, leaving him with the noose still tied around his neck. No doubt they wanted him left alive—but beaten, strangled, and humiliated—to serve as a warning to other slaves who might consider taking up arms against their masters or any American soldier.[32]

CAPTURING THE ENEMY

Although White's plan of attack on the south side of the Santee counted on infantry support from Buford, Buford's regiment failed to show up at Lenud's Ferry. Instead, Buford sent a messenger with a note claiming that he could not send any infantry but that he wished White success in attacking the enemy. Despite this setback, White was determined to go forward with the operation. Following their encounter with the rebellious slave, White and Washington marched their dragoons about twelve miles to Wambaw, a plantation owned by a Tory named Elias Ball Sr. It was a windy, disagreeable day. At about nine a.m. the Americans found their quarry, a detachment from the British 63rd Regiment of Foot, commanded by a Lieutenant Ash and consisting of a sergeant and a dozen privates. Capt. Baylor Hill led the attack and received little opposition. Badly outnumbered, only one redcoat fired a pistol before the rest surrendered.[33]

What was a bloodless American victory nearly turned into a massacre. White and Washington's dragoons were still smarting from their crushing defeat at Moncks Corner and emotions must have been running high among the Americans when they captured the redcoats. Captain Hill had to intervene to protect the British, and only his quick action prevented "many of them being put to the Sword."[34]

Under Captain Hill's protection, Lieutenant Ash and the rest of the British captives were marched to Lenud's

Ferry. The American cavalrymen no doubt rode back to the river exulting over their success. They had used overwhelming force and surprise to capture the enemy and disrupt his ability to supply the besiegers of Charleston. After the disaster of Moncks Corner and three weeks of constant riding but no fighting, the American dragoons had finally taken the war to the enemy. In high spirits, the horsemen probably even joked at the expense of the slave who had tried to obtain a commission from them that morning.

INDISCRETION

Despite the Americans' success in striking at the enemy, White and Washington realized their precarious position. The Santee was a great natural barrier that, once crossed, would immediately protect them. The problem was crossing the river. At the time, the Santee was probably 800 to 1,200 feet across—far wider than the river is today. Then as now, the Santee at Lenud's Ferry is no river for a man to swim across. Beneath its placid waters are a swift current, alligators, and water moccasins. Although swimming the horses across was possible, the only certain way for White and Washington to put more than one hundred men and their horses safely on the north bank would be by ferry boats. That would take time, and while they waited on the south bank to complete their crossing, the Americans were vulnerable.[35]

White sent a messenger ahead to Buford asking him to send troops across the Santee to cover the cavalry's retreat. Buford later claimed he immediately sent 150 infantrymen to cross the river and stand watch while the dragoons and their horses were ferried to the north side. It is not clear how soon Buford marched his men, but the cavalry arrived at Lenud's Ferry long before the infantry. Colonels White and Washington and Major Jameson knew their men were tired and the horses were hungry, but White and Washington disagreed about what to do next. The surprise and rout at Moncks Corner was fresh in Washington's mind, and having his men camp in broad daylight with their back to the river must have made Washington nervous. He strenuously urged White to cross the Santee immediately, but White refused. Instead, White ordered the men to feed the horses and then rest themselves. To maintain a vigil during their halt, the men were ordered to feed only half the horses while the other half covered them. But the Americans were careless, allowing many of the horses that were not feeding to be unbridled or unsaddled.[36]

## Surprise

Within a half hour of the American arrival at Lenud's Ferry, only a single boat was on the south bank, and Buford's infantrymen were nowhere in sight. Captain Hill had turned his prisoners over to Capt. Walker Baylor, who put them in the boat to ferry them to the other side. Unknown to the Americans and their captives, however, Tarleton and 150 dragoons and mounted infantry were very close by. Tarleton had been on an intelligence patrol that day, seeking information on American force levels and movements in the same area. As Tarleton and his dragoons reconnoitered, they encountered Elias Ball, the owner of the plantation where the redcoats were surprised that morning, who told them of the skirmish and that the Americans were now planning to cross the Santee with their prisoners. Ball then guided the Legion to Lenud's Ferry.[37]

Tarleton was emboldened at the prospect of attacking White's forces on one side of the river while they were separated from Buford's troops and at the same time freeing the British prisoners. He spurred the Legion onward to Lenud's Ferry and arrived at the river just as the captured redcoats departed by boat from the south bank. It was three p.m. White's dragoons were still resting, still feeding their horses, and still waiting for boats and

Buford's men to arrive to cover their withdrawal. Suddenly, a warning shot rang out, and the Americans turned around to "see the approach of the Brittish horse in full Speed."[38]

It was a complete surprise. Before the Americans could bridle a single horse, Tarleton's Legion charged into White's men. Caught unaware, and trapped with their backs to the Santee, the Americans on foot faced an onslaught of gunfire and slashing swords from a mounted enemy. The carnage was sickening as the Americans were "cut & hacked . . . in a most shocking manner." Some of those lucky enough to survive the onslaught of British steel were either blinded or disfigured for life, with ears cut off or skulls smashed in.[39]

The redcoats captured that morning immediately took advantage of the surprise attack. The boat they were in had just left the shore. As soon as they saw Tarleton leading the charge, they seized their guards, threw them overboard, rowed themselves back to the south bank, and joined the Legion.[40]

The Americans fled the battlefield in every direction. Some headed to the river. White and Washington, along with Major Jameson, swam for their lives and reached the other side, but other, less fortunate Americans drowned in the attempt. The Legion's dismounted infantry chased other fleeing rebels into the swamps, where many slipped away. Maj. Richard Call and seven others remounted, raced past the British Legion, and escaped on horseback. Captain Hill frantically searched for his horse, but it was not where he had left it. He tried to bridle another horse, but gunfire and the shouts of the Legionnaires frightened the horses and he was unable to mount. When a Legion trooper ordered Hill to surrender, he abandoned any plan for a mounted escape and fled on foot. Hill ran across fields and jumped over fences, chased all the way by a dragoon slashing at him with a saber until he finally surrendered.[41]

Tarleton quickly crushed the Americans on the south bank. In his words, the Americans, "being totally surprised, resistance and slaughter soon ceased." Tarleton claimed the Legion killed or wounded forty-one and captured sixty-seven Americans, but his count is far higher than other sources. As for the British, they lost only two men and four horses, and rescued their captured comrades.[42] Thus, in one short, fierce engagement, the Americans were once again surprised and routed. Unfortunately for them, Lenud's Ferry was a harbinger of worse to come, and would not be the last time an American colonel ran away in the face of an onslaught by Tarleton's dragoons.

## AFTERMATH

In the immediate aftermath of the battle, White and Washington stood on the north bank of the Santee. They were soaking wet and spent, and gazed despondently across the river. Their reversal of fortune was profound. The morning's triumph was swept away by the afternoon's disaster. Men who just minutes earlier had followed their lead now lay dead or dying, or were captured or on the run, and White and Washington were powerless to help. The defeated Americans could only stand by and listen to the cries of the wounded, the shouts of Legion officers and sergeants directed at their men, and the jeers of the enemy. While the British rounded up their prisoners and stripped the dead of uniforms, boots, and weapons, they could see the Americans who had escaped were now huddled on the opposite shore, bedraggled and thoroughly defeated. Tarleton's men would soon hear the details of how their comrades were captured that morning and nearly massacred on the spot. Their story would be repeated again and again, and the thrashing of the Americans at Lenud's Ferry would be just a taste of what the British Legion would dish out to the rebels.

After overcoming the shock of the attack and their narrow escape, White and Washington must have realized the enormity of their defeat. White's regiment of horse was shattered, and no organized cavalry remained in the South. The Americans could no longer mobilize mounted troops to aid in the defense of Charleston. Instead, the British Legion grew stronger, and this latest rout gave Tarleton another forty to fifty captured American horses in addition to those taken at Moncks Corner. The horses lost during the winter's voyage southward were quickly being replenished in the spring, thanks to American miscalculation and lack of preparation. As a result, the British now completely dominated the lowcountry, from the outskirts of Charleston to the south side of the Santee, and no reinforcements could break through to the besieged garrison.

After the battle, Tarleton rode hard back to Cornwallis's camp near Hughes Bridge, a forced march so grueling that it killed twenty horses. The Legion had at least thirty prisoners in tow, including Maj. Cosmo de Medici and Captain Hill. They spent one night there, unguarded after giving their parole. From Cornwallis's camp, the captured Americans were taken to Charleston, where many remained as prisoners until exchanged over the course of the next six to twelve months. A few of the American dragoons refused to wait for an exchange. They made a daring escape from the British by stealing a boat in the harbor, and eventually made their way back to Virginia.[43]

## VINDICATION

With no hope of retaliating against the Legion, White and Washington turned their backs on the Santee and returned to Georgetown, where recriminations on the American side soon began. Ever sensitive to his honor, Lieutenant Colonel White immediately demanded a court of inquiry. The court issued its judgment one week after the battle, and it was everything that White could have hoped for. Surprisingly, the verdict was that "the Court hearing the evidence produced are of the opinion that Colonel White was not guilty of the least neglect or inattention on the 6th instant, and that on the whole he did everything for the troops under his command, that Prudence could dictate."[44]

## RECOVERY AND RECRIMINATION

Around the same time, White received additional good news as more men and horses who escaped from the battle returned to the ranks. On the day of the attack, Pvt. John Gore and five others in White's regiment had fled to a nearby swamp and hid there until night fell. In the darkness, they traveled up the river and then went inland until they came to a house. They knocked on the door seeking food and water, and found inside Captain Murray and seven other men from Colonel Washington's regiment. Before they left their hosts the Virginians commandeered a rickety old canoe. All fourteen of them piled in, paddled to the north side of the Santee, and then marched twenty miles to Georgetown to rejoin White. Fourteen fine horses that White had lost were soon recovered, thanks to two sixteen-year-old boys who stole them back from the British Legion and brought them to White in Georgetown.[45]

The recovered horses were a welcome addition because Washington's forces were so depleted that "we have not at present in my Command twelve Men that are equipped for the Field."[46] White and Washington soon left Georgetown and retreated to Halifax, North Carolina, to rebuild their shattered cavalry. The result of the defeat at Lenud's Ferry was that, for the rest of the spring and summer of 1780, the American cavalry in the South was completely sidelined and no longer an effective combat force.

## BUFORD'S REPORTS

On the day of the battle at Lenud's Ferry, Colonel Buford may not have perceived the effect the cavalry's destruc-

tion would have on his own regiment, but Buford keenly
felt the loss. Buford eventually arrived at Lenud's Ferry to
rendezvous with White and Washington, but by then it
was too late. Seeing the carnage across the river, and sensing that his absence from the battle would be reported
unfavorably, Buford dispatched a letter to Gen. George
Washington to describe what had happened and to
explain his actions. Talk among the men was that one of
Buford's fellow officers, Lt. Col. Samuel Hawes, had
begged Buford to send boats across the river, but that
Buford refused to do so "from some motive believed at
the time to be a bad one." Buford's dispatch to General
Washington, however, insisted, "I immediately detached
150 men with officers to cross the ferry & get into the rear
of the horse to cover their crossing the river."[47]

Buford also used his letter to General Washington to
report on the conditions existing in the lowcountry on the
eve of Charleston's expected surrender. Buford was shak-
en by images of the dead and wounded that he saw in the
aftermath of the British Legion's attack, and the fact that
the enemy had forced American officers to flee ignomin-
iously from the battlefield to save themselves. Buford
thought this was a fate "which is little better than being
killed or taken."[48]

SURRENDER

In his report to General Washington, Buford also confirmed the worst. The mauling the Americans had just
received at Lenud's Ferry, along "with the late surprise at
Monk's Corner has rendered our Cavalry unfit for service
& given the enemy horse very great superiority." The
advantage the British gained at Lenud's Ferry was not lost
on either the British or American commanders. Two days
after Lenud's Ferry, Sir Henry Clinton sent General
Lincoln a summons demanding that he surrender
Charleston. Clinton listed "the destruction on the 6th
instant of what remained of your cavalry" as one of the

reasons why it was now hopeless for the Americans to resist.[49]

Clinton gave Lincoln a deadline to surrender by eight o'clock that night or hostilities would begin again. The Americans temporized and bargained for an extension so they could negotiate terms. After a thirty-six-hour truce, talks collapsed when Clinton rejected Lincoln's proposed surrender terms. The Americans responded with a tremendous cannon barrage and the British promptly returned fire. Each side blistered the other in a nighttime cannonade that shook the city for hours. The thunder of the artillery duel rolled across the lowcountry and could be heard by Buford's men forty miles away at Lenud's Ferry. Vigilant against another surprise attack, the men lay on their muskets that night and listened to the constant thump of the distant cannons.[50]

The besieged defenders could not hold out and risk destroying the city they fought to save. On May 12, 1780, General Lincoln surrendered Charleston to the British. The loss was enormous. An entire army of five thousand men was taken prisoner. With one of the greatest ports in North America now back under British control, the forces of the Crown had tremendous momentum as they spread out from Charleston to conquer South Carolina. In the end, White's attempt to strike the enemy and disrupt the siege of Charleston resulted instead in the destruction of his cavalry and hastened the city's surrender.

ASSESSMENT

There were many causes for the destruction of the American cavalry at Lenud's Ferry. Buford was too slow to respond to White's request for infantry to cover the cavalry's planned return across the Santee. White then gambled and lost when he crossed the Santee without waiting to receive infantry support from Buford. He should have learned from his success ten months earlier at New Rochelle, where his dragoons were saved by crossing a bridge that spanned a creek while being covered by the infantry who guarded the bridge. This was a critical lesson that White should have remembered: when cavalry crosses a river, infantry support is essential to protect the dragoons during the crossing. White's failure to heed this lesson proved devastating to the American cause.

William Washington had had a very recent and painful experience in fighting the Legion, and when they arrived at the Santee, White should have accepted Washington's advice to immediately cross the river by swimming the horses. Overconfident because of his successes in skirmishing with the British Legion in New York the year before, White foolishly let the men rest while waiting for Buford to arrive, making matters worse with simple carelessness. While the Americans were halted on the south bank of the Santee, White and all of his officers were negligent in not maintaining proper vigilance to ensure their men would be ready in case of a surprise attack. It is hard to understand why the Americans failed to learn the right lessons after being surprised and routed just weeks before at Moncks Corner. The American cavalry suffered needlessly at Lenud's Ferry, and Buford's regiment would soon face the dire consequences of being slow and lax in the face of an aggressive, fast-moving enemy like Tarleton.

## BUFORD'S DEFEAT

White's loss at Lenud's Ferry, along with Buford's own mistakes, contributed to the annihilation of Buford's regiment a short time afterward. While White and Washington retreated into eastern North Carolina, a number of White's dragoons remained with Buford but were too few in number to make a difference. Three weeks after Lenud's Ferry, Buford's detachment of nearly 350 men were the only active Continental troops in South Carolina. With the loss of Charleston, however, it was pointless for Buford's small regiment to remain in the area. As they beat a retreat into North Carolina, Tarleton chased them down and launched a ferocious attack near the Waxhaw settlement in the South Carolina backcountry.

Without sufficient cavalry to support him, Buford's infantrymen had to stand their ground in an open wood against the British Legion's combined force of dragoons and dismounted infantry. Some British soldiers were nearly murdered on the spot when White's cavalry had captured them three weeks earlier. They owed their freedom to Tarleton's rapid assault at Lenud's Ferry, and no doubt the British Legion was not inclined to show great mercy to an enemy they despised. Tarleton's surprise attack at the Waxhaws led to a hugely disproportionate British victory, albeit one tainted with the charge of massacre and which handed the Americans a powerful narrative of a bloodthirsty and cruel enemy. In the melee of battle, some Americans raised a white flag of surrender while others fought on. The British Legion cut the Americans to pieces, killing men while they were trying to surrender and then murdering the wounded. Colonel Buford, however, saved himself. Like White and Washington before him, he discovered the merits of self-preservation and fled the field of battle.[51]

## REBUILDING

Even though White was acquitted at his court-martial following the debacle at Lenud's Ferry, the defeat was the low point of his career, and the disastrous results of his failure to protect his men against Tarleton's surprise attack dominated the rest of a bad year for White. By summer, he and William Washington had repaired to Halifax, North Carolina, to rebuild their shattered regiments. This required money, which was in short supply, but his position and background allowed him to take care of his regiment's immediate needs. On July 4, 1780, White advanced, on his own credit, the sum of $150,000 in Continental currency to purchase supplies and equipment that the 1st Dragoons desperately needed. It was a generous gesture, but one that would haunt White for the rest of his life.[52]

After General Lincoln's surrender of Charleston and his army, Maj. Gen. Horatio Gates became commander of the Southern army. In late July, Gates was advised of the miserable state of the American cavalry in the South, that White and Washington had traveled from Halifax to Virginia to procure horses and arms, and that it would be at least six weeks before the dragoons would be fit for service.[53]

White and Washington were successful in recruiting more men and persuading the Virginia General Assembly to foot the bill for more horses and equipment. Gates, however, was not happy that his cavalry was not ready for action, and ordered White's troopers to deploy at once, even if it meant that they were to become infantrymen. In a long explanatory letter to his superior, White very politely objected to Gates's order, explaining that due to "our Melancholy state," in which he and Washington had only twenty horses equipped and fit for duty, the two regiments would be more hindrance than help to the army. The new recruits would have to be trained and outfitted. More important, the recruits had been promised that they would be cavalrymen who could be pressed into service in the infantry only in the greatest emergency. As for the veterans, if an infantry role awaited them, none would reenlist. White pleaded with Gates to countermand his order and warned that "if the Cavalry are called to the field in their present Situation nothing but their ruin can Issue."[54]

Gates got the message and left White and his cavalry alone. As a result, Gates had no cavalry support two weeks later when his army marched into South Carolina and was demolished at Camden—a profound disaster that compelled Gates (like Buford before) to flee the battle on horseback. Two weeks after Gates's defeat at Camden, White was still in Halifax and still writing to Gates about his lack of readiness. This time, the great number of his dragoons who were sick from the ague and fever made it impossible for White to guess when he might be able to comply with Gates's orders. At the very least, White was sympathetic to Gates's devastating defeat and wrote that he was "sorry that the want of Horse should in so great a measure be the Cause of it."[55]

White himself soon fell sick and nearly died. By the middle of October, he was in Halifax trying to recover. White wrote to Gates about his extremely weak condition and also advised that his regiment was not quite ready. But White promised that his men would be prepared to ride in a week.[56] Thus, for nearly six months after Lenud's Ferry, White and the 1st Dragoons were essentially out of commission as meaningful contributors to the war effort. Even worse, the cavalry disasters at Moncks Corner and Lenud's Ferry bore bitter fruit for the infantry, first under Buford at the Waxhaws and then under Gates at Camden.

The challenge of reequipping White's regiment in 1780 was made all the more difficult by accusations leveled against White, a problem that festered into 1781. Despite the court of inquiry in May that had cleared White of any culpability for his defeat at Lenud's Ferry, many of his fellow officers were resolutely against him. White had Lt. Presley Thornton arrested "for attempting, in a base & Ungentleman like manner to assassinate my Character." Thornton was court-martialed and convicted, and White approved the sentence. William Washington wanted White arrested, but because White was his superior, Washington could not do it on his own. Instead, he maneuvered White's arrest through a North Carolina officer, Col. Gideon Lamb, who happened to be passing through Halifax. At Washington's request, Colonel Lamb ordered White arrested and Thornton retried.[57]

In September 1780, a general court-martial convened to try White on the charges pressed by Washington. Maj. Gen. William Smallwood presided, with a jury comprised of the twelve senior Continental officers in the state. Colonel Buford was excused from the court because White intended to call him as a witness. The trial was deferred, however, because one of the parties—presumably Washington—was not able to attend, and White was suspended from his arrest. Finally, in January 1781, when White was tried at a court-martial held in Hillsborough, North Carolina, he was acquitted. Maj. Gen. Nathanael Greene disapproved the judgment, however, because the court considered evidence that was not contained in the charges. Nevertheless, Greene had White released from arrest and placed back on active duty. White then headed west to Salem, home of the Moravians, to obtain fifty horses for the cavalry, before heading north into Virginia to complete his regiment.[58]

## 1781–1782: THE WAR WINDS DOWN

In the last years of the Revolution, White traveled throughout the South, impressing horses, recruiting in Virginia, and fighting in Georgia. By the spring of 1781, White was supporting the Marquis de Lafayette in opposing Tarleton's operations in Virginia. Lafayette knew that Tarleton had mounted a large body of infantry and that it was urgent for White to increase the cavalry under his command. White had two hundred dismounted dragoons under his command and Lafayette pleaded with General Washington that White be allowed to impress two hundred horses and receive the equipment needed to remount his men. These measures were critical to guard against Tarleton's depredations. Lafayette warned Washington that "nothing else will put it in my power to prevent the Enemy from ravaging the Country in small parties." Within a month, White had "two hundred excellent horses" but was still waiting for saddles, swords, pistols, boots, and clothing. If he obtained what he needed, White would have more dragoons than the British.[59] While the Americans were still trying to obtain boots for their troopers, Tarleton raided Charlottesville and nearly captured Virginia's governor, Thomas Jefferson.

Lafayette put Maj. Richard Call in charge of equipping the dragoons while White gathered soldiers who would remain in service for the duration of the war. One recruit recalled enlisting under White in the summer of 1781, in eastern Virginia at an army camp at Chickahominy Swamp: "Col. White of the dragoons came to camp and [we] were paraded. He requested that all men who would enlist for the war would ground their arms and march five paces in front and offered a bounty of $1,000 and half pay during life." White's offer was enticing. Thirty to forty men stepped out and enlisted.[60]

While White was trying to field his regiment, Lafayette was maneuvering Cornwallis into a trap. By October 1781, Cornwallis was surrounded at Yorktown and forced to surrender. At the same time, White's old nemesis Tarleton surrendered his post across the York River at Gloucester. Once the British Army had been defeated in Virginia, White prepared to leave the state and head south to join General Greene in South Carolina. Some were happy to see White leave. Prominent Baltimore politician George Lux, writing to Greene, lamented William Washington's capture at Eutaw Springs, South Carolina, two months earlier and unfavorably compared White with Washington: "Col W-lt-n W—e is not here considered his [Washington's] equal in merit & I am told, he has marched down with a full Corps to join you, adorned with Tarleton's spoils."[61]

Before White left Virginia, there was still an old score to settle. He had a knack for falling into disputes with his fellow officers, and was a magnet for charges that besmirched his reputation. White would not let any accusations slide, even if they were years old. In the fall of 1781, White requested that a court-martial be convened to try him on the charges leveled against him two years earlier by Capt. John Heard, who had served under White in the 4th Light Dragoon Regiment. White's request was granted, and when Heard was called upon to put up or shut up, Heard dropped the charges, claiming that upon investigation he found that his charges were grounded upon misinformation. General Washington wanted to clear the air completely and ordered that Heard's retraction be published to the entire Continental Army so that White would be "totally freed from the aspersions cast on his Character." Washington went further and admonished his troops that "Accusations of so serious a nature should be made with the most scrupulous caution; an Officer's Character being too sacred to be impeached with Levity without a sufficient foundation."[62]

Despite the British surrender at Yorktown, fighting in the South continued, and for White in particular there was still action to be found in Georgia. In early 1782, his cavalry was attached to Brig. Gen. Anthony Wayne's army, which was assigned the task of retaking Savannah from the British and reasserting American control over Georgia. Wayne also had to assert control over his dragoons. General Greene warned Wayne that "Cavalry are difficult to keep in good order, and require much nursing, more than I could have imagined, until I learnt it by experience. I would just hint this matter as worthy your attention in the arrangement of your affairs."[63]

On January 12, 1782, Wayne's army crossed the Savannah River with White and one hundred of his dragoons. After Wayne maneuvered the enemy out of their posts, the British massed for attack. White responded with a "spirited & judicious disposition" that forced the British to retreat. In late January, a body of Creek warriors marched to Savannah in support of the British. A detachment of Wayne's troops "Clothed in Scarlet" tricked the Creeks into believing that they were British dragoons and led them back to Wayne near Ogeechee Ferry, where they were surrounded and disarmed without resistance. The twenty-six Indians soon escaped, but White recaptured most of them.[64]

In February, Wayne was desperate for reinforcements that would allow him to bring his artillery and baggage across the Savannah River. Many of his men were Georgia militia, and his ability to ward off the enemy depended almost entirely on White and his dragoons. During this time, discipline was becoming a problem; the men were disaffected over lack of pay and clothing. Wayne wrote that, except for their worn-out caps, coats, and overalls, White's dragoons were "almost as naked as Nature left them." Wayne thought the task of retaking Georgia was "much more difficult than that of the Children of Israel, they had only to make bricks without straw."[65]

By comparison, Wayne and White had to acquire provisions, forage, and equipment without money; build boats and bridges without materials; make Whigs out of Tories; and overcome the depredations of local bandits. Despite these problems, Wayne was able to take Georgia back from the enemy (except for Savannah) "with the help of a few Regular Dragoons." White and his dragoons also assisted Wayne with a midnight strike against the enemy at the plantation of the royal governor, Sir James Wright. The plantation, located very close to Savannah, was where the British were collecting their forage. Although the farm was within musket range of the British inside Savannah, Wayne's troops were able to sweep in and burn the forage. The fire from Wright's plantation that night "highly Illuminated" the town and had the effect of forcing the enemy to stay within Savannah, possibly from fear that the Hessian troops and new recruits inside the town would desert if sent outside on a mission.[66]

In April, Wayne attacked British outposts and drove the troops back into Savannah. As the British fell back, they resorted to scorched-earth tactics and destroyed whatever could not be carried to the city. Although Wayne's forces were outnumbered, it did not stop him from besieging Savannah. The British called upon their Creek allies for help, and loyalist colonel Thomas Brown dispatched a detachment of his men to march from Savannah to meet the Creeks at Ogeechee Ferry. Wayne discovered their plan and sent White out with an infantry unit to intercept the loyalists. That night the Americans captured an enemy patrol, but one loyalist escaped and rode back to warn Colonel Brown. Brown brought on a greater force of dragoons and infantry and clashed with the rebel cavalry near a swamp. White's forces charged into the loyalist dragoons, who fell back upon their own infantry. Once the enemy was boxed in on a narrow causeway, White and his dragoons, along with the American infantry, attacked the confused mass of loyalists, killing forty, capturing twenty, and forcing the rest of the enemy to flee into the swamp. The Americans had only five killed and two wounded.[67]

On June 24, a band of Creek warriors surprised General Wayne with a nighttime assault five miles from Savannah. Wayne's advance guard retreated and the Creeks seized two artillery pieces. White's cavalry and the infantry counterattacked, and in a close-quarters brawl in which both sides used swords and bayonets, the Americans forced the Indians back. The Creeks kept fighting until their chief was killed, which prompted them to finally quit the battle and retreat. Three weeks later, on July 11, the British evacuated Savannah and sailed to Charleston under a truce, leaving Wayne to occupy Savannah.[68] Five months later, the British surrendered Charleston and the war in the South was over.

EPILOGUE

White's life after the Revolution was a series of promising starts and crushing disappointments. By the summer of 1783, White was out of the Army and settling down in Charleston. While in the city, White met and soon married Margaret Ellis, who was both young and rich, the daughter of a wealthy local merchant. White was thirty-three but she was only fifteen. Margaret was the sister-in-law of Dr. David Ramsay, a leading citizen of Charleston, prominent as a physician and politician, and soon to be the author of a history of South Carolina during the Revolution. In 1785, Ramsay published his history, and without mentioning that White was his brother-in-law, Ramsay wrote that White had issued orders "to proper persons to collect boats, and to assemble a body of infantry at [Lenud's Ferry], to cover the American cavalry in their recrossing the Santee, but they had not been carried into execution. . . . From the want of boats and of infantry, a retreat was impracticable, and resistance unavailing. A rout took place."[69] Ramsay's history, the first of its kind on the American Revolution and influential for decades to come, relieved White of responsibility for the disaster at Lenud's Ferry, and by implication placed the blame on Col. Abraham Buford.

Despite his own personal wealth and that of his young wife, White suffered a series of financial disasters and for much of his life was besieged by creditors. In Georgia, his mercantile house failed. He also guaranteed the debts of his former troopers, who later defaulted, forcing him to liquidate his property at a great sacrifice. White then left Charleston and moved to New York, where he lived on an estate near New Rochelle, not far from where he had skirmished with Tarleton a few years before. More financial disasters followed, and White was forced to use most of his inheritance to pay his creditors.[70] White then moved back to his home state of New Jersey and returned to the town of his birth, New Brunswick. There, he and his wife Margaret had their only child, a daughter named Eliza.

A constant feature in his life at this time was his unpaid war debt, and White was a persistent claimant before the federal government, seeking reimbursement for the money he advanced in 1780 on behalf of his regiment. White literally was seeking an act of Congress in order to be paid, but throughout the 1790s he was repeatedly rebuffed.[71]

White became active again in national military affairs in the 1790s during the Whiskey Rebellion. When the federal government tried to enforce its collection of a new tax on whiskey, the Scotch-Irish settlements in the backcountry exploded. Western Pennsylvania was the center of the insurrection. Rebel militias took over local government, and more than seven thousand insurrectionists gathered in revolt, threatening to burn Pittsburgh to the ground. President George Washington personally took the field at the head of a thirteen-thousand strong militia-based army to crush the insurrection.[72]

White eagerly volunteered to go to war against his fellow Americans. The New Jersey militia would be a key unit in the expedition, and White lobbied to take command of it. Even though he held the rank of brigadier general in the state militia, the perception was that his temper rendered him unfit to lead it in action. White was turned down, but he persisted and was soon put in charge of arresting those accused of treason and bringing the prisoners back to Philadelphia for trial. After marching for weeks through cold, rainy weather over muddy tracks and broken hills, he crossed the Allegheny Mountains and descended upon the four western counties that had rebelled.

The plan of attack involved a coordinated, mass arrest without warrants, which began on November 13, 1794. The locals came to remember the event as the "Dreadful Night." For his part in it, White became known as "Blackbeard" for his brutal treatment of the locals whom he captured, verbally and physically abused, and marched back to Philadelphia for trial on a thirty-day journey through snow and mud. Blackbeard maintained strict discipline on the march. The prisoners trudged on foot, each man between two mounted troopers. White's orders were that his men were always to keep their swords drawn, and if there was any rescue attempt, his troopers were to decapitate the prisoners and bring their heads to Philadelphia. Ultimately, not one of his prisoners was ever convicted.[73]

White's military career was inactive for another five years until America became involved in the "Quasi War" with France, where French privateers attacked and seized hundreds of American ships. In May 1798, Congress authorized President John Adams to raise a provisional army of ten thousand troops in the event of a declaration of war, and President Adams nominated White to be a brigadier general for this paper army. His nomination drew howls of protest from those who had served with White in the South. They harshly criticized him as "totally unfit for command, or anything else, but to dress and parade thro' the Country" and claimed he suffered from "great imbecility of mind, & frivolity of character" such that no one wanted to serve under him. George Washington echoed such sentiments, even referring to his former aide-de-camp and cavalry officer during the Revolution as a "notorious liar." War jitters faded over time, the provisional army never materialized, and White never assumed command.[74]

White's final years were even more difficult. In 1802 he was forced into involuntary bankruptcy. He died the following year at the age of fifty-three without ever receiving payment on his claim to be reimbursed for the debt he had incurred to outfit his regiment in 1780. His young widow continued her husband's quest; she too was unsuccessful during her lifetime, but their daughter persisted. Finally, on March 3, 1859, both the House and Senate approved a bill granting relief for White's only child and heir, Eliza White Evans. The Secretary of the Treasury was ordered to pay her the sum of $3,750 plus forty-one years of interest. It had taken the government nearly eighty years to repay the money White lent to rebuild the U.S. cavalry after its defeat at Lenud's Ferry.[75]

White's turbulent life saw triumph and disaster, much of it self-inflicted, and followed an arc that began with the promise of privileged youth and ardent patriotism but ended in a travesty of the martial spirit and a bankrupt estate. Upon his death, he was buried at Christ Episcopal Church in New Brunswick, New Jersey. The inscription on his monument summed up his life, not in the words of a disinterested historian, but from the vantage point of those who loved him: "He was an affectionate husband, a tender parent, a sincere and generous friend, a zealous and inflexible patriot, and a faithful, active and gallant officer in the Army of the United States during the Revolutionary War."[76]

# SIX

# South Carolina's Backcountry Rangers in the American Revolution
### "A Splendid Body of Men"

## *Michael C. Scoggins*

WHEN MOST PEOPLE THINK ABOUT THE BATTLES OF THE American Revolution, they picture large numbers of British and American foot soldiers facing off against each other in traditional eighteenth-century battle lines. While this is certainly an accurate image for many of the large land battles fought during the Revolution, the struggle in the South Carolina upcountry or "backcountry" was generally a much different type of warfare. Here the conflict was often characterized by small bands of fast-moving troopers mounted on horseback, who traveled quickly from place to place, struck the enemy hard, and then retreated into the woods and hills to fight another day. Although well mounted, these soldiers were not usually trained or equipped to fight like the cavalry or "dragoons" of the regular armies until the final years of the conflict.

For most of the war, these backcountry rangers used their horses to travel to and from the battlefield, but the general lack of true cavalry weapons like sabers, pistols, and short rifles or carbines meant that they usually had to dismount in order to engage in combat. They also performed a vital role for the commanders of the regular armies by acting as scouts, foragers, and "cowboys" or cattle drovers.

During the nine years of the American Revolution, the state of South Carolina fielded one regiment of mounted Continental riflemen, nine state regiments of light dragoons or cavalry, and two state legions that included both light dragoons and infantry. These mounted units were generally divided into troops, the cavalry equivalent of infantry companies. There were also a large number of mounted militia regiments raised on the state establishment between 1775 and 1780, and an indeterminate number of "partisan rangers" who served as unpaid volunteers after the British Army occupied the state in 1780. These mounted soldiers campaigned not only in the upcountry but also in the coastal regions or "lowcountry" and on the frontiers of Georgia and Florida. This study, however, will focus primarily on the mounted troops in the backcountry and not on their counterparts in the midlands and coastal regions. This study will also be confined to the mounted patriot (Whig) soldiers who fought for the South Carolina revolutionary government and not their opponents in the British regular and provincial corps and the loyalist (Tory) militia, who were similarly equipped and deployed.

## THOMSON'S RANGERS

In June 1775 South Carolina's First Provincial Congress began providing for the defense of the state by organizing regiments of both state troops and militia. At the same time the Provincial Congress subdivided the large Ninety Six and Camden judicial districts, created by the colonial government in 1769, into smaller electoral districts so that the backcountry could elect delegates to the new government's legislature. This subdivision also made it easier to raise and organize the South Carolina militia along electoral district lines. The state troops were originally composed of two regiments of infantry, or foot soldiers, drawn mostly from the lowcountry, and a regiment of mounted riflemen, or "rangers," recruited from the backcountry. Although the rangers were not technically cavalrymen, contemporary writers sometimes described them as "light horse," and at one point the Provincial Congress briefly contemplated changing their designation from "rangers" to "light dragoons."[1]

The 1st and 2nd Regiments of infantry were each commanded by a full colonel and a lieutenant colonel, and were assigned to protect Charleston and the coastal region from British attack. As was standard practice for regiments of mounted soldiers in both the American and British armies, the rangers of the 3rd Regiment were commanded by a lieutenant colonel and a major. Their primary mission was to patrol the backcountry and the frontier and guard against loyalist and Indian uprisings. A 4th Regiment of Artillery was established in November 1775 to protect Charleston against invasion from the sea.[2]

When originally established, the 3rd South Carolina Regiment of Rangers was commanded by Lt. Col. William Thomson of the Orangeburg District and Maj. James Mayson of the Ninety Six District. Both men were veterans of frontier warfare and had led provincial rangers and mounted militia during the Cherokee War of 1759–1761; Thomson was also colonel of the Orangeburg District militia regiment. The 3rd Regiment was initially authorized to raise 450 men, organized into 9 companies of 50 privates each, with each company commanded by a captain and two lieutenants. Each sergeant and private of the rangers received a bounty of fifteen pounds currency, in addition to their monthly pay, "for purchasing a pair of leather breeches, and such uniform cap and coat, as the Lieutenant-Colonel shall think proper—which he is required to order."[3]

The rangers' original uniform consisted of blue regimental coats with white facings and white metal buttons, leather horsemen's caps with the words "Liberty or Death" painted on the upturned visor, and leather breeches. Each ranger was expected to provide his own horse, rifle, powder horn, shot pouch, and tomahawk or hatchet, and the men were paid at a higher rate than corresponding foot soldiers of the same rank in order to compensate for the extra expense of horses and riding equipment.[4]

In November 1775 the New York newspaper *Rivington's Gazette* published a description of the three newly raised South Carolina regiments, referring to the 3rd Regiment as a regiment of "light horse": "In South Carolina they have two thousand men in actual pay, and five hundred horse on the frontiers . . . They have twenty tons of powder, and the quantity daily increasing. Two thousand men in uniforms, blue faced with red. Light horse, five hundred, blue faced with white, and well furnished. The militia in the country in fine order; drill sergeants having been sent among them many months past."[5]

Easily the most striking and unique aspect of the 3rd Regiment's original uniform was the leather jockey cap with the "Liberty or Death" motto painted in prominent white letters on the upturned bill. More than fifty years after the end of the war, veterans of the Revolution still vividly recalled the "Liberty caps" worn by Thomson's Rangers. One such testimonial is found in the October 1832 federal pension application of Charnel Durham, who served for three years in the Rangers (1775–1778). In a sworn deposition attesting to Durham's military service, Thomas Parrott of Richland District stated that he once saw Durham in his uniform, "and recollects a plate on his cap bearing the motto inscribed 'Liberty or Death.'" Another veteran who remembered these caps was Joseph Gaston of Chester District, the youngest of nine brothers who served in the Revolution—four of whom (Robert,

Alexander, Hugh, and Ebenezer) served together in the 3rd Regiment. In a Fourth of July speech in 1836, Gaston recalled seeing his older brothers in the Rangers with the "'Liberty or Death' motto . . . inscribed on the front of their military caps."[6]

An interesting example of the effect that the "Liberty caps" had on the loyalists in the backcountry occurred in early November 1775, when the South Carolina Provincial Congress sent a wagonload of gunpowder and lead to the Cherokee Indians as a peace offering. A small detachment of 3rd Regiment rangers under 2nd Lt. Thomas Charleton, of Capt. Eli Kershaw's company, escorted the shipment on its journey from Charleston to the backcountry. On November 3, the wagon was stopped by a large group of armed loyalists under Capt. Patrick Cunningham, and the ammunition was confiscated, ostensibly because the loyalists feared the Cherokees would use it against them. The rangers were riding some distance behind the wagon, and arrived on the scene after Cunningham's party had seized the powder and lead.[7]

Later that day, wagoner Moses Cotter swore a deposition before Justice of the Peace James Mayson (who was also major of the 3rd Regiment), stating that "When the rangers were at some little distance behind the waggon, and were riding up pretty fast, Cunningham's party said, 'there comes the liberty caps; damn their liberty caps, we will soon blow them to hell;' and such like scurrilous language."[8]

As the rangers were surrounded and heavily outnumbered, they were forced to surrender the powder and ammunition to the loyalists. Later in November, loyalist militia under Cunningham and Maj. Joseph Robinson laid siege to Fort Ninety Six, which was occupied by Whig soldiers under Major Mayson of the 3rd Regiment and Maj. Andrew Williamson of the Ninety Six District militia. The siege lasted from November 19 to 21, following which a truce was declared.[9] This was the first armed conflict of the Revolution in the South Carolina backcountry.

In an effort to increase its military readiness, in February 1776 the Second Provincial Congress enacted new resolutions to bring the original three regiments up to full strength and increase their pay and rations. The state also authorized an adjutant and quartermaster for the rangers, and further resolved that "the said regiment of Rangers shall be composed of *expert* Rifle-men, who shall act on horseback, or on foot, as the service may require."[10]

Additional measures included authorizing a regiment of infantry riflemen, composed of seven companies and commanded by a full colonel, to enter service as the 5th South Carolina Regiment. This new regiment was, like the regiment of rangers, to consist of "*expert* Rifle-men," and each recruit was expected to provide, at his own expense, "his own cloaths, except a uniform hunting shirt, and hat or cap, and blanket, to be provided by the public; and also, at his own expence, to be constantly provided with a good rifle, shot-pouch, and powder-horn, together with a tomahawk or hatchet." The Provincial Congress was adamant that "the men to be inlisted in the regiment of Rangers and Rifle-men, be approved of by the commanding officer of each regiment respectively,—*as expert Rifle-men.*" Isaac Huger of Charleston and Alexander McIntosh of St. David's Parish were duly elected colonel and lieutenant colonel of the new regiment of riflemen, which would be raised from the lowcountry.[11]

Commissioners were then appointed to contract for the manufacture or purchase of "any number, not exceeding one thousand stand, of good rifles, with good bridle locks, and proper furniture, not exceeding the price of thirty pounds each," along with an equal number of "good smooth-bored muskets, carrying an ounce ball, with good bridle locks and furniture, iron ram-rods, and bayonets, at a price not exceeding twenty pounds each."[12]

Six days after it created the 5th Regiment, the Provincial Congress authorized a second regiment of riflemen, consisting of five companies, to be designated the

6th South Carolina Regiment. Thomas Sumter of the District Eastward of the Wateree River was elected lieutenant colonel, and William Henderson of the Upper District Between the Broad and Saluda Rivers (later the Spartan District) was elected major of the new rifle regiment. Like Thomson's 3rd Regiment, Sumter's 6th Regiment would be composed primarily of men from the backcountry.[13]

The South Carolina General Assembly, which replaced the Provincial Congress after the colonies declared their independence, placed all six of its state regiments on the Continental establishment in September 1776 and raised their pay rates to match those of the Continental soldiers. The following month, the legislature officially promoted the lieutenant colonel, major, and senior captain of the 3rd Regiment one grade in rank as well, giving the Rangers a full colonel, lieutenant colonel, and major as the unit's field officers. Colonel Thomson was also authorized to add three more companies to his regiment, bringing its total strength to six hundred, although it appears unlikely that the Rangers ever attained this ideal strength. Nonetheless, hundreds of men from the backcountry did serve enlistments ranging from six months to three years in the 3rd Regiment between 1775 and 1780.[14]

In August 1777 Colonel Thomson reorganized his regiment, now reduced by discharges and illness to only three hundred men, in order to make it "of most service to the State." He ordered two hundred French muskets, bayonets, flints, and cartridge boxes so that he could dismount an equal number of soldiers and reequip them as infantry while retaining the other one hundred troopers as "complete Rifle men with good Horses and spears." The spears were apparently issued in lieu of swords, which were in short supply. Thomson also changed the 3rd Regiment's uniforms from blue faced with white to blue faced with red, to match those of the 1st and 2nd Regiments. In July 1773 he completed the reorganization from rangers to infantry, dismounting the rest of his men and reequipping them with French Charleville muskets and bayonets.[15]

The rangers of the 3rd South Carolina Regiment took part in most of the early campaigns of the war, including the defense of Sullivan's Island in June 1776; the Cherokee Campaign of July–October 1776; the aborted expedition to Florida in the summer of 1778; the bloody Battle of Stono Ferry in June 1779; and the unsuccessful, costly attempt to take Savannah from the British in October 1779. During this early period of the war, many of these soldiers served in isolated detachments along the frontiers of Georgia and East Florida, where they were assigned to defend South Carolina from loyalist raiders and hostile Indians. Other detachments were assigned to rotating tours of garrison duty at Charleston, Fort Moultrie, and Purysburg.[16]

In February 1780, Maj. Gen. Benjamin Lincoln, commanding the Southern Department of the Continental Army, completely overhauled South Carolina's Continental Line. By this time regimental strengths were low, with many former Continentals returning home to serve as officers and enlisted men in their local militia regiments or retiring from active service altogether. The state's five infantry regiments were consolidated into three regiments or battalions. The 5th Regiment was consolidated with the 1st, and the 6th Regiment was consolidated with the 2nd.[17]

All three of South Carolina's remaining infantry regiments, along with the 4th Regiment of Artillery and the rest of Lincoln's Southern Army, took part in the unsuccessful defense of Charleston in the spring of 1780. They surrendered to Sir Henry Clinton's British Army on May 12, 1780, and were held as prisoners of war on the islands off the South Carolina coast. The final incarnation of the 3rd Regiment was officially disbanded at Charleston on January 1, 1783, and the state did not officially field any more Continental regiments for the duration of the war.[18]

## MILITIA ORGANIZATION IN THE SOUTH CAROLINA BACKCOUNTRY

At the beginning of the American Revolution, the South Carolina backcountry was divided into two large judicial (circuit court) districts, the Ninety Six District and the Camden District. During the years 1775 and 1776, the First and Second Provincial Congresses subdivided these judicial districts into smaller electoral districts for representation in the provincial government, and these electoral districts in turn became the basis for organizing the militia regiments of the backcountry. The Ninety Six Judicial District was initially divided into two electoral districts, Ninety Six District and the District Between the Broad and Saluda Rivers. The Camden Judicial District was divided into three electoral districts: the District Eastward of the Wateree, the District Between the Broad and Catawba Rivers, and the New Acquisition District. During the nine years of the American Revolution, each electoral district in the South Carolina backcountry fielded at least one regiment of state militia, and some of the larger districts fielded multiple regiments.[19]

Almost all of these backcountry militia regiments were originally commanded by veteran officers who had served in the colonial forces on the frontiers of Pennsylvania, Virginia, and the Carolinas during the French and Indian War (1754–1763). A significant number were also veterans of the South Carolina Regulator War of 1767–1768. When the need arose, companies or battalions from these regiments were often assigned to detached duty under lieutenant colonels, majors, or captains. Most of these field officers also served as representatives in the First and Second Provincial Congresses and the General Assembly between 1775 and 1780. By the summer of 1780, however, many of the original field officers had been killed in battle, had retired due to advanced age, or had been captured and paroled (or in some cases imprisoned) by the British Army following the surrender of Charleston.

These elder officers were then frequently succeeded in command by their sons, nephews, or cousins.[20]

The Ninety Six Electoral District was large enough and populous enough to field two regiments for most of the war. The Upper Ninety Six or Long Cane Regiment (from present-day Abbeville, Greenwood, and McCormick Counties) was commanded initially by Col. John Savage, then by Col. Andrew Williamson, and later by Col. Andrew Pickens. The Lower Ninety Six Regiment or Stephen's Creek Regiment (from present-day Saluda, Edgefield and part of Aiken Counties) was led by Col. LeRoy Hammond.[21]

The District Between the Broad and Saluda Rivers was soon divided into two and later three electoral districts: the Upper or Spartan District, the Middle or Little River District, and the Lower or Dutch Fork District, with provision for three militia regiments. The Spartan District, however, actually raised two militia regiments during the Revolution, which were known as the Spartan Regiment and the Fair Forest Regiment. The Spartan Regiment, from what is now Spartanburg and western Cherokee County, was commanded by Col. John Thomas Sr. Following the surrender of Charleston, Colonel Thomas was imprisoned at Fort Ninety Six, and his son John Thomas Jr., took over the regiment. When the younger Thomas was given command of a regiment of state troops in 1781, Col. Benjamin Roebuck Jr., assumed command of the Spartan Regiment.[22]

The Fair Forest Regiment, from present-day Union County, was commanded by Col. Thomas Brandon. Col. James Williams led the Little River Regiment (from present-day Laurens County) until his death at the Battle of Kings Mountain on October 7, 1780, and was succeeded by Col. Philomen Waters. The Dutch Fork Regiment (from current Newberry County) was commanded initially by Col. John Lyles, Sr., then by Col. Jonas Beard, who was captured at Charleston in 1780, and finally by Col. James Lyles from the summer of 1780.[23]

In early 1775, the Camden Judicial District was organized into three electoral districts with a militia regiment from each: the District Between the Broad and Catawba Rivers, the District Eastward of the Wateree River, and the most recent addition, the New Acquisition District, so called because the territory had been "acquired" from North Carolina following the boundary survey of 1772. These regiments were under the overall command of Col. Richard Richardson Sr., the senior militia officer in the upper part of the state. The first two districts were much larger in size and population than the New Acquisition, and it soon became apparent that organizing a single regiment from each district was an awkward arrangement. In March 1776 the Provincial Congress further divided the regiments in both the District Between the Broad and Catawba Rivers and the District Eastward of the Wateree into upper and lower battalions. Each battalion was commanded by a lieutenant colonel and a major who reported to Colonel Richardson.[24]

By 1778, when Richardson was promoted to brigadier general, the District Between the Broad and Catawba Rivers was actually fielding three militia regiments. The upper portion of the district adjoining the New Acquisition, corresponding to present-day Chester County, was commanded by Col. Joseph Brown and after 1779 by Col. Edward Lacey. The middle portion, corresponding to current Fairfield County, was commanded by Col. John Winn and, after the fall of Charleston, by his brother Col. Richard Winn, who had served as a lieutenant and captain in the 3rd Regiment from 1775 to 1779. The regiment from the lower portion of the district (corresponding to present-day Richland County) was originally commanded by Col. Robert Goodwyn and later by Col. Thomas Taylor.[25]

Following Richardson's promotion to brigadier general, the regimental commander in the District Eastward of the Wateree River (comprising present-day Lancaster,

Kershaw, Lee, Sumter and Clarendon Counties) was Col. Joseph Kershaw of Camden. He was succeeded by his brother Col. Eli Kershaw, a former captain of the 3rd Regiment. Both Kershaws were captured and imprisoned by the British in the summer of 1780, and Col. Robert Patton became senior commander of the militia east of the Wateree.[26]

To the north of the District Between the Broad and Catawba Rivers, along the North Carolina border, lay the New Acquisition Electoral District, corresponding roughly to current York County. Col. Thomas Neel commanded the New Acquisition militia regiment from early 1775 until his death at the Battle of Stono Ferry on June 20, 1779, whereupon he was succeeded by Col. Samuel Watson. When Watson resigned his command in early June 1780, the regiment's members elected Colonel Neel's son Andrew as their senior colonel. Col. Andrew Neel was killed at the Battle of Rocky Mount on July 30, 1780, and was succeeded by Col. William Bratton, who was by then the senior field officer in the New Acquisition. During 1782, the New Acquisition militia was commanded in the field by Lt. Col. James Hawthorne and Col. John Moffitt.[27]

For the first three years of the war all of the backcountry militia units were under the overall command of Colonel Richardson. Richardson led these militia regiments in the so-called Snow Campaign against loyalists in the Ninety Six District during November and December 1775, but that was his last active field command. In March 1778, Gov. John Rutledge organized the South Carolina militia into three brigades. The three most senior militia colonels in the state—Richardson, Andrew Williamson, and Stephen Bull—were promoted to brigadier general and placed in command of these brigades.[28]

This command structure only lasted until May 1780. Richardson resigned his commission in late 1779 due to his age (he was then seventy-five), but was captured by the British when the American army surrendered at Charleston on May 12. Denied parole, his health failed and he was allowed to return home, where he died in September 1780. Bull was also captured at Charleston but was paroled and performed no further military service during the war. Williamson gave his parole to the British at Fort Ninety Six and resigned his command in early June 1780.[29]

In late June 1780 the backcountry militia regiments elected Thomas Sumter, former colonel of the 6th South Carolina Regiment, as their brigadier general. Governor Rutledge made the appointment official in October 1780, and Sumter remained the senior militia commander in the state until he resigned in February 1782. At that point Lt. Col. William Henderson, who had served under Sumter in the 6th Regiment, assumed command of Sumter's brigade and was subsequently promoted to brigadier general himself.[30]

The surrender of the Continental Army at Charleston in May 1780 initially left only the backcountry militia to resist the subsequent British occupation of South Carolina. In early July these regiments, in particular those from the present-day counties of York, Chester, Fairfield, Richland, Lancaster, Kershaw, Spartanburg, Union, Cherokee, Laurens, and Newberry, became the core of Sumter's Camden District militia brigade and began a protracted campaign of raids and attacks against British and loyalist forces in the backcountry.[31]

During the same period Col. Francis Marion, who was promoted to brigadier general in December 1780, organized the militia units east of the Catawba-Wateree-Santee river system into an effective brigade to resist the British and loyalists in the lowcountry. Finally, in March 1781 Andrew Pickens was promoted to brigadier general and given command of the Ninety Six District brigade in the western part of the state. This gave South Carolina three brigades of militia under Sumter, Marion, and Pickens, and these brigades were to remain in the field for the duration of the war. From June 1780 until late 1781, all three commanders raised very effective regiments of "militia light horse" to oppose the British and loyalist forces operating in the backcountry.[32]

There were several independent units of mounted militia also organized in the backcountry in the summer and fall of 1780 that included men from both Carolinas and Georgia. The best known of these was a company of militia light horse organized by Maj. William Richardson Davie. Davie grew up in the Waxhaws, a Presbyterian community that straddled the North Carolina–South Carolina border on the east side of the Catawba River. After serving as a North Carolina militiaman early in 1778, he was commissioned a major in the Continental Line in the spring of 1779 and given command of a brigade of cavalry under Brig. Gen. Casimir Pulaski. Davie was severely wounded at the Battle of Stono Ferry in June 1779 and returned to his home in Salisbury, North Carolina, to recover. Following the British occupation of the South Carolina backcountry in June 1780, Davie once more took to the saddle and organized an independent battalion of mounted militia from Mecklenburg and Rowan Counties in North Carolina and the Waxhaw community (present-day Lancaster County) in South Carolina. Davie fought alongside Sumter's militia at the two battles of Hanging Rock in Lancaster County on July 30 and August 6, 1780.[33]

In recognition of his leadership, Davie was promoted to colonel. Returning to North Carolina in the late summer, he routed British Legion cavalry at Wahab's Plantation in Union County on September 21 and captured a significant number of horses and supplies in the process. His most famous action came at the Battle of Charlotte on September 26, 1780, when he and about 120 of his dismounted horsemen slowed the advance of the British Army under Lt. Gen. Charles, Earl Cornwallis. Armed

Francis Marion crossing the Pee Dee River with his mounted militia to quell a loyalist uprising in June 1782. (*South Caroliniana Library, University of South Carolina, Columbia*)

with rifles and using the buildings of the town for cover, Davie and his men successfully covered the retreat of the main body of North Carolina militia under Brig. Gen. Jethro Sumner and then escaped themselves. Davie's battalion continued to operate independently until joining Maj. Gen. Nathanael Greene's Continental Army in December, following which Davie became Greene's commissary officer.[34]

## MOUNTED MILITIA AND PARTISAN RANGERS

As early as June 1770, South Carolina lieutenant governor William Bull noted in a letter to the Earl of Hillsborough: "In the country almost every militia man marches on Horseback." This practice continued after the Revolution began, and in the upper districts the "country militia" was generally well mounted, although men without horses could serve as teamsters or "waggoners," pack horse handlers, garrison soldiers in forts, and in other dismounted roles. In June 1775 the Provincial Congress went one step further and provided for the organization of "volunteer troops of horse" or "Volunteer Rangers" from within the established district militia regiments. These volunteer companies were independent of the district militia, but in the event of an emergency they would act as auxiliaries to the militia and state troops.[35]

By the end of that summer, several companies of these "volunteer Horse Rangers" had been organized in the Spartan District, the New Acquisition District, the District Between the Broad and Catawba Rivers, and elsewhere. Like the 3rd Regiment, both the mounted militia and volunteer rangers generally fought on foot with muskets and rifles, but they relied on their horses for speed and mobility. Each soldier provided his own equipment, which included a rifle, musket, carbine or smoothbore hunting fusil, a cartridge box or shot bag and powder horn, a tomahawk or knife, and whenever possible a pistol or brace of pistols and a sword, especially for officers. They were also required to provide their own horses, saddles, bridles, stirrups, and other riding gear.[36]

Militia companies were divided into three classes, and generally only one class was called upon to serve at any given time. Enlisted men either volunteered or were drafted to serve specific tours of duty during formal campaigns, and contrary to popular belief, they almost always served out their tours until discharged by their commanding officers. Other men served as substitutes for draftees who were unable or unwilling to serve when called. Field officers often rotated duty as the war progressed, so that they were not required to serve repeatedly on campaign without relief. The colonels were required to muster their regiments into battalions at least once every three months, and drill the men in arms during muster.[37]

Militia officers, unlike officers in the Continental Army, were elected by the enlisted men they commanded and then commissioned by the Council of Safety. After Charleston was captured in May 1780 the state government ceased to exist, but Governor Rutledge continued to issue some officers' commissions from his exile in

Hillsborough, North Carolina. Since it was impractical for every officer to ride to Hillsborough to receive a commission, Rutledge authorized General Sumter to issue brevet commissions and to appoint and remove officers as he thought proper. Many militia officers, however, operated without formal commissions during the last two years of the war; having the support and confidence of their men was always the most important requisite. As one of Sumter's officers, Maj. John Adair, later stated, "they [did] enter into a solemn obligation to place themselves under the command of Genl. Thomas Sumpter and to continue in a body and serve under his command untill the war was at an end, or untill their services were no longer necessary, they were to find their own horses and arms, cloathing and all necessities—it being absolutely necessary that they should act on horseback."[38]

The military records and postwar memoirs of the backcountry militia soldiers make clear distinctions between service as "horsemen" and "footmen." For instance, the pay rate for a mounted private in the South Carolina militia was established early in the war as twenty shillings (one pound) per day, the same as a private in Thomson's Rangers, while the pay for a foot soldier in the militia was only ten shillings per day, the same as a regular infantryman. South Carolina's audited accounts and the United States federal pension applications for Revolutionary War service provide ample proof that most militia service in the backcountry, especially after the fall of Charleston, was on horseback. Many of these troopers were in fact experienced veterans of the 3rd and 6th South Carolina Regiments and had served under colonels Thomson and Sumter during the early campaigns of the war.[39]

Technically, once the South Carolina government was dissolved in May 1780 the state militia ceased to exist; the men who opposed the British and loyalist forces after that were actually partisans, at least until the General Assembly reconvened at Jacksonboro in January 1782. For this reason, both American and British sources during this period often referred to the militiamen as "partisans" or "partizans." Numerous nineteenth- and twentieth-century historians have also described these combatants as "partisans" or "partisan-militia."[40] The nineteenth-century South Carolina historian Edward McCrady confirmed the reasoning behind the use of this terminology:

> Since the fall of Charleston there had been really no militia in the State, though the partisan bands were usually so called; for a militia . . . implies the existence of a government under which the citizens are enrolled and required to do duty. But since [Governor Rutledge's] departure from the State there had been no government except that of the British authorities under the protection of the Royal army. During the four months of June, July, August, and September 1780, in which so much had been done by the partisan bands under Sumter, Marion, Clarke, and Shelby, there had not been even a militia commission in the hands of these leaders . . . These bands were thus purely volunteers fighting from patriotism only, without pay or reward.[41]

As a former Confederate colonel himself, McCrady was no stranger to partisan warfare, which was widely practiced during the War Between the States. Influenced by the successful use of partisan tactics during the American Revolution, the Confederate States (and several border states as well) fielded battalions of "partisan rangers" to operate as irregular cavalry behind federal lines. Employing their horses in lightning-fast raids, they attacked base camps, captured supply convoys, destroyed rail lines and bridges, interrupted communications, and dispersed foraging parties. There was one important difference, however, between the partisan rangers of the 1860s and those of the 1780s: the Confederate partisans were initially authorized by the Confederate States government under the Partisan Ranger Act of 1862. Two years later the act was repealed under pressure from Robert E. Lee and other Confederate generals, who were growing increasingly alarmed at the brutal tactics used by some of the irregulars. Most of the partisans who continued to operate after that time did so without the blessings of the Confederate government, and were true guerrillas.[42]

Along the same lines, historians have drawn numerous analogies between the partisan conflict of the American Revolution and the twentieth-century partisan warfare waged in Nazi-occupied Europe during World War II and in postwar Indochina. In both of these cases, partisans once again waged irregular or guerrilla warfare against occupying armies by impeding the enemy's ability to communicate and to supply and mobilize its forces. One important difference lies in the use of horses, which were not nearly as important in the twentieth century as they were during the eighteenth and nineteenth centuries.[43]

WEAPONS, CLOTHING, AND EQUIPMENT OF THE MOUNTED MILITIA

Unlike the Continental soldiers and state troops, South Carolina's militia soldiers and partisan rangers did not generally wear formal uniforms. One of the few exceptions was Lt. Col. Peter Horry's regiment of militia light horse from the South Carolina lowcountry. Organized in February 1781, this militia regiment was outfitted with light-blue short coats or "coatees," leather horsemen's caps, swords, and various types of firearms. According to historian Fitzhugh McMaster, "Each troop consisted of long term volunteers from one of five infantry regiments and each had its own distinctive color (red, blue, yellow, green, or black) for the flat collar and cuffs of the coatee, which was made of homespun; as the warp was blue yarn and the weft [was] white (or vice versa), the coatee had a light blue appearance."[44]

For most backcountry militiamen, however, clothing consisted of whatever they could provide for themselves. The mounted militia trooper generally wore leather shoes or riding boots, trousers, an undershirt and waistcoat, and the ubiquitous "hunting shirt" of rugged linsey-woolsey or osnaburg, worn over the other clothing to protect the wearer in the brush and woods. Militia soldiers generally favored a wide-brimmed hat for the protection it offered the wearer from rain and sun, but many of the mounted militia sported stiff leather jockey caps with a bill in front and a crest of horsehair along the top. Similar "horsemen's caps" were worn by regular cavalry troopers in both the American and British armies as a badge of mounted service, and by 1780 (if not earlier) the mounted militia in the backcountry had adopted them as well. These caps also had a practical use: they were helmets, in effect, and protected the wearers' heads from sword cuts from opposing dragoons.[45]

Several detailed descriptions of the clothing, weapons, and accoutrements utilized by the militia or partisan rangers of the Carolina backcountry have been preserved. One of the most important accounts comes from the autobiography of James P. Collins, who served under Capt. John Moffitt (Colonel Moffitt) of the New Acquisition District from July 1780 until the end of the war. Note that Collins's comments apply particularly to the period after the fall of Charleston, when the state government had been dissolved and the backcountry partisans had to fend for themselves:

> It will be, perhaps, proper here to mention, that we were a set of men acting entirely on our own footing, without the promise or expectation of pay. There was nothing furnished us from the public; we furnished our own clothes, composed of coarse materials, and all home spun; our over dress was a hunting shirt, of what was called linsey woolsey, well belted around us. We furnished our own hors-

es, saddles, bridles, guns, swords, butcher knives, and our own spurs; we got our powder and lead as we could, and often had to apply to the old women of the country, for their old pewter dishes and spoons, to supply the place of lead; and if we had lead sufficient to make balls, half lead and the other pewter, we felt well supplied. Swords, at first, were scarce, but we had several good blacksmiths among us; besides, there were several in the country. If we got hold of a piece of good steel, we would keep it; and likewise, go to all the sawmills, and take all the old whip saws we could find, set three or four smiths to work, in one shop, and take the steel we had, to another. In this way, we soon had a pretty good supply of swords and butcher knives. Mostly all of our spurs, bridle bits, and horsemen's caps, were manufactured by us.[46]

Private Collins also provided a detailed description of the appearance and construction of the leather horsemen's caps worn by the mounted militia:

We would go to a turner or wheelwright, and get head blocks turned, of various sizes, according to the heads that had to wear them, in shape resembling a sugar loaf; we would then get some strong upper, or light sole leather, cut it out in shape, close it on the block, then grease it well with tallow, and set it before a warm fire, still on the block, and keep turning it round before the fire, still rubbing on the tallow, until it became almost as hard as a sheet of iron; we then got two small straps or plates of steel, made by our own smiths, of a good spring temper, and crossing in the centre above, one reaching from ear to ear, the other, in the contrary direction; the lining was made of strong cloth, padded with wool, and fixed so as to prevent the cap from pressing too hard on the ears; there was a small brim attached to the front, resembling the caps now worn, a piece of bear skin lined with strong cloth, padded with wool, passed over from the front to the back of the head; then a large bunch of hair taken from the tail of a horse, generally white, was attached to the back part and hung down the back; then, a bunch of white feathers, or deer's tail, was attached to the sides, which completed the cap. The cap was heavy, but custom soon made it so that it could be worn without inconvenience. We made the scabbards of our swords of leather, by closing on a pattern of wood, and treating it similar to the cap. Our swords and knives, we polished mostly with a grindstone—not a very fine polish to be sure; but they were of a good temper, sharpened to a keen edge, and seldom failed to do execution, when brought into requisition.[47]

Joseph Graham, who rose to the rank of major in the Mecklenburg County, North Carolina, militia regiment, left another interesting description of the equipment used by the mounted backcountry militiamen:

The principal difficulty was to procure arms. They generally had rifles—carried the muzzell in a small boot fixed to a strop fastened beside the right stirrup leather, & the but[t] run through their shot bag belt so that the lock came directly under the right arm. Near half the swords were made by black smiths—those who had a Pistol had it swung by a strop the size of a bridle rein hung down on the left side over the sword which was hung higher than the modern way of wearing them so as not to entangle their legs when acting on foot. Their equipments were not splendid they were the best [that] could be procured at that time and in the hands of such men ultimately as serviceable as arms that looked much finer. They had at all times all their arms with them whether on foot or horse back and could move individually or colectively as circumstances might require without depending on commissary Quarter master or other Staff.[48]

Material captured from the enemy, whether British or loyalist, also provided an important source of arms, ammunition, and equipment. Again, James Collins provided a description of this mode of "requisition" after a battle with loyalists in the New Acquisition District during the late summer of 1780:

> We then selected a few of the enemy's best rifles and whatever of the swords were deemed sufficient to stand service—breaking the others. We then took all the pistols we could find, and holsters, such as we thought would answer our purpose, breaking the locks of the others and throwing them away, as unfit for further use. We took care of the powder and balls, and the guns we used similar to the pistols—breaking the locks and mainsprings . . . Here I came in possession of a brace of excellent pistols, and the most of our men that lacked swords were furnished. We exchanged two or three of our horses, that were almost tired down for the same number of the best that they had.[49]

Collins also recorded a glimpse of the day-to-day existence of the backcountry mounted militia during the difficult days of late 1780, echoing the words of Joseph Graham:

> There was a small section of country that was united, lying partly in North, and partly in South Carolina. To this we were confined; we kept a flying camp, never staying long in one place—never camping near a public road. We were often invited by our friends, who were able to afford it, to partake of a dinner prepared for us; in these cases there was a long table, prepared of planks, set in an open place, at some distance from the house.

Never stripping off saddles, and only unbitting our bridles, our horses were put to feed, placing a guard over them, and then placing out sentinels; each one sat down with his sword by his side; his gun lying across his lap, or under the seat on which he sat, and so eating in his turn, until all were done, and then often as playful as though there was no danger; we then mounted our horses and moved off. We were sometimes divided into two companies, still keeping up a communication, so as to know the movements of each other.[50]

At hard-fought backcountry battles like Williamson's Plantation (Huck's Defeat), Rocky Mount, Hanging Rock, Musgrove Mill, Kings Mountain, Fish Dam Ford and Blackstock's Plantation in the summer and fall of 1780, the backcountry partisan militia traveled on horseback but mostly fought on foot. In late October 1780 the British commander at Camden, Lt. Col. Francis, Lord Rawdon, noted in a letter to Maj. Gen. Alexander Leslie: "The Enemy are mostly mounted Militia, not to be overtaken by our Infantry nor to be safely pursued in this strong Country by our Cavalry."[51]

By early 1781 these mounted militia units were beginning to look like cavalry and to fight like cavalry when necessary. In their subsequent state audited accounts and federal pension applications, many of these militiamen used the terms "cavalry," "light horse," and even "dragoons," in addition to the earlier term "rangers," to describe their service during the last two years of the war.[52] At the Battle of Cowpens on January 17, 1781, several companies of mounted South Carolina and Georgia militiamen, along with a "regiment of newly-raised South Carolina state troops" under Maj. James McCall, were pressed into service to augment Lt. Col. William Washington's Continental Light Dragoons. Armed with swords and pistols, they exceeded all expectations by fighting as cavalry against similarly armed and equipped British dragoons.[53]

On the evening of February 27, 1781, the core of Sumter's militia brigade went up against a regiment of British provincial cavalry known as the South Carolina Rangers at Fort Watson in present-day Clarendon County, South Carolina. Lord Rawdon described the affair. Referring to Sumter's men at Fort Watson as "the enemy cavalry," Rawdon noted that the rebel troops were "regularly formed" and that they were "all mounted: About a fourth of them were armed with Swords, as Cavalry; & had excellent Horses."[54]

A little over a week later, on March 6, 1781, Sumter's men clashed with a provincial infantry regiment called the South Carolina Royalists, commanded by Maj. James Fraser, at Scape Hoar on Stirrup Branch of Lynches River in what is now Lee County, South Carolina. In the same letter Rawdon provided a classic description of the mounted militia's more typical battle tactics during this period: "When the parties first met, Sumter's men were all mounted; & quickly gave way before the fire of the Infantry: They soon however dismounted; & advanced with tolerable countenance to attack Fraser."[55]

Sumter's brigade during late February and early March of 1781 consisted of about three hundred to four hundred mounted militia from the upper Broad and Catawba River region, commanded by colonels William Bratton and Edward Lacey. Within a few weeks they were joined by similar units under colonels Richard Winn, William Hill, Thomas Taylor, and Henry Hampton.[56] Throughout this period, American and British officers alike described these militia units as "regiments of horse," as when Maj. John Armstrong of the North Carolina militia referred to "Colo[l] Lasseys [Lacey's] horse" in a letter to Maj. Gen. Nathanael Greene.[57] These were the same militiamen who in their own accounts usually referred to themselves as "rangers," which is perhaps the best and most accurate description of their service.

The mounted militiamen from the South Carolina backcountry under Sumter, Marion, Pickens, and Henderson served in all of the later campaigns of 1781 and 1782, and contributed immensely to the defeat of the British Army in the South. Ironically, when the British finally withdrew from Charleston in December 1782, these same South Carolina militiamen were barred from the celebrations in the city because the town authorities considered them to be too dangerous.[58]

## SOUTH CAROLINA LIGHT DRAGOONS

As early as February 1779, the South Carolina General Assembly authorized a regiment of light dragoons or cavalry to be raised on the state establishment. These were full-time state troops, not militia, and enlisted for service terms of sixteen months. Commanded by Col. Daniel Horry of the lowcountry, these dragoons wore leather jockey caps with an upturned visor, dark brown short coats or "coatees," and leather boots, and were equipped with sabers, carbines, and cartridge boxes. In February 1780 the legislature mandated that the officers and men of the "State Light Dragoons and Independent Companies" be allowed the "same additional subsistence money . . .as is allowed by Congress to the troops of the Continental Establishment." Around the beginning of September 1779, the South Carolina government also created a unit of "Provost Dragoons" to serve for twenty-one months on the state establishment, with an enlistment bounty of five hundred dollars per man. Little else is known about these Provost Dragoons, but their name implies that they would have functioned as mounted military policemen.[59]

There is no evidence that the regiment of "State Light Dragoons," also referred to as "Colonel Horry's Horse," ever served in the backcountry, but it did fight alongside the 3rd Regiment of Rangers in the attack on British-held Savannah in October 1779 and participated in the defense of Charleston in 1780. Four troops of this regiment were routed and dispersed by British Legion cavalry at Moncks Corner in April 1780 and Lenud's Ferry in May, while the other two troops were captured when Charleston fell on May 12.[60]

Acting on orders from Governor Rutledge, in the late fall of 1780 Maj. James McCall of the Ninety Six District organized a new battalion of mounted state troops for six months' service. McCall had formerly served as a captain in the 3rd Regiment of Rangers; his battalion of state troops, unlike Horry's regiment, was composed of men from the backcountry who had campaigned all over the northwestern frontier. McCall's troopers joined Brig. Gen. Daniel Morgan's Continental Army corps following the Battle of Kings Mountain in October 1780, and they also served under Sumter at the battles of Fish Dam Ford and Blackstock's Plantation in November. After Sumter was wounded at Blackstock's, Morgan attached McCall to the 3rd Continental Light Dragoons commanded by Lt. Col. William Washington. McCall's state troops fought alongside Washington's regular cavalry at Rugeley's Mill and Hammond's Store in December 1780. At the Battle of Cowpens in January 1781, McCall's battalion and several companies of mounted South Carolina and Georgia militia were armed with sabers, pistols, and carbines, and assisted Washington's troopers in defeating the well-trained and highly experienced British 17th Light Dragoons. McCall was then promoted to lieutenant colonel, and his regiment went on to serve under generals Pickens and Greene during the siege and capture of Augusta, Georgia (May through June 1781), and the siege of Fort Ninety Six in June.[61]

The success of McCall's regiment may have demonstrated to General Sumter the utility of state troops. In late March 1781 Sumter decided to reorganize part of his militia brigade into "light dragoons," to be designated as full-time soldiers serving ten-month tours of duty on the state establishment. Sumter initially organized six regiments of light dragoons in his own brigade, each consisting of four mounted troops from the backcountry under the command of lieutenant colonels William Hill, William Polk, Wade Hampton, Henry Hampton, Charles Myddleton, and John Thomas Jr. Each troop was to consist of a captain, two lieutenants, three sergeants, a trumpeter, and twenty-five privates.[62]

Sumter also instructed Pickens and Marion to raise similar regiments of state dragoons in their brigades. In May 1781 Lt. Col. Samuel Hammond of Pickens's brigade, who had served as a major under Colonel McCall, raised a light dragoon regiment consisting of five troops, and the following month Marion organized two regiments of light dragoons under lieutenant colonels Peter Horry and Hezekiah Maham.[63]

These new state troops were commanded by veterans with years of experience as field officers in the mounted militia. Sumter authorized the new state dragoons to wear uniforms consisting of blue coats faced with scarlet, leather horsemen's caps with scarlet turbans and deer tails on the crests, and waistcoats and breeches of homespun. Since raw materials were in short supply, Sumter authorized his officers to purchase cloth in North Carolina. The dragoons were armed with cavalry sabers manufactured by local blacksmiths, along with pistols, muskets, rifles, or hunting fusils.[64]

It is uncertain whether all of the state dragoons were ever uniformed as originally specified. There is evidence, however, that at least some of them were. In December 1782 Lieutenant Colonel Hampton submitted a receipt to the state government for cloth and equipment he had purchased for his regiment in 1781. The itemized list included "63 sides of harness leather, for Caps, Sword belts, Scabbards &c. purchased for the use of his Reg^t." at three dollars each; "36 swords" at six dollars each; "25 spears made with screws and neatly polished" at two dollars each; and "27 yards of Scarlet Durants for Sashes to Caps & Flags to Spears," at a half dollar each. The total owed Hampton for all items was $468.50. The receipt also includes the following memorial dated December 1, 1782:

> Wade Hampton makes oath that the above Sum of Four hundred, Sixty Eight, & an half Dollars Specie, was paid by him in North Carolina for the articles above mentioned, purchased to Equip his Regiment; having Genl. Sumter's orders for the Same, and an assurance that the money Shou'd be reimbursed by the State. That no part thereof has ever been return'd, nor has he ever received any kind of Satisfaction for it.[65]

Several other vouchers exist in the state records for clothing and equipment issued to Sumter's dragoons in 1781 and 1782, including an account of clothing "received and to be received" by Lt. Col. John Thomas's regiment of light dragoons; two regimental clothing rolls for the 1st Regiment of State Troops commanded by Lt. Col. Wade Hampton; clothing receipts for four officers in Hampton's "regiment of cavalry;" and a petition from Lt. Col. William Polk "requesting reimbursement for expenses incurred in procuring swords for the state brigade."[66]

Since the state government had no money to pay these soldiers, Sumter established a bounty system whereby the state troops would be paid in slaves confiscated from loyalists' estates. Both Sumter and Pickens enlisted troops on this plan, which became known as "Sumter's Bounty" or "Sumter's Law." The bounty system drew criticism from Marion, who refused to implement it, but Sumter's Law remained in effect until the end of the war. Furthermore, in 1784 the South Carolina General Assembly passed an act to indemnify its officers from legal prosecution for utilizing the system. The state also honored the unpaid debts from this bounty system when it settled its military accounts after the war.[67]

General Sumter's state troops, along with his veteran militia regiments, participated in numerous military actions in the spring and summer of 1781. By late summer, these light dragoons were among the most experienced soldiers in the Southern army. As McCrady noted,

> These State troops were not regulars, but they were now veterans, who had seen more actual service and fought more battles than probably any Continental troops in the service, with the exception of [Henry Lee's] Legion, which now accompanied them. It was a splendid body of men, most of whom were volunteers, though veterans, fighting purely for patriotism and not for pay. The best of horsemen, unerring shots, and well disciplined in their rude way, they were most excellently fitted, alike by character and experience, for the service upon which they now entered. With such a body of men Sumter had every reason to expect the most substantial results.[68]

Nonetheless, by August 1781 the logistical difficulties of maintaining the light dragoons in the field had forced Sumter to consolidate his six regiments into three, commanded by Wade Hampton, Charles Myddleton and William Polk. These state troops, under the overall command of Col. William Henderson, distinguished themselves as part of General Greene's army at the Battle of Eutaw Springs near Orangeburg on September 8, 1781. In that monumental battle Henderson's state troops consisted of seventy-two light dragoons, commanded by Hampton, and seventy-three infantrymen, commanded by Myddleton and Polk.[69]

Hampton's dragoons performed extraordinary service under heavy fire during the battle, and when Henderson was severely wounded, Hampton assumed command and rallied his troops, aided by Polk and Myddleton. In his after-battle orders, General Greene commended the troops for their bravery at Eutaw Springs, noting that,

"The state Troops Com$^d$ by Col$^{os}$. Henderson Hampton Middleton Polk & Hammond behaved with that gallantry & firmness which Characterized the advocates for Liberty."[70] Col. Otho Williams of the Maryland Continental Line echoed Greene's comments regarding the courage of the state troops under fire: "Never was the constancy of a party of men more severely tried."[71]

In a letter to Thomas McKean, president of the Continental Congress, Greene noted:

> A most valuable Officer Lieut$^t$ Col$^o$ Henderson got wounded early in the Action, and Lieutenant Col$^o$ Hampton who commanded the State Cavalry, and who fortunately succeeded Lt Col$^o$ Henderson in command, charged a party of the Enemy and took upwards of 100 Prisoners. . . . Lieutenant Colonels Polk and Middleton who commanded the State Infantry, were no less conspicuous for their good conduct than their intrepidity; and the Troops under their command gave a specimen of what may be expected from Men naturally brave, when improved by proper discipline.[72]

Following the Battle of Eutaw Springs, Lt. Col. Samuel Hammond received orders from Governor Rutledge to reorganize his state regiment into four troops of light dragoons and two companies of mounted riflemen for three years' service on the Continental establishment. One of these rifle companies was composed of men recruited from his brother LeRoy Hammond's militia regiment, and the other was made up of former loyalists who had renewed their allegiance to the state.[73]

By December 1781, Sumter's state troops were reduced to one mounted regiment under Wade Hampton and one infantry regiment under Charles Myddleton. In January 1782 Hampton's light dragoons, commanded by Maj. Francis Moore, accompanied Brig. Gen. Anthony Wayne on an extended campaign against British forces and allied

Indians in southern Georgia. On at least one occasion, these dragoons turned their coats inside out in order to mislead a party of Indians into thinking they were British soldiers. This incident provides an interesting detail regarding their uniforms: in addition to being blue with scarlet facings, their coats must have been lined with scarlet cloth as well.[74]

While his veterans were campaigning in Georgia, Hampton began raising a new regiment of light dragoons to replace the original state troops, whose enlistments would soon expire. After adding some infantry companies, he redesignated his unit as a legion, a mixed corps of cavalry and infantry. This new regiment was divided into four troops of eighty men who enlisted for three years of service. In March 1782 South Carolina's new governor, John Mathews, commissioned Lt. Col. James Conyers Jr., to raise another new state dragoon regiment in the lowcountry. Conyers was an experienced officer who had formerly commanded a troop in Peter Horry's regiment of militia light horse.[75]

From January until March 1782, several companies of Samuel Hammond's state troops accompanied General Pickens on a punitive expedition against the Cherokee Indians in western South Carolina and northern Georgia. By the end of that summer, the need for multiple regiments of state dragoons had passed. The three remaining dragoon regiments from Sumter's and Marion's old brigades, now commanded by Hampton, Conyers, and Lt. Col. Hezekiah Maham, were consolidated into a new state legion consisting of two troops of dragoons and two companies of infantry under Conyers. These units saw only limited service from August until December 1782.[76]

The final service of the state dragoons took place in September and October 1782, when Hammond's regiment once again accompanied Pickens on a campaign against the Cherokees in northern Georgia. Due to a shortage of gunpowder on this expedition, Hammond's cavalry employed their swords in battle with the Indians, marking the first time in American military history that cavalry armed with sabers engaged in successful combat against Native Americans.[77]

## POSTWAR RANGERS

Following the British evacuation of Charleston in December 1782, both James Conyers's legion and Samuel Hammond's regiment were disbanded. This decision was somewhat premature, however, as events soon demonstrated. Lawless elements known as "outliers," including many former loyalists, continued to raid the backcountry settlements even after the cessation of hostilities with Great Britain. One of the most hated of these outliers was Maj. William "Bloody Bill" Cunningham, the notorious leader of a troop of mounted loyalist partisans and an excellent horseman in his own right. Cunningham had committed numerous atrocities during the war, including the execution of unarmed Whig prisoners, and in October 1782 he fled to East Florida, which was still a British colony. From this base of operations, he continued to raid settlements in southern Georgia and lower South Carolina. Capt. William Butler, whose father and brother were killed by Cunningham in November 1781, pursued Cunningham and his men throughout most of 1782. In spite of Butler's best efforts, however, Cunningham eluded capture.[78]

During one of his raids in February 1783, Cunningham murdered General Pickens's commissary officer. Brig. Gen. William Henderson immediately recommended to the General Assembly that the state raise a company of mounted rangers to patrol its western frontier. He also recommended that the state offer a reward "to take such Ringleaders and Common disturbers of mankind as Cunningham and others."[79] In March 1783 the General Assembly authorized the raising of "a Company of Twenty well mounted Rangers for Six Months to be

Commanded by Capt$^n$. Rumph and a Lieutenant with an Allowance of Provisions, Forage, Arms & Ammunition together with Pay of Twelve Dollars per month to each man from the public . . . and that the Officers be allowed the same pay &c. as Officers of the same Rank in the Militia." Capt. Jacob Rumph was well qualified to lead these mounted rangers, having commanded a troop of independent cavalry from Orangeburg District during the Revolution.[80]

In order to deal more directly with "Cunningham and his Gang," the assembly authorized a reward of 300 guineas for his capture, dead or alive, and 100 guineas each for his comrades John Lawrence (alias John Lane) and William Lee. The assembly could think of no one better suited to go after Cunningham than Capt. William Butler, so it duly commissioned "a Company to Consist of the same number of Officers & privates to be command-ed by Capt. Butler to Act as Rangers and be on the same footing of pay &c. [as Rumph's company] under the orders of Brigadier Gen$^l$. Pickens."[81]

Cunningham remained in East Florida, out of reach of the South Carolinians, and continued his depredations until March 1785. By then Britain had ceded Florida back to the Spanish, to whom it had belonged before the French and Indian War, and Spanish officials quickly deported Cunningham to Cuba. He returned briefly to Florida later that year and was deported again, this time to the Bahamas. After a brief sojourn in England, Cunningham returned to the Bahamas. He died at Nassau in 1787, under somewhat mysterious circumstances.[82]

Meanwhile, believing that the worst was over, the General Assembly recommended that the two companies of rangers under Rumph and Butler be paid and disband-ed. Butler's company was disbanded in February 1784, but in March word of further trouble in the backcountry prompted the assembly to recommend that Rumph's company "be continued in the Service of the State, so long as his Excellency the Governor with the advice of his Council may think it expedient." They recommended that an identically equipped company "be also enlisted in the Southern Parts of this State."[83]

The news of continuing atrocities in the backcountry came from Gov. Benjamin Guerrard, who forwarded an alarming letter to the House of Representatives that he had received from Col. William Bratton of the New Acquisition District. Dated February 13, 1784, Bratton's letter included the following description of conditions in his district: "There is not one week but what there is a Robbery committed or Horses stolen. They are robbing of Travellers in open Daylight upon the Highway, and it appears to be out of the power of the Law to suppress them at present as we have no Gaol nor place of confinement to commit them to if they were even taken in the act." Bratton offered his services to help bring the situation under control, suggesting to the governor that "If your Excellency thought proper to issue orders to me to raise about Twenty Five Men under the Command of a good Officer and to be continued under pay for about six months to range in the Fork between Broad & Catawba river, I think it would be the only means to clear our Country of such rascals as are now distressing the whole Neighbourhood." Bratton went on to compare the situation with conditions during the Revolution:

> I assure your Excellency that we labour under nearly as much difficulty as when Cornwallis was amongst us. By reason we expected when Peace was declared and the good people in my Neighbourhood was glad to hear the News we returned our Swords to the scabbards hoping to live in peace—but it is so much to the contrary that those Outliers came to the house of a very civil man and took him off & it is supposed they have put him to Death, which act was committed within fifteen miles of my own house. They think noth-

ing to tie up any person that opposes them in their proceedings and whip him as long as they please.[84]

In response to Bratton's plea, the House of Representatives authorized that "an Officer and Twelve men be raised to preserve the Public Peace in the part between Broad and Catawba Rivers, under the direction of the Governor, and continued so long as he with the advice of the Privy Council may think necessary, with the same pay and Rations as Captain Rumph's Company are entitled to."[85]

During the unsettled times of 1783 and 1784, the ranger companies fielded by Rumph, Butler, Bratton, and other veteran officers performed a valuable service by maintaining law and order in the backcountry. When the state government finally established county courts and jails for that region in 1785, peacekeeping duties fell to the newly elected justices of the peace, county sheriffs, and constables. Almost all of these officers were also drawn from the ranks of local Revolutionary War veterans.[86] The experience that these men gained during the years of the Revolution was to serve them in good stead as officers of the peace after the war. Even so, the militia continued to be the state's primary civil and military enforcement arm for much of the nineteenth century, just as it was during the colonial period and the War for Independence.

CONCLUSION

Throughout the nine years of the American Revolution, the mounted troops of the backcountry fought with great bravery and extraordinary dedication. During the first five years of the war, they gained valuable experience in almost constant campaigns against loyalists, Indians, and British forces. After the state capital fell to the British Army in May 1780, these men were left to oppose the occupation of their home state alone and with little support. Relying on their own resources and those they confiscated from the enemy, they took to the field once again. Against overwhelming odds, they frustrated the king's troops, raided British convoys, attacked forts, and engaged British and loyalist soldiers at every turn. Their record of success in battle against British regulars, provincials, and loyalist militia is extraordinary, and their use of mobile warfare paved the way for similar tactics used by nineteenth- and twentieth-century armies. After the war ended, these same men helped keep the peace in the backcountry, rounding up bands of outlaws and disaffected loyalists. Whether serving as Continental riflemen, mounted militia, partisan rangers, or state dragoons, these horse soldiers typified the courage, resolve, and self-sacrifice that helped America win its independence.

# SEVEN

# Continentals in Tarleton's British Legion

## May 1780–October 1781

*Lawrence E. Babits*
*and Joshua B. Howard*

T HIS ESSAY IS AN EXAMINATION OF SEVERAL DIFFERENT but related topics. Why did Lt. Col. Banastre Tarleton's British Legion dragoons fail to charge as ordered at the Battle of the Cowpens on January 17, 1781? Why did people enlist, or even choose a side, during the Revolutionary War? And, finally, what happened if someone switched sides, especially during the next battle or after the war? In some ways, this essay is a classic example of readily available information not being utilized because the right question was not asked. Paraphrasing Thomas Pynchon, "If you don't ask the right questions, you'll never get meaningful answers."[1]

The authors wish to thank Matthew Brenckle for his aid in cross-checking names and numbers used in this paper.

Research began as a logical follow-up to answer why the majority of Tarleton's British Legion dragoons performed badly at the Cowpens. When loyalist Alexander Chesney explained the failure to charge, he noted that "Col Tarleton charged at the head of his Regiment of Cavalry called the British Legion which was filled up from the prisoners taken at the battle of Camden . . . the prisoners on seeing their own Regt opposed to them in the rear would not proceed against it and broke: the remainder charged but were repulsed."[2]

The Chesney account suggests that, after Capt. David Ogilvie's British Legion troop routed North Carolina militia flankers, the reserve dragoons were unwilling to take on Lt. Col. William Washington's counterattacking American cavalry. Chesney's statement does not explain why the reserve did not charge, especially as Ogilvie's troop and the 17th Light Dragoons, British regulars, engaged the Continental cavalry. There seemed more to this combat situation than the Legion troopers simply seeing their old regiment arrayed against them. If these men were concerned about being "caught in arms" fighting against their former comrades, they presumably would have been more willing to win and ensure that they would not be captured and subjected to reprisal.

The starting point in unraveling this mystery was Michael Dockerty's (also spelled Daugherty) explanation as to why he, as a former Continental soldier, joined a British Legion infantry company. In the Battle of Camden on August 16, 1780, Dockerty noted, "our Regiment was cut up . . . my unfortunate self wounded and made prisoner." His "prejudices against a jail" led Dockerty "to be persuaded and [en]listed in the infantry of Tarleton's Legion." At Cowpens, he declared, "wee were taken one and all."[3]

Alexander Garden reported that Americans evacuating Salisbury Hospital in North Carolina included men in red and green coats, the latter the color worn by the soldiers of Tarleton's Legion. Garden recalled one doctor saying, "Our party had, indeed, a very equivocal appearance. Many soldiers wore scarlet, and some green, taken from the field of battle."[4] Garden's 1781 account can mean different things; first, that coats were looted from British wagons and the dead; second, that British soldiers joined Brig. Gen. Daniel Morgan's "Flying Army" after the Battle of Cowpens; or third, that Americans taken prisoner at Camden served in the British Legion and then rejoined their old units when given an opportunity after Cowpens.

There is no doubt that all three explanations are possible. The British raised a unit of Continental Army deserters in New York as early as 1777. Dockerty's statement provides clear evidence of Americans switching sides in the South and Continentals enlisting in Tarleton's Legion. The fear of incarceration on a prison ship in Charleston Harbor was a strong motive for doing so, one well expressed by Pvt. Henry Wells of the Delaware Continentals in his pension application. "Two of my Cosins fell into the hands of the enemy at Camden, and died from the Severity of their treatment," Wells declared. "The other lived to be exchanged, but he returned with a Shattered Constitution."[5]

Maj. Gen. Nathanael Greene, who commanded the Continental Army in the South from December 1780 until the war's end, allegedly reported in late spring 1781 that he was fighting with British soldiers while the British were fighting him with Americans. The quote is not found in Greene's published papers and may well be apocryphal. It apparently originated in William Johnson's 1822 biography of Greene, and Johnson did not provide a source for the statement.[6]

OUTLINE HISTORY OF THE BRITISH LEGION

The British Legion was organized at New York during the summer of 1778. Composed of loyalist provincial companies, including the Caledonian Volunteers; Bucks County, Pennsylvania, Light Dragoons; and other units, the Legion continued recruiting even after it went south in 1779. Information on individual troops and companies is scanty, but tracing various commanders suggests that many original British Legionnaires came from occupied Pennsylvania when the British evacuated Philadelphia in the late spring of 1778. The British Legion was a provincial unit, one composed of Americans and not regular British Army troops during the Southern campaigns.[7]

In the South, Tarleton and his men acquired a bloodthirsty reputation, in part the result of the May 1780 engagement at the Waxhaws, South Carolina. One Legion officer, Capt. Christian Huck, was detached from the British Legion at the time he met his end after a short career of looting and burning rebel farmsteads. The Legion's field commander, Lt. Col Banastre Tarleton, was an officer in the British Army and had a colorful and controversial wartime career.[8]

CONTINENTAL UNITS AND RECRUITMENT

Continentals were the regular army soldiers of the new United States. Gen. George Washington wanted a professional army, trained well enough to beat the British in open combat. By 1777, enlistments were for three years or the duration of the war, and this resulted in the longer service needed to make the recruits competent soldiers. There were several groups of people who served in the Continental Army. Early in the war, most enlistees were highly motivated and patriotic. Later, after the glamour wore off, drafts were instituted, along with a more intensive recruiting effort that swept up men considered "surplus" in their communities. Men were encouraged to enlist or hire a substitute to take their place. Those who did not want to serve and could afford to buy their way out of service did so. Other encouragements were given by state governments and the Continental Congress in the form of cash bounties and promises of land grants when the war was over.[9]

## CAMDEN AND PRISONERS OF WAR

The Battle of Camden was an American disaster. On August 16, 1780, the American army suffered a traumatic defeat at the hands of Lt. Gen. Charles, Lord Cornwallis. After the militia fled, the Maryland and Delaware troops in the two Continental brigades, supported by a single North Carolina militia regiment, stayed and fought until they were nearly surrounded. The surviving Continentals finally fled the field in small groups, leaving behind some 650 men killed or captured.[10]

Enlisted prisoners were taken to Camden and then marched off to Charleston in groups of 150 men each, beginning as early as August 23. So demoralized were the prisoners that of one group released by partisan leader Francis Marion on August 25, some eighty-five men refused to accept their liberation and claimed that, as prisoners, they were duty bound to continue to Charleston. Col. Otho Holland Williams of the Maryland Line later noted that "of the 150 men retaken by Marion, only about 60 rejoined their corps—some were sick but most of them just departed." One Maryland county reported that its men "returned from captivity in South Carolina in a distressed state." Others were listed as deserters or defectors in September 1780 after American leaders learned that they had survived the battle but were neither prisoners nor back in the ranks of their units.[11]

## RECRUITMENT OF PRISONERS BY THE BRITISH LEGION

As most British Legion officers and men *were* Americans, they were not reluctant to enlist other Americans. Offering the well-trained Continentals the same familiar lifestyle they had experienced, and perhaps even enjoyed, in the Continental Army, British Legion officers were able to induce many prisoners to enlist. Faced with

Battle of Camden, Death of De Kalb. (*South Caroliniana Library, University of South Carolina, Columbia*)

a choice between a slow death on a prison hulk or service with a British unit that would feed, clothe, and pay them, more than one hundred Continentals chose the latter option.

Given earlier references to Continentals in the British Legion, published Legion muster rolls were searched for names that could be positively identified as Continental soldiers. One such individual was Thomas Tyac, whose last name recalls a Maryland Native American group, the Piscataway, from southern Maryland. A search of published Maryland records revealed Tyac's continuous Continental service record even though he was reported missing on August 16, 1780. That date became a key indicator for identifying other Maryland and Delaware soldiers.[12]

The British Legion generated a list of eighty-one men enlisted before October 25, 1780. That roll provided the comparative list from which at least forty-six names were cross-matched with Maryland and Delaware casualties.

British Legion muster rolls with names out of alphabetical sequence indicated additional enlistees who might have joined the Legion after August 16. Tyac is not on the pre-October enlistment roll but his name does appear out of sequence in Capt. Charles McDonald's company roll. Many additional "out of sequence" enlistees probably had enlistment dates in August 1780, as these names include thirty-two prisoners or missing soldiers from the Maryland and Delaware regiments. Combining the two lists yielded at least 78 out of 113 names (69 percent). The 81 names of August–October 1780 enlistees and 32 names cross-matched that were out of alphabetical sequence provided the lists on which this research data are based.[13]

These numbers are somewhat generalized because of the difficulty of confirming identities, so they should not be considered definitive. Working through additional sources such as American veterans' pension applications and loyalist material in Canadian archives may solidify the data. Nevertheless, there are far too many correlations between the names and units to suggest that the links are coincidental.

The next step was to list Maryland and Delaware Continentals reported missing on August 16. The Continental rolls exist, so names could be compared with those in the British Legion. In comparing the names of men enlisted in the Legion prior to October 25, at least eighty-three matches were found. The listing was then expanded to include Legion names out of alphabetical sequence. For Legion companies where rolls have survived, anywhere from 10 to 30 percent of their strength at Cowpens was composed of former Maryland or Delaware Continentals. The total would be higher if Virginia, Continental Light Dragoon, and Continental Artillery muster rolls were available.

Matching names is a subjective process. Common names such as John Smith, James Smith, John Hill, and John Taylor might be found in virtually any Revolutionary

War unit. However, unusual last names, spellings, and unusual first names are good indications that the same person is being referenced. Once names were matched, they were checked to see when they were listed as missing from the Continental Army and when they enlisted in the British Legion. Similarity of names listed as missing or captured on August 16 and as British Legion enlistees between August 25 and 29 was solid circumstantial evidence for considering the names as indicating the same men.

Initially, the search tried to match names of Continental prisoners and missing soldiers with the pre–October 25 British Legion enlistments. Matches with unusual first or last names were considered as being probable; more common names were considered possible. In some instances, the same first and last names appeared twice in the Continental rolls and also in two different Legion units. This complicated matters, but if two men were missing or known to have been prisoners, they might well be the same two Continentals later serving in the Legion.

Another step was to identify patterns in the Continental names appearing on the Legion rolls. For example, did men from a particular Continental regiment join a particular British Legion company, or is there any suggestion that the British averted a potential mass desertion by not putting men with prior associations together? Finally, was there any possibility that Legion companies or troops with the highest Cowpens losses were also those units with the highest percentages of former Continentals?

The numbers suggest that while men from the 1st or 2nd Continental Brigades were recruited together, the British distributed them throughout different Legion companies. This can be seen in Legion units that had only a few members of one brigade and several from the other. There was also little recruiting of Continental non-

commissioned officers. Only five corporals and two sergeants were tentatively identified. It seems that at least
one corporal and four men from the 6th Maryland
Regiment, plus six other 2nd Brigade men (c. 30 percent)
ended up in Captain McPherson's infantry company.
Similarly, seven of ten possible Continentals (25 percent)
in Capt. John Rousselet's infantry company were from the
1st Brigade, including a sergeant; the company also enlisted a 2nd Brigade corporal.

Another source is to compare probable Continental
names and look for them in the National Archives'
Pension-Bounty-Land Warrant files. This underutilized
data is an outstanding source of minutiae about the
Revolution. Roughly one in five veterans survived to
claim a pension.[14] Many more obtained land, or assigned
their rights to land to others. This evidence is limited, in
part because of archival fires, but it dates after the war.
Some missing or captured Continental names appearing
in British Legion muster rolls did obtain postwar land
warrants based on their American service.

Very few Tarleton's Legion names appear in Bobby G.
Moss's list of South Carolina Patriots, suggesting that men
who joined the Legion after Camden were Maryland or
Delaware Continentals rather than militia. Searching the
Virginia, Continental Light Dragoon, and Continental
Artillery muster rolls should also prove fruitful in identifying American soldiers who joined the Legion. The key
might well be to abstract the Revolutionary War muster
rolls, pension, bounty, and land warrant records in a fashion similar to that done for Civil War soldiers.[15]

OGILVIE'S TROOP

The failure of the British Legion troopers to charge at
Cowpens occurred when the Americans counterattacked
Ogilvie's troop on the American right flank. One partici-
pant, Thomas Young, recalled: "We made a most furious
charge, and cutting through the British cavalry, wheeled

and charged them in the rear. In this charge, I exchanged my tackey for the finest horse I ever rode."[16]

Young's recollection reveals several things. First, the Americans made a "furious charge" and cut "through the British cavalry." He also swapped horses, apparently capturing a riderless horse on the return trip. The phrase "cutting through" might be variously interpreted that William Washington had given orders to use sabers, not pistols, so cutting is a particularly appropriate term. Since American dragoons had just routed the 17th Light Dragoons on the opposite flank, the Americans' ardor was high and it was reflected in Ogilvie's casualties (see Table 1).[17]

TABLE I

Ogilvie's Troop

|  | Dec. 1780 | Feb. 1782 | Former POWs | Continental Cross-Match |
|---|---|---|---|---|
| Officers | 3 | 1[a] | 1 | |
| Sergeants | 3 | 3 | | |
| Quartermaster | 1 | | | |
| Corporals | 3 | 3 | | |
| Trumpeters | 2 | 2 | | |
| Farrier | 1 | 1 | | |
| Privates | 58 | 22[b] | 35 | 9[c] |

a. in England
b. includes 9 privates in South Carolina
c. 1 prisoner of war, 4 no record, and 4 in South Carolina
From Murtie June Clark, ed., *Loyalists in the Southern Campaign of the Revolutionary War*, 3 vols. (Baltimore, MD: Genealogical Publishing Co., 1981) 2:222-228, 230–231. December 1781 numbers include only those names shown on the December 1780 roll.

Specifically, Ogilvie's troop went into battle at Cowpens with fifty-eight privates on their December 24, 1780, muster roll. Of these fifty-eight, nineteen names (33 percent) appear on the August to October enlistee list. Of the fifty-eight privates, thirty-one were captured at

"Battle of Cowpens," by Frederick Kemmelmeyer, c. 1809. (*Yale University Art Gallery*)

Cowpens (53 percent) and six were probably killed, as their names are missing from the next muster roll, giving a casualty rate of 64 percent. Nine others were later reported as being "in Charleston," probably as wounded prisoners on parole. Of those nine names, four cross-match with former Continentals.[18]

Most accounts claim that Ogilvie had forty men when his troop made its ill-fated charge, but of the fifty-eight privates on the Cowpens muster roll, forty-six names (79 percent) were no longer present at Yorktown, Virginia, in the fall of 1781. Since the British Legion dragoons were not heavily engaged after Cowpens, most of Ogilvie's casualties probably occurred at Cowpens. Of the seventy-two officers, noncommissioned officers, and privates on the December 1780 muster roll, fifty-six were no longer present—a loss of 78 percent of all ranks. If Ogilvie had only forty privates at Cowpens, his unit suffered an effective loss rate of 95.8 percent. Short of three companies that participated in Pickett's Charge during the Civil War Battle of Gettysburg on July 3, 1863, this would be the highest loss the authors have seen documented for a single engagement, except the 1876 Battle of the Little Big Horn and a few other battles of the Indian Wars. Comparing names for Ogilvie's troop at Yorktown is confusing because the troop was reconstituted with infantrymen transferred to make up dragoon losses suffered at Cowpens.[19]

The numbers suggest that William Washington did not decimate Ogilvie's troop. In less than two minutes, American dragoons inflicted between 78 percent and 95 percent casualties on the unit, destruction far more severe than the term "decimation" implies. If the Legion dragoons in reserve saw this occur, it is no wonder that they were unwilling to engage. The American cavalry gained the upper hand in part because they outnumbered the British about four to one, and then hacked through and over any opponent they encountered. There should be no doubt why the remaining dragoons failed to charge. They feared retribution, and the Americans increased their fears of retaliation by screaming "Buford's Play," a reference to the Legion's alleged massacre of Col. Abraham Buford's Virginians at the Waxhaws.

A comparison between Ogilvie's troop and another troop of Legion dragoons may prove instructive. Of all the other British Legion dragoon troops, only Capt. Richard Hovenden's participated to any extent in the Cowpens fighting. It was the lead troop during the approach march to the battlefield, and it captured American videttes and then apparently located the American skirmish line with a reconnaissance by fire. Hovenden went into Cowpens with sixty-three officers and men, including at least eight privates who were probably listed as missing or captured at Camden, plus another three possible former Continentals. Of the eleven, six no longer appear on the rolls after Cowpens and one was captured. Another was captured sometime after Cowpens but before Yorktown. One was promoted to corporal, served at Yorktown, and was taken prisoner there along with three privates (see Table 2).

TABLE 2

Hovenden's Troop

|  | Dec. 1780 | Dec. 1781 | No Return | POW at C | POW at Y | POW at Ch |
|---|---|---|---|---|---|---|
| Officers | 4 | 4 |  |  | 1 |  |
| Sergeants | 4 | 3 |  |  | 1 |  |
| Corporals | 3 | 3 |  |  | 2 | 1 |
| Trumpeters | 2 | 2 |  |  |  |  |
| Privates | 50 | 45 | 14 | 6 | 9 | 4 |
| Totals | 63 | 57 | 14 | 6 | 13 | 5 |

C=Cowpens; Y=Yorktown; Ch=Charleston. From Clark, 2:202–205. December 1781 numbers only include those names shown on the December 1780 roll.

ROUSSELET'S COMPANY

For comparative purposes, an infantry company is included in this analysis. Capt. John Rousselet was probably acting as Legion infantry commander at Cowpens because Maj. George Hanger was absent sick. Rousselet's company had eighty-two names on its last pre-Cowpens muster roll. Of this total, there were three officers, three sergeants, three corporals, two drummers and seventy-one privates. Included among these men were thirteen names of Continentals who had fought at Camden (18.3 percent).[20]

The next muster roll still identified the company commander as Rousselet even though he had been badly wounded at Cowpens, and was then a prisoner on parole in Charleston. Only one officer listed on the Cowpens roll was still present in December 1781. Similarly, only one sergeant and no corporals were present at Yorktown, although both drummers were there. The Yorktown figures are misleading, however, because many companies only surrendered an officer, a noncommissioned officer, and a drummer, sending the other survivors home on cartel ships so as to avoid their prosecution or punishment by the victorious Americans. Of the seventy-one privates shown on the Cowpens muster roll, thirty-two do not appear thereafter, indicating that they were probably killed. Thirty-one more are shown as prisoners. Only eight names were still carried at Yorktown from the Cowpens roll (see Table 3).

TABLE 3

Rousselet's Company

| | Dec. 1780 | Dec. 1781* | No Return | POW at C | POW at Y | Other |
|---|---|---|---|---|---|---|
| Officers | 3 | 1 | 2 | | 1 | |
| Sergeants | 3 | 1 | 2 | | | |
| Corporals | 3 | | 1 | 1 | | 1[a] |
| Drummers | 2 | 2 | | | | |
| Privates | 71 | 6 | 32 | 31 | | 2[b] |
| Totals | 82 | 10 | 37 | 32 | 1 | 3 |

*The greatly reduced unit strength of December 1781 was the result of heavy losses suffered at the Battle of Cowpens, South Carolina, on January 17, 1781.

C=Cowpens; Y=Yorktown

a. transferred to British Legion cavalry

b. reported dead June 1781

From Clark, 2:232–235. December 1781 numbers only include those names shown on the December 1780 roll.

Rousselet's company was destroyed at Cowpens, suffering possibly thirty-two killed and thirty-one captured (88.7 percent casualties). Another two men may have been so badly wounded that they were among eighty-seven seriously wounded British prisoners paroled to Charleston, where both died in June 1781. Whether they were killed or not, sixty-five of seventy-one privates were no longer with the British Legion in the fall of 1781. This works out to a casualty rate of 91.5 percent. Of thirteen Continentals in Rousselet's company, seven were captured at Cowpens, two were no longer recorded and one was "in Charleston." Three surrendered at Yorktown.

For these thirteen probable Continentals, of whom eight names are listed as Maryland prisoners or missing at Camden, six do not appear on the rolls after Cowpens. Six others are shown as having been taken prisoner at Cowpens. The last man, Morris Reagle (or Neagle), was transferred to another company in which he served until captured on June 24, 1781.[21]

IMPLICATIONS OF CONTINENTALS SERVING IN THE BRITISH LEGION

Given the number of Continentals who served in the British Legion, is it possible that several former Continentals feigned being wounded at Cowpens? British lieutenant Roderick McKenzie opened speculation about sham injuries when he described the South Carolina militia's volley fire at the second line at Cowpens. "Two-thirds of the British infantry officers, had already fallen, and nearly the same proportion of privates," McKenzie asserted. "Fatigue, however, enfeebled the pursuit, much more than loss of blood."[22]

The casualty figures in Rousselet's company support McKenzie's contention, as two out of three officers and noncommissioned officers were lost. If McKenzie was right about soldiers being fatigued, it is possible that some men dropped to the ground, hoping they would be able to rejoin the Continental Army if the Americans got the upper hand in the fighting. Now out of the fight, they were not "bearing arms," a critical distinction that determined how they would be treated if captured by their former unit.

McKenzie stated that some men who went down were "fatigued." A case in point is the sworn pension deposition of Robert McLeod, who stated that he was "in the battles of Monmouth and Camden" but "at the battle of Cowpens."[23] Clearly the shift in preposition from "in" to "at" was very important to McLeod's notion of honor involved with his sworn testimony about his military service.

British Legion soldiers later reported as being in Charleston without an entry indicating that they had "escaped" or "returned" are likely some of the eighty-seven wounded men paroled and left at Cowpens.[24] Men whose names do not appear after Cowpens seem to be those known to have been killed or, possibly, those known to have switched sides. There are specific references to men killed in action on January 17, 1781, so missing names may well represent those who changed sides.

Of the 123 men who enlisted in the British Legion from August to October 1780, 88 (71.5 percent) do not appear on the rolls after Cowpens. Some thirty-five (28.4 percent) of the enlistees were still present at Yorktown and later. Three men were either captured or killed between Cowpens and Yorktown. This suggests that a Continental who changed sides did not always do it simply to avoid the prison hulks. Another possibility is that once a man joined the British Legion, he either changed loyalties, felt bound to his new comrades, or was afraid to return to the Continental forces for fear of retribution (see Table 4).

The last option seems to be what motivated the men who deserted the Legion while it was besieged at Yorktown. Once the British were trapped in their fortifications and capture appeared imminent, these men left their arms behind, crossed the siege lines, and surrendered. Because they were not "taken in arms," they were apparently considered returned to service. However, there may have been some retribution. At least one former Continental who deserted at Yorktown was taken back into the Maryland Line but ended up serving until the end of the war.

TABLE 4

August–October 1780 Enlistees' Disposition

| Troop/Company | Number | C Loss | At Y | Other |
|---|---|---|---|---|
| Hovenden | 11 | 7 | 4 | |
| James | 18 | 10 | 8 | |
| Sandford | 8 | 6 | 1 | 1 |
| Ogilvie | 19 | 18 | 1 | |
| Kinlock/Vernon | 19 | 5 | 12 | 2 |
| Stewart | 16 | 13 | 3 | |
| Rousselet | 12 | 9 | 3 | |
| Miller | 2 | 2 | | |
| McDonald | 5 | 4 | 1 | |
| McPherson | 16 | 14 | 2 | |
| Totals | 125 | 88 | 35 | 3 |

C=Cowpens; Y=Yorktown.
Based on Clark, 2:197–251.

Some men who survived to claim land or pensions are interesting in that they provide clues about attitudes toward changing sides. Four men from Prince George's County, Maryland, were killed at Camden, nine captured and a further twenty-one listed as missing. Seven of those reported captured or missing later appear in British Legion muster rolls.[25]

The case of Pvt. Morris Neagle of the 4th Maryland Regiment, and later of the British Legion, provides additional clues. Neagle's will was probated on May 17, 1794. His United States land warrant for service in the Maryland Line was issued after his death, on December 22, 1794, so it is unlikely that he filed his claim for the land, unless he had done so before his death; his one hundred acres were assigned to a Henry Purdy. Neagle's service was recorded as having "continued to the end of the war."[26]

Benjamin Biggs also obtained a land warrant. Four former prisoners had their wills probated in 1793 and 1794, as did seventeen soldiers who had once been listed as missing, six of whose names appear in the British Legion rolls. These men all seem to have had their wills probated to obtain bounty lands in western Maryland. It may be that no Camden prisoners who changed sides came back to Prince George's County. They may have been declared dead by their families in order to obtain the western land warrants, as it is unlikely that a poor man from southern Maryland made a will when he joined the Continental Army. Probating their wills may have effectively declared these men legally dead and allowed land speculators to approach their kin with an offer to purchase the land warrant (see Table 5 for an accounting of Continentals from Prince George's County).

Thomas Tyac was paid by the Continental Army for his time in the British Legion and was presumably also paid other compensation after the war, indicating that it was believed that he had faithfully served throughout the conflict.[27]

Changing sides was a complicated affair. Not all ex-Continentals changed sides after Cowpens, or in the aftermath of later battles, when they had a chance to do so. Of the 123 men who entered the Legion between August and October 1780, about 35 were still serving in the unit at Yorktown. Obviously, their motivations for serving changed after the Battle of Camden and enlistment into the British unit. The very concept of enlisting needs more examination. If recruiters gathered up the unemployed and landless, and local boards drafted surplus men with no ties to the community, why would anyone expect loyalty from these men when they were faced with confinement in disease-ridden prison hulks? Once they shifted to the other side, where would their loyalties then lie?

Only thirty-five probable Camden Continentals served until Yorktown. This is a small sample, and no names checked thus far appear in Canadian pension files. British Legion muster rolls for February and May 1780 do not exist. The earliest Legion muster rolls from before the

TABLE 5

## Continentals from Prince George's County, Maryland

| Name | Regiment | At C[a] | Postwar | Ref.[b] |
|---|---|---|---|---|
| Allcock, Martin | 4th MD | MIA | | 4 |
| Allen, Barnaby | 1st MD | POW | Will, Mar. 4, 1793 | 5 |
| Allen, Gilbert | 5th MD | POW | Will, Mar. 4, 1793 | 5 |
| Allison, Thomas | 1st MD | POW | | 5 |
| Ayers, Frederick | 6th MD | KIA | Will, Nov. 28, 1792 | 8 |
| Biggs, Benjamin | 7th MD | MIA | Warrant, 1790s | 29 |
| Butt, Zachariah | 2nd MD | KIA | | 55-56 |
| Cannon, Patrick | 6th MD | MIA | Will, Mar. 22, 1794 | 57 |
| Carman, James | 5th MD | MIA | Will, Mar. 22, 1794 | 58 |
| Carney, Patrick | 6th MD | MIA | Will, Mar. 22, 1793 | 58 |
| Coffin, Daniel | 5th MD | MIA | Will, Mar. 15, 1793 | 71 |
| Connolly, Benjamin | 3rd MD | KIA | | 74 |
| Corker, John | 5th MD | MIA | Will, Mar. 22, 1794 | 77 |
| Craig, Michael | 5th MD | MIA | Will, Mar. 22, 1794 | 79 |
| Davis, Thomas | 4th MD | MIA | Will, Jan. 18, 1793 | 85 |
| Downes, William | 4th MD | MIA | Will, Dec. 13, 1804 | 90 |
| Duffey, John | 4th MD | MIA | Will, Mar. 15, 1793 | 95 |
| Duly, William | 7th MD | MIA | Will, Jan. 18, 1793 | 95 |
| Ferguson, John | 2nd MD | POW | | 112 |
| Hilliary, Rignal | 3rd MD | POW | Will 1786, died 1783 | 149 |
| Hinness, John | 2nd MD | POW | | 150 |
| Hoskins, John | 1st MD | MIA | Will, Oct. 10, 1790 | 155 |
| Jenkins, Isaac | 1st MD | MIA | | 166 |
| Johnson, George | 6th MD | MIA | Will, Mar. 21, 1793 | 168-169 |
| McManis, Barney | 7th MD | KIA | Will, Feb. 20, 1792 | 213 |
| Mooney, Patrick | 6th MD | MIA | Will, Mar. 7, 1793 | 220 |
| Neagle, Morris | 4th MD | POW | Will, May 17, 1794 | 230 |
| Rawlings, John | 2nd MD | POW | | 250 |
| Satterfield, William | 7th MD | MIA | Will, Mar. 10, 1794 | 263 |
| Shean, Timothy | 4th MD | MIA | Will, Mar. 10, 1794 | 268 |
| Townley, Henry | 3rd MD | MIA | | 299 |
| Turner, Richard | 3rd MD | POW | Will, Mar. 10, 1794 | 305 |
| Wade, James | 3rd MD | MIA | Will, Mar. 22, 1794 | 309 |
| Williams, William | 4th MD | MIA | Will, Jan. 24, 1797 | 337 |

*(Table 5 continued)*
a. C=Camden; KIA=killed in action; MIA=missing in action; POW=prisoner of war.
b. Numbers refer to pages in Henry C. Peden Jr., *Revolutionary Patriots of Montgomery County, Maryland, 1775–1783* (Westminster, MD: Willow Bend Books, 2001)

British capture of Charleston in May 1780 are from October and December 1779, before the Legion began campaigning in South Carolina.[28] This makes it difficult to identify the possible presence of Continental soldiers captured at Charleston.

There are intriguing implications about the Charleston prisoners of war. For Rousselet's company, only twenty-one of seventy-nine enlisted men on the December 1780 muster roll were found on the October 1779 roll. Thirteen enlisted after Camden and have already been discussed. Of the sixty October 1780 names, seven correspond with Virginia, North Carolina, or South Carolina Continentals or militiamen captured when Charleston fell. Some names are extremely uncommon, such as John Ederington and John Turnipseed.

In Capt. James Edwards's British Legion infantry company, four names on the October 1780 muster roll are likely Charleston Continentals or militia prisoners, including John Snatt and John Lynch. Lynch is a particularly interesting case because his American military records ceased when Charleston surrendered. At that time he was serving in Lt. Col. Benjamin Roebuck's militia battalion from Spartanburg District, South Carolina. He appears on the October 1780 British Legion roll and then is noted as a prisoner at Cowpens. Roebuck commanded a Spartanburg militia battalion at Cowpens. Lynch may have enlisted in the Legion to avoid confinement on a prison ship and then changed sides as soon as the Legion was close enough to his home for him to make his escape and rejoin his former comrades.[29]

Finally, while this effort concentrates on the British Legion, there is evidence that other British units, specifically the Volunteers of Ireland, also recruited Continental prisoners taken at Camden. One, drummer Benjamin Jones, may be the man who informed Lt. Col. Francis, Lord Rawdon, that Nathanael Greene's army outside Camden did not have any artillery or militia; this information encouraged Rawdon to attack and defeat Greene at the Battle of Hobkirk's Hill on April 25, 1781.

# EIGHT

# Cavalry Operations at the Battle of Eutaw Springs

## A Novelist's View

### *Charles F. Price*

IN JUNE 2005 MY FRIEND AND RESEARCH COLLEAGUE LEE F. McGee sent me an e-mail that contained what was, for me, an exciting revelation. For months he and I had been rummaging through every primary and secondary source we could find in an effort to discover what manual, if any, governed the organization and tactics of the dragoons of the Continental Army.

Our purpose was to define, if we could, the practice of the Continental horse in camp, in the field, and on the battleground, so that I could portray these activities as accurately as possible in a novel I was writing, *Nor the Battle to the Strong*. One of the novel's characters was to be a private in the 1st Regiment of Continental Light Dragoons during the summer of 1781.

Until that day, our search had borne scant fruit. We knew, of course, that the Continental Congress had reorganized the Continental cavalry on January 1, 1781, converting the prior system of four all-mounted dragoon regiments into a structure whereby each regiment would consist of four mounted and two dismounted troops, to be called a legionary corps.[1]

We had known early on, from a letter of Maj. Richard Call of the 3rd Dragoons to Col. William Davies, Virginia's commissioner of war, that by the late summer of 1781 attempts were under way in the field, at least in that state, to conform the cavalry regiments to this new system. We also knew that in 1780, Inspector General "Baron" Friedrich von Steuben had begun writing, but had never finished, a drill manual for a proposed legionary corps, doubtless based on his knowledge of the widespread use of such a concept in the European armies of the time. We even had a partial abstract of that incomplete manual, courtesy of 3rd Dragoon historian C. F. William Maurer, which had been drawn up for the use of dragoon reenactors during the Revolutionary War Bicentennial. The abstract was based on records in the Steuben Papers in the collections of the New-York Historical Society.[2]

While the Steuben manual was quite explicit about the operation of a legionary corps, we had no way of knowing whether any of its directives had ever been put into practice. The fact that it was unfinished suggested that they had not been applied. I laid the manual aside as a possible valuable but still unverified resource. Eventually, as we continued to work, Lee examined a microfilm copy of the Steuben Papers, but since much of the collection was written in French, a language neither of us knew, and since all of it was extremely difficult to decipher, it was quickly put aside.

I continued searching through other relevant primary and secondary sources of the eighteenth and early nineteenth centuries, mostly British, in an effort to locate information I thought might have been adapted by the Americans from the cavalry usage of the mother country, and I also consulted a number of relevant recent studies. I learned that until 1796 the British cavalry service had no standardization of the sword exercise, and that even the type of sword used—broadsword or saber—varied according to the whims of individual regimental commanders. Also, multiple manuals appear to have been used for British regimental cavalry drill, again presumably reflecting the personal preferences of regimental commanders.[3]

Of course, until Steuben began training the Continental Army at Valley Forge in 1778, there was no standard *infantry* drill for American forces. Battalions followed whatever colonial-era manuals had come to hand, sometimes Humphrey Bland's *A Treatise of Military Discipline* of 1717; the "Sixty-Fourth" or the British Army Manual of 1764; or the so-called Norfolk discipline of 1759, as later revised by Timothy Pickering as *An Easy Plan of Discipline for a Militia*.[4] Consequently, I should not have been surprised, but was, when Lee turned up evidence that the same was true of the Continental cavalry.

Meanwhile, Lee had begun to examine the Steuben documents in detail. The collection contained not just the truncated legionary corps manual, but also some of Steuben's official correspondence. Among these letters was one from Lt. Col. Francis Mentges, deputy inspector general of the Continental Army in the South, to Steuben, who was serving as inspector general for the entire Continental Army. Writing from James Island, South Carolina, on January 9, 1783, Mentges was reporting on the condition of the Virginia, Maryland, and Pennsylvania infantry, Lee's Partisan Legion, the artillery of the army, and the 1st Regiment of Continental Light Dragoons, and remarked: "No system or treatise being adopted by congress for the order and discipline of the caveraly I therefore only observed their martial appearance the care and attention paid by the officers to the men and horse the regularity of the keeping their books and their uniformity that prevails amongst them."[5]

If, as late as January 1783, "no system or treatise . . . for the order and discipline" of the cavalry had been adopted and put into practice, obviously none had existed in 1781, either. Looking back on all this, I can now see that I should have known from the start that this would be the case. But I did not, and at any rate the search itself had been instructive. In at least one respect—that of cavalry drill—Colonel Mentges had loosed me from the constraints of known fact; I was free to indulge in imaginative fiction. But whatever I imagined could also be usefully informed by the historical plausibilities born of my research.

A reasonable person might ask why a novelist like me became so enmeshed in matters that are more properly associated with the historian than with the writer of fiction. Why not just get on and tell a rattling good tale, and to hell with all the details? Few readers would notice any number of anachronistic howlers, or care about them if they did notice. Well, I may deal in fiction, but I *do* care. I deal in *historical* fiction, and I take my history seriously.

But it's true that I'm not a historian. I'm a novelist, and the novelist is a storyteller. I must tell my story in a convincing and consistent way, and unlike pure history, which is often murky and messy, my story must have a clear contour that will be satisfying to the reader. Conflicts must be resolved, loose ends neatly tied, plot lines rounded out. Having made my various leaps of faith over the gaps and obstacles in the record, I can decide what I *believe* might have happened, whereas the historian is forced to stop short of such unverifiable speculation.

With that issue disposed of, I could set to work building a conjectural, but still plausible, idea of what the day-to-day life of a Continental dragoon recruit might have been like—how he might have been trained, taught horsemanship, and drilled; by whom he would have been trained; and how his unit might have been organized.

The very large question of dragoon tactics, however, remained to be addressed, and it was a topic beset by the woes of which Colonel Mentges had relieved me in regard to drill. Luckily, Lee tackled this one; he has written persuasively and extensively about the European influences on the dragoon tactics of Lt. Col. William Washington, specifically the Prussian influences as possibly gained through contact with Steuben, Casimir Pulaski, and other European officers. It is an absorbing topic and one deserving serious study. It lay totally unexplored, so far as I know, until Lee ventured into it, beginning as a consultant for my novel and continuing until now as an independent researcher.[6]

I'll address the tactical issues Lee studied in a moment; for now, I want to discuss the assumptions I made about training, organization, and drill. First, taking my cue from Major Call's letter to Colonel Davies, I assumed that the cavalry regiments in Virginia during the spring and summer of 1781 were in fact making good-faith efforts to implement the legionary corps structure. Lee later found evidence in a return of March 7, 1781, confirming this assumption.[7]

At that time, Steuben shared command of the Continental forces in Virginia with the Marquis de Lafayette. One source tells us that Steuben personally devoted himself to instructing recruits in basic infantry drill while at the Point of Fork Arsenal in May and early June 1781. It is also clear from that summer's archived correspondence that he was deeply involved with the details of recruiting and equipping troops of the 1st and 3rd Dragoons.[8]

I assumed, therefore, that Steuben may also have influenced the organization and training of the newly recruited 1st and 3rd Regiments, either personally, as he did with some of the infantry, or through directives to Major Call and Col. Anthony Walton White, commander of the 1st Dragoons, and that the ideas set forth in his manual were the ones he drew upon. This assumption enabled me to use his abstracted manual as my guide to the organization and functioning of the Continental cavalry of 1781, at least in Virginia.

So I placed the protagonist of my novel, Pvt. James Johnson, in a troop of the 1st Dragoons at the camp of instruction at Manakin Town on the James River, fifteen miles upstream from Richmond. The 1st at this time was a regiment in transition to a legionary corps. Based on the mounted organization for a legionary corps as outlined in the Steuben manual, in my novel the six-troop, all-mounted regiment of 1777 now has four mounted troops and is waiting to receive its two dismounted troops (companies), currently being recruited and trained elsewhere. Johnson's horse troop is one of the two that comprise a squadron. His troop consists of two divisions, each composed in turn of two platoons. Each platoon has two sections composed of two ranks of at least four and no more than five riders.[9]

Private Johnson is taught horsemanship by a riding master who is assisted by several horse handlers called roughriders, who break and train the newly impressed horses. The principles of horsemanship and the means of horse breaking are as set forth in two eighteenth-century British instructional manuals.[10]

He is taught the sword exercise, first on foot and then on horseback, by a noncommissioned officer acting as fugleman, demonstrating the various movements with the aid of a circular pane like a sandwich board on which is painted a human face, the panel divided, like a pie sliced for serving, into the lines of the several designated sword cuts. The sergeant also instructs Johnson in the operation of the pistol and the carbine.[11]

In my novel, Johnson's training is interrupted when he is detailed to travel to South Carolina as part of an escort for a wagon train of clothing destined for Maj. Gen. Nathanael Greene's Southern Army. He arrives just in time to be thrown into the battle at Eutaw Springs with the small contingent of the 1st Dragoons serving with William Washington's command.

This brings us to the tactical issues studied by Lee. A corollary to our surmise about the Virginia troops being organized according to Steuben's plan for legionary corps was that the detachment of dragoons under Washington, engaged in active operations against the British in South Carolina, enjoyed little leisure to attend to the fine details of the Steuben scheme, and instead continued to function as it had since General Greene had taken command of the Southern Army in December 1780—that is, as a body of horse composed mainly of 3rd Dragoon troopers but also including a small party of men from the 1st Dragoons, sometimes operating in conjunction with the light troops of Delaware or Virginia.

We remembered that Greene had traveled with Steuben from New York on his way to take up the southern command. Lee conjectured that the two men had ample time during this journey to discuss Steuben's military experience and ideas about the legionary corps concept. We don't know for certain that this happened. What we do know is that soon after taking command in the South, Greene tended to employ cavalry and light infantry together somewhat in the general mode of the legionary system, but less formally and less frequently than was called for in Steuben's plan.[12]

Greene's arrangement strongly resembles a field adaptation of the congressional mandate, tailored to suit combat conditions. Colonel Washington's detachment was small, averaging only between 80 and 100 troopers, not even enough to form two full troops of 120 mounted men. Furthermore, the Delaware or Virginia light infantrymen served with his dragoons only on certain occasions, not as a permanent element of his command as Steuben directed. Nor, as Lee has pointed out, is there any primary-source evidence that Washington's force contained any dismounted troopers.[13]

The cumulative effect of both our assumptions and our proofs was that in Virginia, where the dragoons were only lightly involved in combat, White and Call were trying to rebuild the 1st and 3rd Regiments according to the legionary corps model, while in South Carolina a more flexible approach was used that better suited both Greene's need for strategic mobility and Washington's bold temperament, as well as the pressing contingencies of nearly constant active operations. As Lee has said, the differences "are less attributable to what Greene and Washington had *than to what [they] wanted to have.*" What they wanted, and used effectively, was pure horse cavalry.[14]

Thus, when Private Johnson mounts up and takes his place in the ranks of Washington's command on the morning of September 8, 1781, for the Battle of Eutaw Springs, he finds himself in unfamiliar circumstances. For one thing, he is alone in carrying a carbine; that cumbersome weapon has fallen out of use in the Southern Army. The troopers around him rely mainly on the sword. Then, just before advancing on Maj. John Marjoribanks's position on the British right flank, when Washington orders the dragoons to form by sections, Johnson expects to see a formation of two ranks of no more than five troopers, as he has been taught to look for in Virginia. Instead, he sees what he (and Steuben's manual) would have called a platoon front—that is, a party composed of two ranks of eight to ten men, a broader section front than he's used to.[15]

Also, the whole force is in a column twelve ranks deep, whereas Steuben's manual called for them to have displayed in line of battle, two ranks deep. A conflict arises here, because in another place—a letter to George Washington from October 23, 1780—Steuben asserts that cavalry, when attempting to break a line of infantry, generally should advance by troops or squadrons, "or in column in *echiquier* (checker-wise). The deeper they are, the surer they are to break through.[16]

However this may be, we do have the eyewitness testimony of 3rd Dragoon trooper George Hood describing the twelve-deep column, and I used it in my novel. I believe it would have been a formation alien to Private Johnson's training, but one adopted by William Washington for reasons of his own that we cannot now know any more than we can know why he frontally charged infantry strongly posted in a wooded position, a maneuver ordinarily considered contrary to cavalry usage. It may even be, as Lee has suggested, that the term "column" is a misnomer, implying as it does a single dense block of horsemen; in Europe at the time, and perhaps in America, too, a so-called column would have been understood as a squadron in two-deep ranks, with successive squadrons behind them, the whole forming a column.[17]

Lee's analysis of all known primary and secondary sources suggests the possibility that Washington may have made more than one charge that day, perhaps even into the main British battle line as well as against Marjoribanks's position on the flank.[18] He drew these conclusions some time after I had completed my novel and it had been accepted by a publisher—too late for me to amend my original assumption based on the more standard sources. So in my book, Private Johnson participates in one assault on the blackjack thicket, which veers to the left along the front of the British grenadiers and light infantrymen posted there, exposing the rightmost files and the officers and noncoms on the right of the formation to a destructive fire.

But before that happens, I make one change that falls wholly into the realm of fictional license. I find it very hard to believe that Washington, bold as he was, would have attacked the thicket headlong without first reconnoitering it. There is no evidence that he did so. In my novel, he does. Why? The only answer is that I thought he should have. Ever since the full-scale battle began, South Carolina state troops under Col. William Henderson—and later under Col. Wade Hampton after Henderson was wounded—had been posted opposite Marjoribanks.

Undoubtedly they had skirmished with the British flank battalion. That they took fire is proven by Henderson's wound. That they begged permission to charge Marjoribanks, to relieve themselves from this fire, and were denied it by Greene, is asserted by Col. Otho Williams.[19]

So I write that Washington suspends his advance and rides forward with Hampton to study Marjoribanks's position. Why then, given the difficult nature of the British flank—a deep ravine covered by impenetrable thickets that Washington should have seen during this survey—does he resume his frontal charge? My own belief (and I think Lee's, too) after viewing the ground at Eutaw Springs, is that Marjoribanks's skirmishers were deployed well in advance of his main line, occupying a hummock that obscured a swale behind it and then a second rise, covered by a steadily thickening growth of blackjack, where the main force of Marjoribanks waited. I assumed that the state troops had never penetrated beyond the enemy skirmish line and thus possessed no knowledge of the strong position behind it; consequently Hampton, during their reconnaissance, could not warn Washington of it. Perhaps Washington saw only Marjoribanks's skirmishers and took them for the whole flank force of the enemy, which he believed he could disperse, thus gaining the British rear.

So the charge resumes.

For what happens next, you'll have to read the novel.

# NINE

# The "Black Dragoons"

## Former Slaves as British Cavalry in Revolutionary South Carolina

### *Jim Piecuch*

L ATE ON THE NIGHT OF JANUARY 17, 1782, WILLIAM Mathews was disturbed by the sounds of a large party of mounted men surrounding his house outside Charleston, South Carolina. Sensing danger, Mathews refused to leave the building to investigate, but finally opened the door in response to shouted threats to break it down. To his horror, the uniformed British cavalry he confronted were not white soldiers but a unit of "Negroe Dragoons" commanded by "one John Jackson." The troops demanded "some refreshment," and Mathews—a slaveowner accustomed to being served by blacks, not serving them—reluctantly complied. After eating and drinking, the dragoons left, "swearing that had I not been an Invalid they would have fired the House & cut me in Peices." Mathews complained bitterly of his treatment to British officials in Charleston, insisting that as a supporter of the Revolution who had remained peaceful since the surrender of Charleston, he was entitled to protection from such disturbances.[1] His rage at the activities of the black cavalrymen illustrated the difficulties that the British faced in using former slaves as soldiers: these men could provide valuable military service, but their activities provoked a severe backlash among whites who saw black soldiers as a threat to the very foundations of South Carolina's slavery-based social and economic system.

From the outset of the American Revolution, British officials recognized that the large number of African American slaves in the Southern colonies could be a valuable asset in any effort to regain control of the region. Many Britons, from army officers to West Indies planters, sent King George III's ministers various proposals to arm slaves and employ them against the rebels.[2] British leaders, however, were reluctant to adopt such a drastic measure; only Virginia's royal governor John Murray, Earl of Dunmore, possessed sufficient boldness to form an "Ethiopian Regiment" of former slaves in 1775. The London government gave Dunmore's actions lukewarm approval, but the experiment ended in 1776 when Dunmore gave up his efforts to subdue Virginia's rebels. The black regiment was then disbanded and the men assigned to pioneer duties.[3] In the fall of 1779, British major general Augustine Prevost armed about two hundred slaves to help defend Savannah from French and American attack, a measure that aroused the ire of Georgia loyalists.[4]

After the British captured Charleston in May 1780, no effort was made to arm the thousands of South Carolina slaves who fled to the Royal Army in hopes of gaining their freedom. Lt. Gen. Charles, Earl Cornwallis, preferred to rely on regular troops and the loyal militia to secure the province, a policy that proved relatively successful until January 1781. Following the American victory at the Battle of Cowpens that month, Cornwallis pursued the Americans into North Carolina with much of the

British Army, including all of the regular cavalry, and eventually marched to Virginia. Thus, when Maj. Gen. Nathanael Greene led his Continental Army back to South Carolina in April, the British were left without mounted troops to counter the regular cavalry under Henry Lee and William Washington and the mounted partisans of Francis Marion, Thomas Sumter, and Andrew Pickens. Efforts to convert some infantry from the South Carolina Royalists and New York Volunteers to cavalry, and to create new units of loyalist dragoons, proved insufficient to overcome the Americans' numerical advantage. By October 1781, Greene had driven the British back to the vicinity of Charleston, and the Royal Army still desperately needed mounted troops to patrol outside their defensive lines, procure intelligence of American positions and movements, and gather badly needed supplies for the troops, residents, and loyalist refugees in the town. Shortly afterward, British officers turned to the only resource of manpower available to them and formed a cavalry unit of former slaves who became known as the Black Dragoons.

No record exists indicating exactly when the Black Dragoons were organized. In fact, other than one pay abstract, no trace of the unit appears in official British records, and with the exception of one loyalist officer, neither Maj. Gen. Alexander Leslie, who replaced Cornwallis as British commander in the South, nor his subordinates ever directly mentioned the Black Dragoons, although Leslie on one occasion praised those African Americans who had fought for the British in South Carolina. Perhaps Leslie's reticence was the result of the unit's having been created without official permission from his superiors in New York and London.

Historians, too, have largely neglected this unique cavalry unit. They cannot be blamed for doing so, because in addition to the absence of British records, the several American accounts of the Black Dragoons are few and widely scattered. Only by piecing together these often-disconnected references can the story of the Black Dragoons be re-created, although it remains incomplete.[5]

The Black Dragoons were most likely formed in November or December 1781.[6]

They were definitely organized and equipped by early January 1782, when Benjamin Thompson, a former aide to Lord George Germain, arrived in Charleston. Thompson, a New Hampshire loyalist, had procured a commission as lieutenant colonel in the King's American Dragoons and sailed for New York, but chose to remain in Charleston, his ship's first stop, when bad weather delayed the remainder of the voyage.[7] There Major General Leslie appointed him commander of the army's cavalry. On January 11, Thompson wrote that his corps consisted of "five weak Troops" of regular cavalry, which would soon be augmented by a troop of South Carolinians. He also commanded "Two strong Troops of Mounted Militia, and a Seapoy Troop (Gens de Couleurs) that will act with us occasionally."[8]

Thompson spent nearly two weeks training his men before leading them on a foray against the rebels on January 23. "The principal objects of the expedition were to practice the Cavalry in marching in Regular order in the Enemys Country, and to accustom them to act with the mounted militia," Thompson wrote. In addition to carrying out that exercise, Thompson's cavalry surprised one American party, killing two and capturing three; dispersed a second rebel force later in the day, capturing another five prisoners; and gathered three wagonloads of forage and some livestock. The Black Dragoons, commanded by a former slave named Smart who had been commissioned a captain, participated in the operation, although they were assigned to the rear of the marching column and probably did not take part in the skirmishing. Thompson praised all of his men for their performance, not distinguishing between whites or blacks, militia or provincials.[9]

After Thompson departed for New York, the Black Dragoons continued to serve, making important contributions to the British cause. They helped alleviate Charleston's supply problems by keeping the town's markets "supplied with the greatest plenty of everything they want."[10] They also skirmished occasionally with American forces.

The British use of armed former slaves infuriated the Americans—Southerners and Northerners alike. Clearly there was more to the Americans' resentment of the Black Dragoons than the mere fact that they were African American soldiers. Blacks had enlisted in Continental units in many states, although both Georgia and South Carolina officials rejected Congress's suggestion that they offer freedom to slaves who would serve in those states' Continental regiments. Some blacks also served in the various state militias, although in the two southernmost states their roles were limited to musicians and personal servants. However, in the American forces blacks always served under white officers.[11] The Black Dragoons, on the other hand, were led by former slaves commissioned as British officers and frequently served independently, unaccompanied by white units. It was this unique aspect of the unit—armed former slaves acting without white supervision—that angered and terrified the Americans.

Thomas Sumter, a South Carolinian who believed that the best military use for slaves was as enlistment bounties for Whig recruits, denounced the British use of black soldiers. Giving former slaves weapons, he declared, was "sufficient to rouse and fix the resentment and detestation of every American."[12] Col. Lewis Morris of New York, an aide to Greene, shared Sumter's views. When his fiancée, Ann Elliott, met the Black Dragoons outside Charleston, Morris denounced the "rude treatment" that Elliott had allegedly received from "those vile dragoons." Four weeks later, Morris was still infuriated by the incident and begged Elliott not to travel without an escort.[13]

Such intense, racially motivated hatred ensured that American troops would react violently whenever they encountered the Black Dragoons. On April 21, a patrol of twenty-five to thirty American cavalry of Lt. Col. Henry Lee's Legion encountered a British mounted force between Dorchester and the Quarter House. The British horsemen fell back, and the Americans were in pursuit when another British unit, consisting of both white troops and some of the Black Dragoons, ambushed them. The rebels were driven back with losses but regrouped and attacked again.[14] In the ensuing combat the Americans encountered March, a former slave who had been "extremely active, & very troublesome" in British service, along with two or three other armed blacks. When March refused to surrender, the American soldiers "cut him" and his fellows "to pieces."[15] According to one account, which stated that March held the rank of major, the black officer attempted to escape, but an American cavalryman pursued him into a swamp "and with one blow of his sword severed his head from his body."[16] Edward Rutledge praised the rebel soldiers' behavior. "Besides dispatching so infamous a fellow, I have my hopes that others will be prevented from following his Example, if they are not, I hope they will meet his Fate," Rutledge wrote.[17] The Americans may have confused March (who was listed on a pay abstract as serving in the summer and fall of 1782) with Smart, since Capt. Walter Finney of the Pennsylvania Continentals probably referred to the same battle when he recorded an encounter between a rebel party and "a Negroe Captn. Nam'd Smart, and some of his Affrican Banditty," which had resulted in the Americans "Dissecting" Smart.[18]

Rutledge's hope that Smart's death might discourage the Black Dragoons from further service went unfulfilled, as they remained one of the most active British units, frequently operating outside Charleston's defensive lines. Charles Cotesworth Pinckney complained in mid-August that these troops were "daily committing the most horrible depredations and murder in the defenceless parts of our Country."[19]

Marion encountered the Black Dragoons, operating with Maj. Thomas Frazer's loyalist cavalry, in a late August skirmish near Biggin Bridge. Having received reports that British forces were in that vicinity, Marion led his troops to meet them. Frazer with about one hundred loyalist cavalry and "some Coloured Dragoons" charged the Americans, but Marion had posted some of his men to fire into the British right flank, which halted the charge and forced Frazer to withdraw.[20]

In addition to their frequent raiding and the skirmishes that often ensued, the Black Dragoons performed outpost duty and other routine military tasks, an indication of the extent to which they had come to be seen by British officers as just another unit of the army. When Captain Finney arrived at the Quarter House on December 2 with a flag of truce to conduct some business, he was met by "Majr. Mengus of the Black Dragoons" (possibly the officer listed on the pay abstract as Lieutenant Mingo). Because it was too late in the day to complete his task, the captain had to return to the Quarter House the next day, where he found that the Dragoons had been relieved by the New Jersey Volunteers.[21]

Another important duty assigned to the Black Dragoons was the capture of deserters, an essential function given the low morale and inactivity of the Charleston garrison. During the month of October 1782, forty-six men deserted from the three Hessian regiments in the town, but the problem diminished after three deserters from the Von Benning Regiment "were pounced upon by the Black Dragoons in the early morning" of October 31. Two of the deserters were killed and the third escaped, but in the wake of the incident the Hessian commander reported that "desertions have ceased." The Dragoons received a bounty of two guineas for each deserter, living or dead, whom they brought back to the British lines.[22]

The Black Dragoons continued their operations to the very eve of Charleston's evacuation. They were also "kept constantly patrolling" to prevent loyalists and British deserters from leaving the town. During these operations, "a party of the British Negro Horse, consisting of ten men," battled an American detachment under Col. Thaddeus Kosciuszko on November 4, in which eight of the black troops were reported to have been killed or wounded.[23] Just over a week before the British and their supporters left the city, Thomas Bee wrote Gov. John Mathews "at the request of several inhabitants of the Goose Creek neighborhood," soliciting protection "from the ravages of the Black Dragoons who have been out four times within the last ten days plundering & robbing between the Quarter House and this place." On the night of December 8, the Dragoons raided the home of a Mrs. Godins, taking all her livestock and a large quantity of provisions, and told her they would soon be back to "pay a visit to Mr. Parker & Mr. Smith," her neighbors. Godins estimated that there were at least one hundred dragoons in the party, but others who followed the dragoons' tracks put their strength at fifty. Bee requested that Mathews send a party of state cavalry to patrol the area and asked the governor to seek help from Greene as well.[24]

One of Greene's officers, Kosciuszko, had become obsessed with defeating the Black Dragoons and was already doing everything in his power to intercept them and bring them to battle. With the exception of the November 4 skirmish, however, Kosciuszko failed in his efforts. As he explained to Greene on November 29, "[T]he Black dragoons some time come up to the Country for forage but cannot be know well their road what they take as they vary their roads and the time Some time in the night some in the day some time fut [foot] path some time brawd road and sometime go trow [through] the woods."[25] Clearly, the officers of the Black Dragoons had acquired a thorough knowledge of the region and of how to deceive the enemy, frustrating Kosciuszko while successfully carrying out their own missions.

When the British evacuated Charleston on December 14, the Black Dragoons were among the thousands of British troops, white loyalists, and African Americans who preferred an uncertain fate under King George III than submission to the American authorities. Although no records survive of the men's destination, some evidence indicates that they went to the West Indies, where they became the nucleus of the Carolina Black Corps of former slaves. General Leslie, without specifically mentioning the Black Dragoons, informed his superior, Gen. Sir Guy Carleton, that the military service performed by some South Carolina slaves "will engage the grateful attention of Government to which they will continue to be useful."[26]

The career of the Black Dragoons demonstrated both the potential and the limitations of British use of African American troops. Despite their lack of military background and limited opportunities for training, the Black Dragoons performed well, filling the British Army's urgent need for cavalry. They were almost constantly in the field in the final months of 1782. Their raids provided badly needed supplies for the people in Charleston and they performed guard duty in the lines, pursued deserters, and occasionally fought the rebels, albeit with limited success. These achievements indicate that a large force of well-trained African American troops, employed early in the southern campaign, might have enabled the British to retain control of Georgia and the Carolinas.

On the opposite side of the ledger, the operations—even the very existence—of the Black Dragoons inflamed the rebels by challenging the existing social order in the South. Americans responded with anger and violence, the implication being that any large-scale British effort to employ former slaves as soldiers might have produced so severe a backlash among whites as to render the measure counterproductive, perhaps even causing many slave-owning loyalists to switch allegiance to the rebels.

As for the African American soldiers themselves, their motives and attitudes can only be conjectured, since they left no records. All of the Black Dragoons were volunteers, so they must have welcomed the opportunity to ensure their freedom by bearing arms for Britain. By becoming soldiers, they demonstrated their equality with whites on one level, and to be made an officer must have infused those who received commissions with great pride. Furthermore, many of the dragoons would have welcomed the opportunity to strike back at representatives of a system that had exploited them for so long. In that regard, the Black Dragoons were far more than just cavalry: they were a physical, armed, uniformed reminder of the dangerous frailty of South Carolina's slave society.

TABLE I.

Pay Abstract Nr 163, Independent Troop of Black Dragoons, for 92-days pay, 1 July to 30 Sept 1782*:

| | |
|---|---|
| Captain | March |
| Lieutenant | Mingo |
| Adjutant | Garrick |
| Qtr-Mstr | Robin |
| | |
| Sergeant | Mayham, John |
| | Scippio |
| | Davy |
| | |
| Private | Jamie |
| | Peter |
| | Lynch |
| | January |
| | Cane |
| | Primus |
| | Minos |
| | Mingo |
| | Prince |
| | Jacob |
| | Samuel |
| | Isaac |
| | Dawey |
| | Toney |
| | Jeffry |
| | Pompey |
| | Gilbert |
| | Dick |
| | Aberdeen |
| | Tom |
| | Peter |
| | Hammond |
| | Charles |

*This abstract lists a total of thirty officers and men who served for the pay period. Men who left the unit as a result of death, wounds, or capture during this time span, and their replacements, were obviously not included, so that the unit's estimated strength of fifty men, as stated in some documents, was probably accurate.

From Murtie June Clark, *Loyalists in the Southern Campaign of the Revolutionary War*, 3 vols. (Baltimore: Genealogical Publishing Co., Inc., Vol. 3, 1981), 409.

# Notes

CHAPTER TWO: EUROPEAN INFLUENCES ON CONTINENTAL CAVALRY

1. Charles Howell Cureton, "The Virginia Cavalry, 1646–1783: A History of Organizational Development," unpublished PhD dissertation (Miami University, 1985), 13. Cureton also discusses the cavalry of Connecticut, Massachusetts, and South Carolina.

2. James Titus, *The Old Dominion at War: Society, Politics and Warfare in Late Colonial Virginia* (Columbia: University of South Carolina Press, 1991), 42; Oliver L. Spaulding, "The Military Studies of George Washington," *American Historical Review* 29, no. 4 (1924), 675–680. As commander of the Virginia Provincial Regiment, Washington had charge of Robert Stewart's troop of horse.

3. Spaulding, 675–680; Casimir Pulaski to George Washington, December 19, 1777, in *The Papers of George Washington, Revolutionary War Series*, ed. Philander D. Chase (Charlottesville: University Press of Virginia, 2002), 12:637.

4. Pulaski to Washington, January 9, 1778, in *Papers of George Washington* (2003), 13:192–193; Robert K. Wright, *The Continental Army* (Washington, DC: US Army Center of Military History, 1983), 121, 128, 132–133.

5. Francis Mentges to Baron Friedrich von Steuben, January 9, 1783, Friedrich von Steuben Papers, New-York Historical Society, New York, NY.

6. Sir John Fortescue, *A History of the British Army* (East Sussex, England: Naval and Military Press, 2004), 3:530. This author's work on Continental cavalry in the South in 1781 confirms Fortescue's view. See Lee F. McGee, "The Battle of Rugeley's Fort: 'A Spirit of Enterprize and Intrepidity Still Prevails,'" *Southern Campaigns of the American Revolution* 2, no. 6 (June 2005), 11–15; "'The Better Order of Men': Hammond's Store and Fort Williams" Ibid., 2, no. 12, 14–21; "'Most Astonishing Efforts': William Washington's Cavalry at Eutaw Springs," Ibid., 3, no. 3 (March 2006), 15–33; "'The Object Was Worthy of the Cast': The Patriot Cavalry Re-Examined at the Battle of Hobkirk's Hill," Ibid., 3, no. 4 (April 2006), 13–19; "Cavalry Actions at the Battle of Hobkirk's Hill—Remounted," Ibid., 5, no. 2, (February 2008), 36–37.

7. Cureton, "The Virginia Cavalry," *passim*.

8. H. C. Wylly, *XVth (The King's) Hussars, 1759–1913* (London: Caxton Publishing, 1914), 398–399; Fortescue, *British Army*, 3:530–533; David Dundas, *Principles of Military Movements, Chiefly Applied to Infantry* (East Sussex, England: Naval and Military Press, 2004), 12.

9. Fortescue, *British Army*, 3:529–532; Dundas, *Principles*, 11–12.

10. Cureton, "The Virginia Cavalry," *passim*.

11. Fortescue, *British Army*, 3:531, 599–600.

12. Dundas, *Principles*, 12.

13. Stephen Brumwell, *Redcoats: The British Soldier and War in the Americas, 1755–1763* (Cambridge, UK: Cambridge University Press, 2002), 262–263.

14. Gùy Chet, *Conquering the American Wilderness: The Triumph of European Warfare in the Colonial Northeast* (Amherst: University of Massachusetts Press, 2003), 147.

15. Fortescue, *British Army*, 3:530.

16. C. E. Warnery, *Remarks on Cavalry*, trans. G. F. Koehler (London: Constable and Co., 1997), viii.

17. Edward Barrington de Fonblanque, *Political and Military Episodes in the Latter Half of the Eighteenth Century Derived from the Life and Correspondence of John Burgoyne, General, Statesman, Dramatist* (London: Macmillan and Co., 1876), 63–64.

18. Ira D. Gruber, "British Strategy: The Theory and Practice of Eighteenth-Century Warfare," in *Reconsiderations on the Revolutionary War: Selected Essays*, ed. Don Higginbotham (Westport, CT: Greenwood Press, 1978), *passim*, esp. 17; Gruber, "The Education of Sir Henry Clinton," *Bulletin of the John Rylands University Library of Manchester* 72, no. 1 (1990), *passim*, esp. 148–149.

19. Gruber, "British Strategy," 17–18.

20. Robert Hinde, *The Discipline of the Light Horse* (London: W. Owen, 1778), 1; Fonblanque, 15.

21. Wylly, *Hussars*, 2; Marquess of Anglesey, *A History of the British Cavalry, 1816–1919* (London: Leo Cooper, 1873), 1:38, 41.

22. Anglesey, *British Cavalry*, 42.

23. Sir John Fortescue, *A History of the 17th Lancers (Duke of Cumberland's Own)* (London: Macmillan and Co., 1895), 4; Allan Mallinson, *Light Cavalry: The Making of a Regiment* (London: Leo Cooper, 1993), 10.

24. Silas Deane to George Washington and the Continental Congress, October 17, 1776, www.footnote.com/image/#396913; Benjamin Franklin to John Hancock, January 20, 1777, www.footnote.com/image/#245869; http://mottindelabalme.monsite-orange.fr/page1/index/html. All accessed July 8, 2011.

25. George Washington to John Hancock, May 9, 1777, in *Papers of Washington*, ed. Dorothy Twohig (1999), 9:371; Mottin de la Balme to George Washington, undated 1777, George Washington Papers, Library of Congress (hereafter LOC), Washington, DC.

26. Mottin de la Balme to the Continental Congress, October 3, 1777, www.footnote.com/image/#427385, accessed July 8, 2011; *Papers of Charles Lee*, New-York Historical Society, New York City, 3:287. Lee contradicts himself to some extent in his remarks on Pulaski. It is the author's opinion that Lee's mention of Pulaski's "principle of exercise" may have been a reference to Prussian doctrine and the effect Michael Kovats was having as exercise master. See also Lee Papers, 2:387.

27. General Orders, October 3, 1777, in *Papers of Washington*, eds. Philander D. Chase and Edward G. Lengel (2002), 373; Samuel Smith to George Washington, October 14, 1777 (Ibid., 511); Washington to the Marquis de Fleury, July 18, 1779, George Washington Papers, LOC.

28. Richard Peters, Report to the Board of War, April 1, 1779, www.footnote.com/image/#380915; William Galvan to the Continental Congress, December 28, 1779, www.footnote.com/image/#179704, both accessed July 8, 2011; George Washington to William Galvan, December 31, 1780, George Washington Papers, LOC.

29. Benjamin Stoddart to the Board of War, December 27, 1779, www.footnote.com/image/#382207, accessed July 8, 2011; William Galvan to George Washington, December 24, 1780, Galvan to the Continental Congress, November 30, 1780, and Washington to Galvan, December 26, 1780, George Washington Papers, LOC.

30. "Expédition Particulière," http://www.xenophongroup.com/mcjoynt /ep_web.htm, accessed November 29, 2011; Johann Ewald, *Diary of the American War*, trans. Joseph P. Tustin (New Haven, CT: Yale University Press, 1979), 199, 214–215, 217; Bernhard A. Uhlendorf, ed., *The Siege of Charleston* (Ann Arbor: University of Michigan Press, 1938), 185; Banastre Tarleton, *A History of the Campaigns of 1780 and 1781 in the Southern Provinces of North America* (North Stratford, NH: Ayer Company, 1999), 8–9.

31. John Eager Howard to John Marshall, undated c. 1804, Bayard Papers, Maryland Historical Society, Baltimore; Daniel Morgan to Nathanael Greene, December 31, 1780 and January 19, 1781 and Greene to James M. Varnum, January 24, 1781, in *The Papers of General Nathanael Greene*, eds. Richard K. Showman and Dennis M. Conrad (Chapel Hill: University of North Carolina Press, 1994), 7:30, 155, 187; Greene to Richard Henry Lee, August 22, 1785, in *Papers of Greene* (2005), 13:567; John C. Dann, *The Revolution Remembered: Eyewitness Accounts of the War for Independence* (Chicago: University of Chicago Press, 1980), 209–210; Patrick O'Kelley, *Nothing but Blood and Slaughter*, vol. 3 (Harnett County, NC: Blue House Tavern Press, 2005), 160–161,

32. Francis Casimir Kajencki, *Casimir Pulaski: Cavalry Commander of the American Revolution* (El Paso, TX: Southwest Polonia Press, 2002), 214–215; Casimir Pulaski to George Washington, November 23, 1777, in *Papers of Washington*, ed. Philander D. Chase, 12:367–368.

33. Pulaski to Washington, November 23, 1777, and December 19, 1777, *Papers of Washington*, 12:367, 637–638; Pulaski to Washington, December 29, 1777, Ibid., 13:48.

34. Pulaski to Washington, December 29, 1777, Ibid., 13:49.

35. Pulaski to Washington, December 29, 1777, Ibid., 13:48–49.

36. Pulaski to Washington, December 29, 1777, January 9, 1778, and January 20, 1778; Washington to Pulaski, December 31, 1777, and January 20, 1778, Ibid., 13:49, 89, 193, 239–240, 299.

37. Henry Lutterloh to John Laurens, January 15, 1778, http://memory. loc.gov/mss/mgw/mgw4/046/1000/1036.jpg, accessed July 8, 2011; Pulaski to Washington, February 4 and February 28, 1778, *Papers of Washington*, 13:452, 697–698.

38. Francis Skelly, "Journal," *Magazine of American History* 24, (1891), 153.

39. Aladar Poka-Pivny, "A Hungarian under Washington," *Hungarian Quarterly* 12, no. 2 (1939), 366–368; Laszlo Eszenyi, *Faithful Unto Death* (Washington, DC: Hungarian Reformed Federation of America, 1975), x, 13–21.

40. Christopher Duffy, *The Army of Frederick the Great* (Chicago: Emperor's Press, 1996), 157.

41. Mark M. Boatner, ed., *Encyclopedia of the American Revolution* (New York: David McKay Co., 1966), 81; Francis B. Heitman, *Historical Register of Officers of the Continental Army* (Baltimore, MD: Clearfield Co., 1997), 92, 105, 116, 317, 536, 574, 585.

42. Kajencki, *Pulaski*, 27–30. For a detailed study of Anthony Walton White, see chapter 5 of this volume.

43 Gruber, "British Strategy" and "Education of Clinton," *passim*.

44. Joseph Johnson, *Traditions and Reminiscences, Chiefly of the American Revolution in the South* (Charleston, SC: Walker & James, 1851), 300–305; James Simons, *A New Principle of Tactics, Practised by the Armies of the Republic of France* (Charleston, SC: Timothy M. Mason, 1791); Jerome La Brun de Bellecour, Baptiste Verdier, and Louis de Beaulieu to Benjamin Lincoln, March 24, 1780, copy courtesy of Sam Fore.

45. Nathanael Greene to Abner Nash, December 6, 1780, *Papers of Greene* (1991), 6:535; Greene to Baron Friedrich von Steuben, September 17, 1781, *Papers of Greene* (1997), 9:360 (quotation).

46. Greene to Alexander Hamilton, January 10, 1781, *Papers of Greene*, 7:89.

47. Greene to Daniel Morgan, January 8, 1781, Ibid., 7:73.

48. Henry Lee, *The Revolutionary War Memoirs of General Henry Lee*, ed. Robert E. Lee (New York: Da Capo Press, 1998), 588; John Eager Howard to unknown, c. 1822, copy courtesy of Sam Fore.

49. Warnery, *Remarks on Cavalry* (1997), xxvi, xxxiv–xxxv; Warnery, *Remarks on Cavalry* 1798 edition (London: J. Barfield), viii, and *passim*.

50. Howard to Marshall, 1804; Richard Call to Thomas Jefferson, March 29, 1781, both in Julian P. Boyd, ed., *The Papers of Thomas Jefferson* (Princeton, NJ: Princeton University Press, 1952, 5:274–275 (quotation).

51. Warnery, *Remarks on Cavalry* (1997), 133, 165.

52. McGee, "'Most Astonishing Efforts,'" 15–33 ; Warnery, *Remarks on Cavalry* (1997), 79.

53. Duffy, *Frederick the Great*, 148, 150.

54. Lawrence E. Babits, *A Devil of a Whipping: The Battle of Cowpens* (Chapel Hill, University of North Carolina Press, 1998); Daniel Murphy, "The Cavalry at Cowpens: Thinking Inside the Box," *Southern Campaigns of the American Revolution* 3, no. 2 (2006), 23–27; James Simons to William Washington, November 3, 1803, copy courtesy of Lawrence E. Babits.

55. McGee, "The Object Was Worthy of the Cast," 13–19.

56. Charles Cotesworth Pinckney to Alexander Hamilton, December 12, 1799, in *The Papers of Alexander Hamilton*, ed. Harold C. Syrett (New York: Columbia University Press, 1969), 15:96–98.

CHAPTER THREE: CAVALRY ACTION AT POUNDRIDGE, NEW YORK

1. George Hanger, *The Life, Adventures, and Opinions of Col. George Hanger, Written by Himself*, ed. William Combe, 2 vols. (London: J. Debrett, 1801), 2:432.

2. Joseph C. M. Goldsmith, "Letter to the Editor," *Southern Campaigns of the American Revolution* 4, no. 2 (April–June, 2007), www.southerncampaign.org (Accessed 9/16/2007). By this strident position taken by a son of the Palmetto State, the author is reminded of James Louis Pettigu's famous description of his home state during the Secession Crisis of 1860: "South Carolina is too small for a republic and too large for an insane asylum."

3. Lewis Pinckney Jones, quoted in Nat and Sam Hilborn, *Battleground of Freedom: South Carolina in the Revolution* (Columbia, SC: Sandlapper Press, Inc., 1970), xv–xvi.

4. James A. Roberts, comp., *New York in the Revolution as Colony and State* (Albany, NY: Brandow Printing Company, 1898), 8, 10.

5. Washington Irving, *Wolfert's Roost and Other Papers, Now First Collected* (New York: G. P. Putnam & Co., 1855), 17.

6. Ibid.

7. David Humphreys, *Life of the Honorable Major-General Israel Putnam* (New York: M'Carty and White, 1810), 175–176.

8. Charles M. Lefferts, *Uniforms of the American, British, French, and German Armies in the War of the American Revolution* (New York: The New-York Historical Society, 1926), 216; Bernhard A. Uhlendorf, ed., *Revolution in America: Confidential Letters and Journals 1776–1784 of*

*Adjutant General Major Baurmeister of the Hessian Forces* (New Brunswick, NJ: Rutgers University Press, 1957), 263–264.

9. William S. Hadaway, ed., *The McDonald Papers, Including Biographical Notes of the Author*, 2 vols. (White Plains, NY: Westchester County Historical Society, 1926, 1927), 2:5.

10. Pension Application of William Patchin, in John C. Dann, ed., *The Revolution Remembered: Eyewitness Accounts of the War for Independence* (Chicago: University of Chicago Press, 1980), 72–73.

11. George Washington to Benjamin Tallmadge, June 27, 1779, in Jared Sparks, ed., *The Writings of George Washington*, 8 vols. (Boston: Russell, Odiorne and Metcalf and Hilliard, Gray and Co., 1834–1835) 6:279; Quoted in Sotheby's, *Four Battleflags of the Revolution, Captured by Lt.-Col. Banastre Tarleton in 1779 and 1780, The Property of Capt. Christopher Tarleton Fagan* (Hong Kong: Sotheby's, Inc., 2006), 19.

12. William Abbatt, ed., *Memoirs of Major-General William Heath by Himself* (New York: William Abbatt, 1901), 191; James B. Lockwood, "The Skirmish at Poundridge, Westchester, 1779," *Magazine of American History* 3, no. 12 (December, 1879), 687 (note).

13. J. Thomas Scharf, ed., *History of Westchester County, New York*, 2 vols. (Philadelphia: L. E. Preston & Co., 1886) 2:565.

14. Washington to Tallmadge, June 27, 1779, in Sparks, *Writings of Washington*, 6:279.

15. Alexander Rose, *Washington's Spies: The Story of America's First Spy Ring* (New York: Bantam Books, 2006), 112–113; Henry B. Dawson, *Battles of the United States, by Land and Sea*, 2 vols. (New York: Johnson, Fry & Company, 1858), 1:506; Hadaway, *McDonald Papers*, 2:36–37. Robert D. Bass, *The Green Dragoon: The Lives of Banastre Tarleton and Mary Robinson* (New York: Henry Holt and Company, 1957), 55.

16. Bass, *Green Dragoon*, 55; Dawson, *Battles of the United States*, 1:506; Gary Corrado, *The Black Hussars: A Brief and Concise History of Frederick Diemar's Hussars* (Westminster, MD: Heritage Books, 2005), 9.

17. Dawson, *Battles of the United States*, 1:504. Hadaway, *McDonald Papers*, 2:36; Banastre Tarleton to Sir Henry Clinton, July 2, 1779, *Henry Clinton Papers: 1736–1850*, 304 vols. (Ann Arbor: University of Michigan) volume 65 (quotation).

18. Charles Swain Hall, *Benjamin Tallmadge: Revolutionary Soldier and American Businessman* (New York: Columbia University Press, 1943), 39; Dawson, *Battles of the United States*, 1:504. Kinnicutt reportedly was the model for James Fenimore Cooper's *The Spy*. Hadaway, *McDonald Papers*, 2:38; Tarleton to Clinton, July 2, 1779, *Clinton Papers*, volume 65.

19. Scharf, *History of Westchester County*, 2:565. Hadaway, *McDonald Papers*, 2:38.

20. Dawson, *Battles of the United States*, 1:506; Tarleton to Clinton, July 2, 1779, *Clinton Papers*, volume 65.

21. Scharf, *History of Westchester County*, 2:565; Hadaway, *McDonald Papers*, 2:38–39; F. W. Beers, A. D. Ellis, G. G. Soule, map: "Town of Poundridge, Westchester County, N.Y." (1867).

22. Scharf, *History of Westchester County*, 2:565; Beers, Ellis, Soule, map. Hadaway, *McDonald Papers*, 2:39.

23. Scharf, *History of Westchester County*, 2:565; Dawson, *Battles of the United States*, 1:506.

24. Hadaway, *McDonald Papers*, 2:39–40; Dawson, *Battles of the United States*, 1:506.

25. Dawson, *Battles of the United States*, 1:505; Hadaway, *McDonald Papers*, 2:40; Tarleton to Clinton, July 2, 1779, *Clinton Papers*, volume 65, (quotation).

26. Scharf, *History of Westchester County*, 2:565.

27. Robert W. Chambers, *The Hidden Children* (New York: D. Appleton and Company, 1914), 86.

28. Hadaway, *McDonald Papers*, 2:40.

29. Scharf, *History of Westchester County*, 2:566; Hadaway, *McDonald Papers*, 2:41.

30. Scharf, *History of Westchester County*, 2:566; Hadaway, *McDonald Papers*, 2:40–41.

31. John T. Hayes, *Prelude to Glory: Tarleton and Simcoe, 1779* (Fort Lauderdale, FL: Saddlebag Press, 1996), 35–36.

32. Tarleton to Clinton, July 2, 1779, *Clinton Papers*, volume 65; Scharf, *History of Westchester County*, 2:566.

33. Hall, *Benjamin Tallmadge*, 39.

34. Scharf, *History of Westchester County*, 2:566; Hayes, *Prelude to Glory*, 34–35. Lockwood, "Skirmish at Poundridge," 687.

35. Hadaway, *McDonald Papers*, 2:42; Susan Cochran Swanson, *Between the Lines: Stories of Westchester County, New York, During the American Revolution* (Pelham, NY: Junior League of Pelham, 1975), 41.

36. Scharf, *History of Westchester County*, 2:566.

37. Dawson, *Battles of the United States*, 1:505–506; Tarleton to Clinton, July 2, 1779, *Clinton Papers*, volume 65, (quotation); Hadaway, *McDonald Papers*, 2:41.

38. Scharf, *History of Westchester County*, 2:565; Hadaway, *McDonald Papers*, 2:42.

39. Hall, *Benjamin Tallmadge*, 39.

40. Hadaway, *McDonald Papers*, 2:43.

41. Dawson, *Battles of the United States*, 1:506; Hadaway, *McDonald Papers*, 2:43–44.

42. Abbatt, *Memoirs of William Heath*, 191.

43. Benjamin Tallmadge, *Memoir of Col. Benjamin Tallmadge, Prepared by Himself, at the Request of his Children* (New York: Thomas Holman, 1858), 32; Jeptha R. Simms, *History—Schoharie County—Border Wars of New York* (Albany, NY: Munsell & Tanner, 1845), 539.

44. George Washington to Benjamin Tallmadge, July 5, 1779, in Sparks, *Writings of Washington*, 6:284–285.

45. Bass, *Green Dragoon*, 55–56; Abbatt, *Memoirs of William Heath*, 191; Tarleton to Clinton, July 2, 1779, *Clinton Papers*, volume 65; Dorothy Humphreys Hinitt and Frances Riker Duncombe, *The Burning of Bedford, July 1779: As Reported in Contemporary Documents and Eyewitness Accounts* (Bedford, NY: Bedford Historical Society, 1974), 25–26.

46. Peter Blum, *Military Miniatures* (New York: Odyssey Press, 1964); 23. George Washington to Samuel Huntington, July 9, 1779, in Sparks, *Writings of Washington*, 6:286.

47. Gregory J. W. Urwin, *The United States Cavalry: An Illustrated History* (New York: Blandford Press, 1983), 21.

48. Robert W. Chambers, *The Painted Minx* (New York: D. Appleton & Company, 1930), 260; Swanson, *Between the Lines*, 41, 44.

49. Hall, *Benjamin Tallmadge*, 39, 63–64.

50. Bass, *Green Dragoon*, 56.

51. Sotheby's, *Four Battleflags*, 6. Glenn Collins, "Remnants of the Revolution, $17 Million," *The New York Times*, June 15, 2006, A20.

CHAPTER FOUR: CAVALRY BATTLES IN NEW YORK AND NEW JERSEY

1. *British Orderly Books, Miscellaneous Units, 16th and 17th Light Dragoons*, www.revwar75.com/crown.misc.htm, accessed July 11, 2011; Donald J. Gara, *Biographical Sketches of the Cavalry Officers of the British Legion, 1778-1782*, accessed July 11, 2011, www.home.golden.net/~marg/bansite/odds/bl_cavalry.html; Gara, *Biographical Sketches of the Cavalry Officers of the Queen's American Rangers, 1778–1782*, accessed July 11, 2011, www.home.golden.net/!marg/bansite/odds/qr_cavalry.html.

2. Robert K. Wright Jr., *The Continental Army* (Washington, DC: US Army Center of Military History, 2000), 345–349.

3. "Kingsbridge, Bronx," accessed July 11, 2011, http://en.wikipedia.org/wiki/Kingsbridge_Bronx; "Boston Post Road," accessed July 11, 2011, http://en.wikipedia.org/wiki/Boston_Post_Road.

4. Stephen Jenkins, *The Story of the Bronx* (New York: G.P. Putnam and Sons, 1912), 127, 133–134, 156–159.

5. Ibid., see map opposite page 126; "New York State Military Forts," accessed July 11, 2011, www.dmna.state.ny.us/forts.

6. John Graves Simcoe, *Simcoe's Military Journal: Journal of the Operations of the Queen's Rangers* (New York: Arno Press, reprint edition, 1968, originally published 1844), 105; Stephen Jarvis, "An American's Experience in the British Army," ed. Charles M. Jarvis, *Connecticut Magazine* 11 (1907), 204; Maj. Gen. Robert Howe to George Washington, August 8, 1779, *Records Pertaining to Military Affairs, including Transcripts of Letters from Military Officers, 1775–1783* (National Archives, Washington, DC)

Record Group 360.2.4; Johann Ewald, *Diary of the American War* (New Haven, CT: Yale University Press, 1979), 173.

7. Howe to Washington, August 8, 1779, *Records*, 360.2.4

8. Simcoe, 105; Jarvis, 204; Howe to Washington, August 8, 1779, *Records*, 360.2.4.

9. Simcoe, *Military Journal*, 105; Jarvis, "An American's Experience," 204; "Return of [Queen's Rangers] Killed, Wounded and Taken Prisoner, November 1777 to October 15, 1780," *Henry Clinton Papers: 1736–1850*, 304 vols. (Ann Arbor: University of Michigan), volume 126; Ewald, on page 173 of his diary, states that "30 horsemen (of the advance guard) were all shot dead or cut down." Simcoe only records one man dead and three wounded. Since Ewald did not personally observe the skirmish, I consider his statement in error, especially when he reports such a large number of casualties. Ewald also records that von Wurmb's Jaeger Corps came upon the scene after this setback and immediately attacked and dislodged the American infantry. Simcoe and Jarvis make no mention of von Wurmb's presence at this action, and again I believe that Ewald is recording inaccurate information told to him by a third party.

10. Simcoe, *Military Journal*, 106.

11. Ibid.

12. Ibid.

13. Jarvis, "An American's Experience," 204.

14. Simcoe, *Military Journal*, 107; Ewald, *Diary*, 174.

15. Simcoe, *Military Journal*, 107, 110.

16. Jenkins, 167-168; "New York State Military Forts."

17. Jenkins, *Story of the Bronx*, 168–169; Mark M. Boatner III, *Encyclopedia of the American Revolution* (New York: David McKay Co., 1966), 291.

18. Robert D. Bass, *The Green Dragoon: The Lives of Banastre Tarleton and Mary Robinson* (Columbia, SC: Sandlapper Press, 1957, reprint edition 1973), 55–56. For a detailed account of the Poundridge Raid, see chapter 3.

19. Simcoe, *Military Journal*, 109.

20. Ibid.; Simcoe to Sir Henry Clinton, undated letter, 1779, *Henry Clinton Papers*, volume 82.

21. Simcoe, *Military Journal*, 111.

22. Ibid., 110; Frank Moore, editor, *Diary of the American Revolution from Newspapers and Original Documents* (New York: Charles Scribner, 2 vols., 1858–1859), 2:233–234.

23. Simcoe, *Military Journal*, 110–111.

24. Ibid., 111–112.

25. Ibid., 113.

26. Ibid., 112.

27. Ibid., 112–113; Henry Lee, *The Revolutionary War Memoirs of General Henry Lee*, ed. Robert E. Lee, reprint edition (New York: Da Capo Press, 1998), 301–302.

28. Simcoe, *Military Journal*, 112–113.

29. Ibid., 113.

30. Ibid., 114; Moore, *Diary of the American Revolution*, 2:235.

31. Simcoe, *Military Journal*, 114–115; Moore, *Diary of the American Revolution*, 2:235.

32. Simcoe, *Military Journal*, 115–116; Bernard A. Uhlendorf, ed., *Confidential Letters and Journals, 1776–1784, of Adjutant General Major Baurmeister of the Hessian Forces* (New Brunswick, NJ: Rutgers University Press, 1957), 316.

33. Simcoe, *Military Journal*, 116; Jarvis, "An American's Experience," 205; Robert V. Hoffman, *Revolutionary Scenes in New Jersey* (New York: American Historical Society, 1942), 147.

34. Simcoe, *Military Journal*, 116–118; Hoffman, *Revolutionary Scenes*, 147; "Middlebush, New Jersey," accessed July 11, 2011, http://en.wikipedia.org/wiki/Middlebush,_New_Jersey.

35. Simcoe, *Military Journal*, 116–117; Jarvis, "An American's Experience," 205; "Return of [Queen's Rangers]," *Clinton Papers*, volume 126.

36. Simcoe, *Military Journal*, 117–118.

37. Simcoe, *Military Journal*, 118; Jarvis, "An American's Experience," 205.

38. Simcoe, *Military Journal*, 118; Jarvis, "An American's Experience," 205; Moore, *Diary of the American Revolution*, 2:235.

39. Simcoe, *Military Journal*, 118; Jarvis, "An American's Experience," 206; "Return of [Queen's Rangers]," *Clinton Papers*, volume 126.

40. Simcoe, *Military Journal*, 118–119; Moore, 2:236; Uhlendorf, *Confidential Letters*, 316–317.

41. Simcoe, *Military Journal*, 265, 268; Jarvis, "An American's Experience," 206; "Return of [Queen's Rangers]," *Clinton Papers*, volume 126.

42. Simcoe, *Military Journal*, 264–265, 316; Hoffman, *Revolutionary Scenes*, 148; Andrew D. Mellick, Jr., *Story of an Old Farm or Life in New Jersey in the Eighteenth Century* (Somerville, NJ: The Unionist Gazette, 1889), 508.

43. Simcoe, *Military Journal*, 266–268.

44. Ibid., 268–272.

45. Ibid., 279–280; John McGill, *Journal, Simcoe Family Fonds*, 63 vols. (Archives of Ontario, Toronto, Canada), Correspondence, 1779–1781, 47-3-1.

46. Simcoe, *Military Journal*, 119–120, 285–286.

47. Boatner, *Encyclopedia*, 1010; Hoffman, *Revolutionary Scenes*, 149; Mellick, *Story of an Old Farm*, 509.

48. Carl P. Borick, *A Gallant Defense: The Siege of Charleston–1780* (Columbia: University of South Carolina Press, 2003), 23; Henry Clinton, *The American Rebellion: Sir Henry Clinton's Narrative of His Campaigns, 1775–1782, With An Appendix of Original Documents*, ed. William B. Willcox (New Haven, CT: Yale University Press, 1954), 167; Simcoe, *Military Journal*, 231.

49. Simcoe, *Military Journal*, 140; Jared C. Lobdell, ed., "Action at Hopperstown, April 15, 1780," *Proceedings of the New Jersey Historical Society* 80 (1962), 261–262: "New Jersey in the Revolution, Newspaper Extracts," *Royal Gazette*, no. 371 (April 19, 1780), in *Documents Relating to the Colonial, Revolutionary and Post-Revolutionary History of the State of New Jersey*, 47 vols. (Paterson, NJ: Archives of the State of New Jersey, 1880–1949), second series, 4:306.

50. Simcoe, *Military Journal*, 140; Lobdell, "Action at Hopperstown," 80:263.

51. Moore, *Diary of the American Revolution*, 2:265; Lobdell, "Action at Hopperstown," 80:264–266.

52. Simcoe, *Military Journal*, 140; Lobdell, "Action at Hopperstown," 80:264–266; *Royal Gazette*, "New Jersey in the Revolution," 4:306-307; Jared C. Lobdell, "Hopperstown, April 16, 1780," *New Jersey History* 88, vol. 1 (Spring 1970), 47–48, including a sketch from the Clinton Papers drawn by Cornet George Spencer. The report on the action at Hoppertown included in Simcoe's *Military Journal* was prepared by Captain Wickham who lifted his account, almost verbatim, from a separate account written by Spencer. Spencer's account was located by Lobdell in the Clinton Papers. This account was reprinted in Lobdell's "Action at Hoppertown"; "In-Depth History of Ho-Ho-Kus," Borough of Ho-Ho-Kus, New Jersey, accessed July 11, 2011, www.ho-ho-kus.com. This site indicates that the correct spelling of the town's name in the colonial era was Hoppertown, not Hopperstown, and that the name of the road over which Spencer and his men traveled was then called the Hoppertown Road and is now called Sheridan Avenue.

53. Simcoe, *Military Journal*, 140.

54. Ibid., 141; Moore, *Diary of the American Revolution*, 2:266.

55. Simcoe, *Military Journal*, 141, Lobdell, "Action at Hopperstown," 80:264, Lobdell, *New Jersey History*, 48.

56. Simcoe, *Military Journal*, 142.

57. Ibid.; "Return of [Queen's Rangers]," *Clinton Papers*, volume 126; Lobdell, "Action at Hopperstown," 80:265–266.

58. Simcoe, *Military Journal*, 142; Moore, *Diary of the American Revolution*, 2:266; *Royal Gazette*, "New Jersey in the Revolution," 4:307; *Royal American Gazette*, April 20, 1780, Newspaper Collections, New-York Historical Society, New York City.

59. *Royal Gazette*, "New Jersey in the Revolution," 4:307–308.

60. Simcoe, *Military Journal*, 142; Lobdell, "Action at Hopperstown," 80:266; Moore, *Diary of the American Revolution*, 2:266.
61. Simcoe, *Military Journal*, 142, 150, 162; Peter J. Guthorn, *British Maps of the American Revolution* (Monmouth Beach, NJ: Phillip Freneau Press, 1972), 43–44.

CHAPTER FIVE: ANTHONY WALTON WHITE, A REVOLUTIONARY DRAGOON

1. Anna M. W. Woodhull, "Memoir of Brig. Gen. Anthony Walton White of the Continental Army," *Proceedings of the New Jersey Historical Society* 7, second series (1882), 107–115; William Nelson, "Anthony White, I, II, and III," *The Magazine of History with Notes and Queries* 4 (July–December 1906), 73, 74.
2. Nelson, "Anthony White," 74–77.
3. Biographical sketches of Lewis Morris III can be found in John Sanderson, *Biography of the Signers of the Declaration of Independence*, 2 vols. (Philadelphia: W. Brown and C. Peters, 1828), 2:159–180, and Martha Morris Lawrence, *The Boundary Line and Other Bits of Biography and History* (Deckertown, NJ: Sussex Independent, 1895), 33–37. There have been two recent biographies of Gouverneur Morris. One is Richard Brookhiser's elegantly written work, *Gentleman Revolutionary: Gouverneur Morris, the Rake Who Wrote the Constitution* (New York: Free Press, 2003). Another excellent biography is James J. Kirschke's *Gouverneur Morris: Author, Statesman, and Man of the World* (New York: Thomas Dunne Books, 2005).
4. George Clinton to George Washington, July 27, 1775, *Public Papers of George Clinton, First Governor of New York*, 10 vols. (New York: State of New York, 1899–1914), 1:208–209; George Washington to George Clinton, August 25, 1775, in John C. Fitzpatrick, editor, *The Writings of George Washington from the Original Manuscript Sources, 1745–1799*, 39 vols. (Washington, DC: US Government Printing Office, 1931–1944), 3:447; George Washington to Anthony White, August 25, 1775, in Fitzpatrick, *Writings*, 37:514.
5. George Washington to Anthony White, October 28, 1775, in Fitzpatrick, *Writings*, 4:50.
6. George Washington to Joseph Reed, November 28, 1775, and January 23, 1776, in Fitzpatrick, *Writings*, 4:126, 269.
7. Arthur S. Lefkowitz, *George Washington's Indispensable Men: The 32 Aides-De-Camp Who Helped Win American Independence* (Mechanicsburg, PA: Stackpole Books, 2003), 13–14.
8. Philip Schuyler to George Washington, August 18, 1776, in Philander D. Chase and Edward G. Lengel, eds., *The Papers of George Washington: Revolutionary War Series*, 16 vols. (Charlottesville: University Press of

Virginia, 1985–2010), 6:68; George Washington to Philip Schuyler, August 24, 1776, George Washington Papers, 1741–1799, Letterbook 2, 31–34, Library of Congress, Washington, DC (hereafter LOC); Anthony Walton White to Philip Schuyler, September 16, 1776, in Lefkowitz, *Indispensable Men*, 317 n. 40; Ebenezer Elmer, "Journal Kept During an Expedition to Canada in 1776 by Ebenezer Elmer, Lieutenant in the 3rd Regiment of the New Jersey Troops in the Continental Service, Commanded by Colonel Elias Dayton," *Proceedings of the New Jersey Historical Society* 3 (Edison: New Jersey Historical Society, 1848–1849), 30, 32, 41; Ebenezer Elmer, "The Lost Pages of Elmer's Revolutionary Journal," A. Van Doren Honeyman, ed., *Proceedings of the New Jersey Historical Society* 10 (October 1925), 412.

9. Lefkowitz, *Indispensable Men*, 220–221.

10. George Washington to Anthony Walton White, March 20, 1777, Letterbook 1, 34–35, Washington Papers, LOC.

11. Anthony Walton White to George Washington, in Chase and Lengel, eds., *Papers of Washington*, 11:278.

12. Ibid.

13. George Washington to Alexander Hamilton, September 21, 1777, and Hamilton to Anthony Walton White, September 23, 1777, in Chase and Lengel, eds., *Papers of Washington*, 11:282–283.

14. George Washington to Count Pulaski and Cols. Theodorick Bland, Elisha Sheldon, George Baylor, and Stephen Moylan, October 25, 1777, Letterbook 4, 234–235, Washington Papers, LOC.

15. George Washington to Philemon Dickinson, June 20 and June 24, 1778, Series 4, 254, 256, 405–408, Washington to Charles Scott, June 24, 1778, Series 4, 438–439, Washington Papers, LOC; White's receipt to Bowen is dated July 1, 1778. It is not clear when Bowen complained, but there was a delay at headquarters in contacting White. Hamilton did not send his letter to White until March 1779. Hamilton to White, March 4, 1779, Series 3b, 156, Washington Papers, LOC.

16. Burt Garfield Loescher, *Washington's Eyes: The Continental Light Dragoons* (Fort Collins, CO: Old Army Press, 1977), 111, 124, 133.

17. Ibid., 113.

18. *Virginia Gazette* (Dixon), August 8, 1779 (extract of a letter dated August 7, 1779 from an undisclosed American officer); John Graves Simcoe, *Simcoe's Military Journal, A History of the Operations of a Partisan Corps, called the Queens Rangers* (New York: Bartlett & Welford, 1844), 105. A fuller description of the action at New Rochelle, also called Poundridge, appears in chapter 4 of this volume.

19. Stephen Jarvis, "Revealing the Life of the Loyalists Who Refused to Renounce Their Allegiance to the King and Fought to Save the Western Continent to the British Empire," *Journal of American History* 1, no. 3, (1907), 441–464, information cited is on 453; *Virginia Gazette* (Dixon),

August 8, 1779; Simcoe, *Military Journal*, 105–106; George Washington to William Heath, August 9, 1779, Series 4, 917, Washington Papers, LOC (quotation).

20. *Pennsylvania Gazette*, September 22, 1779.

21. George Washington to Anthony Walton White, January 28, 1780 and Washington to Stephen Moylan, February 3, 1780, Series 4, 26, 172–173, Washington Papers, LOC; "February 28, 1780," *Journals of the Continental Congress, 1774–1789* 16 (Washington, DC: US Government Printing Office, 1910), 210.

22. General Orders, August 25, 1777, and March 26, 1780, Series 3g, 217–218, 369–372, Washington Papers, LOC.

23. Charles Stedman, *The History of the Origin, Progress, and Termination of the American War*, 2 vols. (London: J. Murray, 1794), 2:181; John W. Fortescue, *A History of the 17th Lancers* (London: Macmillan, 1895), 51.

24. Banastre Tarleton, *A History of the Campaigns of 1780 and 1781 in the Southern Provinces of North America* (London: T. Cadell, 1787), 16–17.

25. Tarleton, *Campaigns*, 16; Stedman, *History*, 2:183; Baylor Hill, *A Gentleman of Fortune: The Diary of Baylor Hill, First Continental Light Dragoons, 1777–1781*, John T. Hayes, ed., 3 vols. (Fort Lauderdale, FL: Saddlebag Press, 2002), 3:63–64.

26. Tarleton, *Campaigns*, 16–17; "A Journal of the Operations before Charlestown, to the Day of its Surrender to the British Forces," author unknown, in Franklin Benjamin Hough, *The Siege of Charleston by the British Fleet and Army Under the Command of Admiral Arbuthnot and Sir Henry Clinton, Which Terminated with the Surrender of That Place on the 12th of May, 1780* (Albany, NY: J. Munsell, 1867), 132.

27. Hill, *Gentleman of Fortune*, 3:76.

28. Lenud's Ferry (pronounced Lenew's or Lenoe's) was named after its operator, who was apparently of Huguenot descent. Tarleton wrote the name as Lenew. Tarleton, *Campaigns*, 19. Captain Baylor Hill, whose diary shows that he spelled most words the way they sounded, spelled it as "Lenoes ferry." Hill, *Gentleman of Fortune*, 3:78–80. Lenud's Ferry was situated on the Santee River approximately forty miles north of Charleston, about one mile from the present-day village of Jamestown and where South Carolina State Highway 17 crosses the Santee. A ferry appears to have operated at this site from the colonial era into the late antebellum period. In 1840, Congress considered running a post route from Lenud's Ferry to the "Thirty-two Mile House," between Georgetown and Charleston. "May 18, 1840," *Journal of the House of Representatives of the United States, 1839–1840* 34 (New York: Francis Childs and John Swain, n.d.), 950; John Rutledge to unnamed, April 25, 1780, in Walter Clark, ed., *State Records of North Carolina*, 16 vols. (Raleigh, NC: P. M. Hale, 1896), 14:805.

29. Henry Lee, *The Revolutionary Memoirs of General Henry Lee*, Robert E. Lee, ed. (New York: Da Capo Press, 1998), 156; John Lewis Gervais to

Henry Laurens, May 13, 1780, in David R. Chesnutt, ed., *The Papers of Henry Laurens: December 11, 1778–August 31, 1782*, 16 vols. (Columbia: University of South Carolina Press, 1968–2003), 15:291–292.

30. Hill, *Gentleman of Fortune*, 3:78–79; John Lewis Gervais to Henry Laurens, May 13, 1780, in Chesnutt, *Papers of Henry Laurens*, 15:291–292.

31. Hill, *Gentleman of Fortune*, 3:79–80; Anthony Allaire, "Diary of Lieutenant Anthony Allaire," in Lyman C. Draper, *King's Mountain and Its Heroes: The Battle of King's Mountain, October 7th, 1780, and the Events Which Led To It* (Cincinnati, OH: P. G. Thomson, 1881), 494.

32. Hill, *Gentleman of Fortune*, 3:79–80. In the fall of 1780, Tory marauders in Westchester County, New York, used this method of "half hanging" as a way to compel local farmers to disclose where they had hidden their money. James Thacher, an American army surgeon, recorded the description given him by one of these victims of what it felt like to be hanged but not killed: "the last sensation, which he recollects, when suspended by his neck, was a flashing heat over him, like that which would be occasioned by boiling water poured over his body; he was, however, cut down, and how long he remained on the ground insensible, he knows not." James Thacher, *Eyewitness to the American Revolution, The Battles and Generals as Seen by an Army Surgeon* (Stamford, CT: Longmeadow Press, 1994), 238. Half hanging seems to have been a common way for the Whigs in the South to deal with loyalists. One veteran who served in a North Carolina militia unit operating in the Yadkin Valley remembers how he "assisted in half hanging William Combs whom they let off on promise of better behavior," Pension Application of Elihu Ayers, R335, National Archives (hereafter NA). Another Wilkes County militiaman who served under Col. Benjamin Cleveland recalled capturing a Tory "from whom they endeavoured to procure information as to other persons who were suspected, but who positively refused to give any, until Colonel Cleveland adopted the expedient of hanging him for a while to the limb of a tree or a bent down sampling, but which did not produce the desired effect until the dose was repeated a second time with more severity than the first." Pension Application of William Lenoir, S7137, NA.

33. John Lewis Gervais to Henry Laurens, May 13, 1780, Chesnutt, *Papers of Henry Laurens*, 15:291; John Peebles, *John Peebles' American War: Diary of a Scottish Grenadier, 1776–1782*, ed. Ira D. Gruber (Mechanicsburg, PA: Stackpole Books, 1998), 370; Tarleton, *Campaigns*, 19; Allaire, "Diary," in Draper, *King's Mountain*, 494; Abraham Buford to George Washington, May 6, 1780, Series 4, 198–199, Washington Papers, LOC.

34. Hill, *Gentleman of Fortune*, 3:80.

35. The Santee is considerably narrower today than it was in 1780 due to hydroelectric projects started in the area in 1938. These projects control

the flooding that routinely occurred when the Santee was in its natural state. Although the river was wider in 1780, the speed of the current today is probably about the same as it was then. Today, the current speed averages two feet per second (and possibly as fast as three feet per second), with the channel velocity higher at three to four feet per second. Information on the Santee River was obtained by the author from John C. Delude in a telephone interview with him on June 9, 2006. At the time of the interview, Mr. Delude was the manager of FERC relicensing for the SanteeCooper Project, a water and electric utility.

36. Pension Application of Lawrence Everheart, S25068, NA; Buford to George Washington, May 6, 1780, Series 4, 198–199, Washington Papers, LOC; John Lewis Gervais to Henry Laurens, May 13, 1780, *Papers of Henry Laurens*, 15:291–292.

37. Hill, *Gentleman of Fortune*, 3:81; Tarleton, *Campaigns*, 19. Tarleton did not identify the loyalist who told him of the capture of his men by White's dragoons. John Lewis Gervais, in a letter written one week later, identified Elias Ball as Tarleton's informant and guide. John Lewis Gervais to Henry Laurens, May 13, 1780, *Papers of Henry Laurens*, 15:292–293. At the time of the Revolution, Elias Ball (II) lived at Wambaw Plantation and his son, Elias Ball (III) lived at Comingtee Plantation at the confluence of the east and west branches of the upper Cooper River near Strawberry Ferry at Childsbury. Both Elias Balls accepted commissions as South Carolina Loyalist militia colonels. Robert Stansbury Lambert, *South Carolina Loyalists in the American Revolution* (Columbia: University of South Carolina Press, 1987), 113. The Ball family owned many plantations and slaves in the South Carolina lowcountry, and their story is told by a descendant. See Edward Ball, *Slaves in the Family* (New York: Ballantine Publishing Group, 1998). One of White's dragoons remembered the genesis of White's sortie across the Santee somewhat differently, including Elias Ball's role that day, identifying Ball as "Harris": "At Lanew's Ferry we found Col. Bluford and Lieutenant Col. Hawes. Bluford ordered Col. White's command to cross the river in search of the enemy, he Bluford promising to send to our aid over the river 500 men and some artillery if needed. When we crossed the river we could hear no intelligence of the enemy until Col. White and Major Jimmeson with servants in disguise went among the tories, where they soon received information of the British. They were thereby enabled to surprise a foraging party of the British at the house of one Harris, which was commanded by a British colonel named Ash or Nash. The Col. with sixteen privates, a Sergeant & Harris were taken. The Sergeant and Harris made their escape and informed Col. Tarleton of British Army. The sequel may well be guessed at." Pension Application of John Gore, W160, reprinted in John Frederick Dorman, *Virginia Revolutionary Pension Applications*, 51 vols. (Washington, DC: J. F. Dorman, 1957–1994), 44:62.

38. Tarleton, *Campaigns*, 19–20; Hill, *Gentleman of Fortune*, 3:81 (quotation).

39. Buford to George Washington, May 6, 1780, Series 4, 198–199, Washington Papers, LOC (quotation); Pension Application of Albion Gordon, W7548, in Dorman, *Pension Applications*, 45:77 (Quartermaster Sergeant Gordon was blinded at Lenud's Ferry); Pension Application of Francis Gray, W7557, Ibid., 46:49–52 (Private Gray had a wound "inflicted with a broad sword which took off the greater part of his left ear and entered his skull. He was paroled and left on the ground, after which he remained with the regiment until they got to Halifax, N.C." A later medical examination showed "a large portion of the skull bone deeply indented and consequently very much disfigured.").

40. Allaire, "Diary," in Draper, *King's Mountain*, 494; Tarleton, *Campaigns*, 20. Years later, one American recalled the attack this way: "We retreated to the ferry with all the haste we could. When we got to the ferry we could not obtain a boat for some hours. When the boat came the prisoners and a Sergeant was put in it to cross the river and as they were putting off from the Shore the British came up, shot the Sergeant in the head, retook the prisoners. A battle ensued in which we were sorely defeated. After loosing all our horses, with thirteen men killed and wounded." Pension Application of John Gore, W160, in Dorman, *Pension Applications*, 44:62–63.

41. Tarleton, *Campaigns*, 20. British general Sir Henry Clinton described the action this way: "They [the Americans] were most spiritedly charged, and defeated. Most of the riders fled to the morasses, or threw themselves into the river, from whence few have extricated themselves." Clinton to Lord George Germain, May 13, 1780, in Tarleton, *Campaigns*, 42; Mellen Chamberlain, *Memorial of Captain Charles Cochrane, A British Officer in the Revolutionary War, 1774–1781* (Cambridge: John Willson and Son, University Press, 1891), 7; David Ramsay, *History of the Revolution of South Carolina, From a British Province to an Independent State*, 2 vols. (Trenton, NJ: Isaac Collins, 1785), 2:65–66; Hill, *Gentleman of Fortune*, 3:81–82.

42. Tarleton, *Campaigns*, 20. Tarleton's number of casualties and prisoners, a total of 108 killed, wounded, and captured Americans, far exceeds those reported in contemporaneous accounts. One American and two British accounts each tallied the number of American prisoners at about thirty, which is less than half the number claimed by Tarleton. For a contemporaneous American account, see Hill, *Gentleman of Fortune*, 3:81–82 (all the captured Americans were privates, except for Captain Baylor Hill and Brigade Major Cosmo de Medici). For two contemporaneous loyalist accounts, see Allaire, "Diary," in Draper, *King's Mountain*, 494, and the Diary of Uzal Johnson, May 6, 1780, in Bobby Gilmer Moss, *Uzal Johnson, Loyalist Surgeon: A Revolutionary War Diary* (Blacksburg, SC:

Scotia-Hibernia Press, 2000), 30. Allaire and Johnson served together in the same unit and both reported that the Legion "took a Major and thirty privates." Sir Henry Clinton's numbers are also less than Tarleton's: "Fifty or sixty men were killed or taken, and every horse of the corps, with the arms and appointments, fell into our hands." Clinton to Lord George Germain, May 13, 1780, in Tarleton, *Campaigns*, 42. Clinton also reported that "Tarleton's loss was only one man killed, one lost in the swamp & two horses wounded." Clinton to Germain, May 7, 1780, Papers of Charles, Earl Cornwallis,    (Public Record Office, London, UK), Section 30/11/72, 6–7. A captain in the British Army recorded that there were twenty killed and wounded, thirty-two prisoners and one hundred horses taken. As for the balance of White's corps, the Legion "drove the rest into a great Swamp." Peebles, *Peebles' American War*, 370. Buford's report to George Washington stated that "I expect the loss will be about thirty men (killed wounded and missing) and from forty to fifty horses." Buford to Washington, May 6, 1780, Series 4, 198–199, Washington Papers, LOC. David Ramsay's history, published five years after the battle, is consistent with Buford's initial report: "About thirty were killed, wounded or taken." Ramsay, *History of the Revolution*, 2:66. Years later, one of William Washington's sergeants stated that the number of American prisoners ranged from twenty to forty. Pension Application of Lawrence Everheart, S25068, NA. Another veteran of Lenud's Ferry remembered that there were "thirteen men killed and wounded." Pension Application of John Gore, W160, in Dorman, *Pension Applications*, 44:62–63.

43. Hill, *Gentleman of Fortune*, 3:82. Captain Hill described the march to Charleston as one involving treatment that ranged from privations to genuinely cordial hospitality, in which the men were sometimes lightly guarded (or not at all) but on occasion closely guarded. On the second night of their captivity, Captain Hill, Major de Medici and the rank-and-file prisoners slept in a church near Lampriere's Point. It was "hard lodging" in which Hill slept on a bench in the church without any covering. Ibid., 83. When they were taken to Charleston, the Americans were strictly guarded by a Hessian unit, but the colonel who commanded it invited Hill and de Medici into his room, gave them wine, supplied them with bedding, and left them unguarded. Ibid., 85. Ultimately, the Americans were placed on board the *Union*, a British transport ship anchored in the harbor, where they remained for about ten days before being sent to Haddrell's Point. Ibid., 85–89. Hill and other American captives were confined to a six-mile radius of Haddrell's Point and seemed to have spent much of their time fishing, crabbing, reading, and drinking. De Medici remained a prisoner at Haddrell's Point until April 20, 1781. He left and returned to North Carolina almost a year to the day of being taken prisoner at Lenud's Ferry. Petition of Cosmo de Medici,

July 22, 1787, *Papers of the Continental Congress*, 204 vols. National Archives, M247, 5:403. Captain Baylor Hill remained a prisoner until January 1781, when he was paroled as part of an exchange. Hill, *Gentleman of Fortune*, 3:170. Pvt. Richard Gulley, a member of Captain Barnett's company in the 3rd Continental Light Dragoons, was a prisoner in Charleston for about a year before he and some other prisoners "took by stratagem a Brigg lying in the harbour" and made good their escape. In July 1781 he reached his home in Virginia. Pension Application of Richard Gulley, S38781, NA.

44. Lt. Col. Hezekiah Maham, of the South Carolina State Dragoons, served as presiding officer of the Court of Inquiry. The Court convened in Georgetown and issued its judgment on May 13, 1780. The judgment is reprinted in C. F. William Maurer, *Dragoon Diary: The History of the Third Continental Light Dragoons* (Bloomington, IN: AuthorHouse, 2005), 256.

45. Gore and the others stayed in Georgetown for a few days before being marched to Halifax, North Carolina. They arrived there a month later, in July 1780. Pension Application of John Gore, W160, in Dorman, *Pension Applications*, 44:62; Alexander Garden, *Anecdotes of the Revolutionary War in America, With Sketches of Character of Persons the Most Distinguished, in the Southern States, For Civil and Military Services* (Charleston: A. E. Miller, 1822), 384–385; William Dobein James, *A Sketch of the Life of Brig. Gen. Francis Marion and A History of His Brigade From Its Rise in June 1780 until Disbanded in December, 1782, With Descriptions of Characters and Scenes Not Heretofore Published* (Marietta, GA: Continental Book Co., 1948), 37. While both sources, originally published just a year apart, generally tell the same story, Garden's is the more detailed account. James identifies the boys as Francis G. Deliesseline and Samuel Dupre. Garden does not mention their first names but gives their ages. Garden also mentions that, at the time Garden was publishing his book, Deliesseline was serving as the sheriff of Charleston District. The names of the boys and their mission are memorialized on the state historical marker at the site of Lenud's Ferry.

46. William Washington to unknown recipient, May 5, 1780, in Clark, ed., *State Records of North Carolina*, 14:807. The date of this letter is one day before the battle at Lenud's Ferry. Consequently, Washington's biographer has questioned whether Washington was at Lenud's Ferry. Stephen Haller, *William Washington: Cavalryman of the Revolution*, (Bowie, MD: Heritage Books, 2001), 61. There are several reasons to believe that he was. First, Washington's statement, in connection with the location at which he wrote it, suggests that the letter was actually written soon after the battle. Second, at least one contemporaneous source confirms that William Washington was present, Buford to George Washington, May 6, 1780, Series 4, 198–199, Washington Papers, LOC. Finally, a much later

source also confirms it. Pension Application of Obed Britt, S1499, in Dorman, *Pension Applications*, 10:48. Referring to Lenud's Ferry, Britt stated that "At this place colonels Washington and White took a number of British prisoners, and brought them over to the side of the river. . . . Washington swam the river and made good his escape to Col. Bluford's marker. Britt saw him when he reached the shore."

47. Pension Application of John Gore, W160, in Dorman, *Pension Applications*, 44:63; Buford to George Washington, May 6, 1780, Series 4, 198–199, Washington Papers, LOC. One of Buford's men confirms this claim: "Col. Bluford [*sic*] detached about 150 men to aid in bringing the prisoners over to the side of the river upon which he was stationed, but before they could be brought over Col. Tarleton who was in close pursuit, came upon them, retook his men and forced the American party to retreat." Pension Application of Obed Britt, S1499, in Dorman, *Pension Applications*, 10:48.

48. Buford to George Washington, May 6, 1780, Series 4, 198–199, Washington Papers, LOC.

49. Ibid.; Henry Clinton to Benjamin Lincoln, May 8, 1780, in Tarleton, *Campaigns*, 58.

50. Carl P. Borick, *A Gallant Defense: The Siege of Charleston, 1780* (Columbia: University of South Carolina Press, 2003), 207–214; Pension Application of Frederick Padgett, S8930, in Lenora Higginbotham Sweeny, *Amherst County, Virginia in the Revolution* (Lynchburg, VA: Mrs. William Montgomery Sweeny, 1951), 157.

51. David K. Wilson, *The Southern Strategy: Britain's Conquest of South Carolina and Georgia, 1775–1780* (Columbia: University of South Carolina Press, 2005), 246–250.

52. H. R. 152, Twenty-Fourth Congress, Second Session, January 14, 1836.

53. Richard Call to Horatio Gates, July 22, 1780, in Clark, ed., *State Records of North Carolina*, 14:507–508.

54. Anthony Walton White to Horatio Gates, July 26, 1780, in Ibid., 14:510–512.

55. White to Gates, August 31, 1780, in Ibid., 14:582–583.

56. White to Gates, October 18, 1780, in Ibid., 14:702–703.

57. White to Nathanael Greene, December 28, 1780, in Maurer, *Dragoon Diary*, 284–285.

58. William Smallwood Orderly Book, September 24 and 26, 1780, Peter Force Collection, LOC; Nathanael Greene to Henry Lee, January 26, 1781, reprinted in Richard K. Showman, Dennis M. Conrad, and Roger N. Parks, eds., *The Papers of General Nathanael Greene*, 13 vols. (Chapel Hill: University of North Carolina Press, 1996–2005), 7:203.

59. Marquis de Lafayette to Nathanael Greene, May 18, 1781; Lafayette to George Washington, May 29, 1781; Lafayette to Washington, June 24,

1781; Lafayette to Thomas Jefferson, July 1, 1781, all in Maurer, *Dragoon Diary*, 322, 324, 327, 328–329.

60. Pension Application of Thomas Brown, S3060, NA.

61. George Lux to Nathanael Greene, November 3, 1781, in Showman, et al., eds., *Papers of Greene*, 9:525.

62. General Orders, October 31, 1781, Series 3g, 85–89, Washington Papers, LOC.

63. Nathanael Greene to Anthony Wayne, February 9, 1782, in Showman, et al., eds., *Papers of Greene*, 10:340.

64. Wayne to Greene, January 26, February 1, and February 11, 1782, in Ibid., 10:301–303, 356–357.

65. Wayne to Greene, February 22, 1782, in Ibid., 10:397–398.

66. Wayne to Greene, February 28 and March 4, 1782, in Ibid., 10:423–424, 442–443.

67. William Gordon, *The History of the Rise, Progress and Establishment of the Independence of the United States of America: Including an Account of the Late War, and of the Thirteen Colonies, From Their Origin to that Period*, 4 vols. (London: privately published, 1788), 4:258, 299; Patrick O'Kelley, *Nothing But Blood and Slaughter: The Revolutionary War in the Carolinas*, 4 vols. (Harnett County, NC: Blue House Tavern Press, 2005), 4:54, 68–70.

68. Gordon, *History*, 4:300; John Frost, *The Pictorial History of the United States of America: From the Discovery by the Northmen in the Tenth Century to the Present Time* (Philadelphia: B. Walker, 1844), 171; O'Kelley, *Nothing But Blood*, 4:78–80.

69. David Ramsay to Benjamin Rush, August 22, 1783, in Robert L. Brunhouse, "David Ramsay, 1749–1815, Selections from His Writings," *Transactions of the American Philosophical Society, New Series* 55, no. 4 (August 1965), 76 and n. 3; see also Ramsay to Rush, July 29, 1774, Ibid., 51; Ramsay, *History of the Revolution*, 1:65 (quotation).

70. Nathanael Greene to Jeremiah Wadsworth, May 24, 1783, and Greene to Robert Morris, June 4, 1783, in Showman, et al., eds., *Papers of Greene*, 13:8–9, 23–24. White went into business with Maj. Richard Call and Capt. William Pierce, and operated a trading house selling merchandise at stores in Augusta and Savannah. The Pierce, White, and Call partnership sank into debt for goods it had purchased and was forced to sell off valuable lands to pay its obligations. The firm dissolved about one year after it formed; Pierce sold his interest to Call, and Call sued Pierce in 1785. Richard Call to Nathanael Greene, September 30, 1784, in Ibid., 13:399; William Pierce to Nathanael Greene, September 24, 1784, in Ibid., 13:396; Grace Gillam Davidson, *Historical Collections of the Georgia Chapters Daughters of the American Revolution, Records of Richmond County, Georgia, Formerly Saint Paul's Parish* 3 vols. (Baltimore, MD: Clearfield, 1995), 2:78. Regarding White's guaranty of his troopers' debts, see John Frost, *The American Generals, from the Founding of the*

*Republic to the Present Time, Comprising Lives of the Great Commanders and other Distinguished Officers Who Have Acted in the Service of the United States* (Hartford, CT: Harford, Case, Tiffany & Co., 1850), 436–437.

71. See, for example, "May 5, 1792," *Journal of the House of Representatives of the United States*, 219 vols. to date (Washington, DC: US Government Printing Office, 1826), 1:599.

72. William Hogeland, *The Whiskey Rebellion: George Washington, Alexander Hamilton, and the Frontier Rebels Who Challenged America's Newfound Sovereignty* (New York: Scribner, 2006), 207–218; Richard Brookhiser, *Alexander Hamilton: American* (New York: Free Press, 1999), 117–120. These two works offer contrasting views of Alexander Hamilton, then Secretary of the Treasury and the driving force behind the tax and the government's response to the rebels. Hogeland is very critical of Hamilton's role in precipitating a crisis over the whiskey tax and the government's response, while Brookhiser is sympathetic to Hamilton.

73. Hogeland, *Whiskey Rebellion*, 216–221, 325, 330; William Findley, *History of the Insurrection in the Four Western Counties of Pennsylvania in the Year 1794* (Philadelphia: Samuel Harrison Smith, 1796), 210.

74. Harold C. Syrett, ed., *The Papers of Alexander Hamilton* 27 vols. (New York: Columbia University Press, 1961–1987), 22:387; William Heth to George Washington, August 14, 1798, (quotation) and Washington to James McHenry, September 14, 1798, Series 4, 1013–1017, 1225–1230, Washington Papers, LOC (quotation). McHenry was President Adams's Secretary of War.

75. Mark Edward Lender, *"This Honorable Court": The United States District Court for the District of New Jersey, 1789–2000* (New Brunswick, NJ: Rutgers University Press, 2006), 38–39; H.R. 932, 35th Congress, 1859. The sum of $3,750 was considered the equivalent in US funds of the $150,000 in Continental currency that White had advanced on behalf of the 1st Dragoons.

76. Woodhull, "Memoir of Brig. Gen. Anthony Walton White," 112.

CHAPTER SIX: SOUTH CAROLINA'S BACKCOUNTRY RANGERS IN THE AMERICAN REVOLUTION

1. "Journal of the First Provincial Congress," 3–17 June 3–17, 1775, June 1–2and 17–18, 1775, and June 6, 1775, in William E. Hemphill and Wylma A. Wates, eds., *Extracts from the Journals of the Provincial Congresses of South Carolina, 1775–1776* (Columbia: South Carolina Archives Department, 1960), 36–55, 33–35. 54–57; *Rivington's Gazette*, New York, November 9, 1775, quoted in Frank Moore and John Anthony Scott, eds., *The Diary of the American Revolution, 1775–1781* (New York: Washington Square Press, 1968), 82–83; "Journal of the Second Provincial Congress," February 21, 1776, in Hemphill and Wates, *Provincial Congresses*, 200.

2. The officers appointed to command the 1st and 2nd Regiments were all from the lowcountry, while those appointed for the 3rd Regiment were from the midlands and upper districts of the state. "Journal of the First Provincial Congress," June 10–12, 1775, in Hemphill and Wates, *Provincial Congresses*, 45–48; *Rivington's Gazette*, in Moore and Scott, *Diary*, 82–83; A. S. Salley Jr., *The History of Orangeburg County, South Carolina* (Baltimore, MD: Regional Publishing Company, 1978), 279; "Journal of the Second Provincial Congress," November 13, 1775, in Hemphill and Wates, *Provincial Congresses*, 124–126.

3. "Journal of the First Provincial Congress," June 10, 1775, in Hemphill and Wates, *Provincial Congresses*, 45; Walter B. Edgar and N. Louise Bailey, *Biographical Directory of the South Carolina House of Representatives, Vol. II: The Commons House of Assembly, 1692–1775* (Columbia: University of South Carolina Press, 1977), 669; N. Louise Bailey and Elizabeth Ivey Cooper, *Biographical Directory of the South Carolina House of Representatives, Vol. III: 1775–1790* (Columbia: University of South Carolina Press, 1981), 490; "Journal of the First Provincial Congress," June 9, 1775, in Hemphill and Wates, *Provincial Congresses*, 43–44 (quotation).

4. *Rivington's Gazette*, in Moore and Scott, *Diary*, 82–83; Fitzhugh McMaster, "South Carolina Heritage: The Horse Troops," *Sandlapper* 9, no. 9 (October 1976), 47; Fitzhugh McMaster and Darby Erd, "The Third South Carolina Regiment (Rangers), 1775–1780," *Military Uniforms in America*, Plate No. 494, Company of Military Historians, accessed September 1, 2011, http://military-historians.org/company/plates/images/494.htm; "Journal of the Second Provincial Congress," February 22, 1776, in Hemphill and Wates, *Provincial Congresses*, 203.

5. *Rivington's Gazette*, in Moore and Scott, *Diary*, 82–83.

6. Charnel Durham, Federal Pension Application (hereafter FPA) W9418, Microfilm Roll M804, National Archives and Records Administration; Joseph Gaston, "A Reminiscence of the Revolution," *The Southern Presbyterian*, May 22, 1873, in Thomas Sumter Papers, 9VV, 159–160, Lyman C. Draper Manuscript Collection, Wisconsin Historical Society.

7. "Journal of the Second Provincial Congress," November 7–9, 1775, in Hemphill and Wates, *Provincial Congresses*, 101–107; William Moultrie, *Memoirs of the American Revolution*, 2 vols. (New York: David Longworth, 1802), 1:97–98; Salley, *Orangeburg County*, 304–307.

8. Moses Cotter's deposition dated Ninety Six District, November 3, 1775, in Moultrie, *Memoirs*; Salley, *Orangeburg County*, 306.

9. "Journal of the Second Provincial Congress," November 7–9 and 25–26, 1775, in Hemphill and Wates, *Provincial Congresses*, 101–107, 151–153; Salley, *Orangeburg County*, 306–12.

10. "Journal of the Second Provincial Congress," February 22, 1776, in Hemphill and Wates, *Provincial Congresses*, 203–204.

11. February 23, 1776, in Ibid., 207.

12. February 24, 1776, in Ibid., 208–209.

13. February 28, 1776, in Ibid., 212–214; Robert D. Bass, *Gamecock: The Life and Campaigns of General Thomas Sumter* (Orangeburg, SC: Sandlapper Publishing Company, 2000), 33–34, 53. For the residences of specific soldiers serving in the Sixth Regiment, see their abstracted service records in Bobby G. Moss, *Roster of South Carolina Patriots in the American Revolution* (Baltimore, MD: Genealogical Publishing Company, 1983).

14. "Journal of the South Carolina General Assembly," September 20, 1776, and October 18, 1776, in William E. Hemphill, Wylma A. Wates, and R. Nicholas Olsberg, eds., *Journals of the General Assembly and House of Representatives, 1776–1780* (Columbia: South Carolina Department of Archives and History, 1970), 165. The extant muster rolls and several order books of the 3rd Regiment have been transcribed and published by the late Alexander S. Salley Jr., former director of the South Carolina Historical Commission. See A. S. Salley Jr., ed., *An Order Book of the Third South Carolina Regiment, South Carolina Line, Continental Establishment, December 23, 1776–May 2, 1777* (Columbia: Historical Commission of South Carolina, 1942); A. S. Salley Jr., ed., *Records of the Regiments of the South Carolina Line in the Revolutionary War* (Baltimore, MD: Genealogical Publishing Company, 1977); and "Colonel Thomson's Order Book—June 24th, 1775, to November 3rd, 1778," in Salley, *Orangeburg County*, 385–465. Field officers are those commissioned officers who rank above captain and below brigadier general, i.e., majors, lieutenant colonels, and colonels.

15. "Thomson's Order Book, August 13, 1777," in Salley, *Orangeburg County*, 452–453 (quotation); McMaster, "Horse Troops," and "Third Regiment," 47–48.

16. Salley, *Orangeburg County*, 278–387. For a more complete treatment of the 3rd Regiment's history, see Michael C. Scoggins, "Brothers in Arms: A History of the Third South Carolina Regiment," *Military Collector and Historian* 58, no. 2 (Summer 2006): 79–82.

17. A. S. Salley Jr., "[William] Thomson," *South Carolina Historical and Genealogical Magazine* 3, no. 2 (July 1902): 177–179; Salley, *South Carolina Line*, 1; Robert K. Wright, Jr., *The Continental Army* (Washington, DC: U.S. Army Center of Military History, 1983), 305–311.

18. Wright, *Continental Army*, 305–307.

19. "Journal of the First Provincial Congress," June 18 and November 8, 1775, in Hemphill and Wates, *Provincial Congresses*, 57, 102–104; "Journal of the Second Provincial Congress," February 10, 20, and March 23, 1776, in Ibid., 181–183, 198–199, 251; electoral district maps in Bailey and Cooper, *Biographical Directory*, 794–795.

20. For examples of colonial war veterans who commanded militia regiments during the Revolution, see the biographies of Edward Lacey,

John Lyles, Thomas Neel, Andrew Pickens, John Savage, John Thomas, Philomen Waters, and Andrew Williamson in Bailey and Cooper, *Biographical Directory, Vol. III*. For those who served as South Carolina district representatives, see also Hemphill and Wates, *Provincial Congresses*, 6–8, 75–78, and Hemphill, Wates, and Olsberg, *General Assembly*, 305–326.

21. Bailey and Cooper, *Biographical Directory*, 301–303, 552–555, 635, 769–771; Moss, *South Carolina Patriots*, 408, 771, 846, 998.

22. "Journal of the First Provincial Congress," June 18, 1775, in Hemphill and Wates, *Provincial Congresses*, 57; "Journal of the Second Provincial Congress," February 10 and March 23, 1776, in Ibid., 182–183, 210; Salley, *Orangeburg County*, 469; Bailey and Cooper, *Biographical Directory*, 708–709; Moss, *South Carolina Patriots*, 827, 925.

23. Bailey and Cooper, *Biographical Directory*, 86–87, 447–449, 752–753, 766–768; Moss, *South Carolina Patriots*, 95, 569, 969, 995. These boundaries are approximate, as present-day Cherokee County was formed out of parts of Spartanburg, Union, and York counties in 1897.

24. "Journal of the First Provincial Congress," January 11–17, 1775, November 7–8 and 26, 1775, in Hemphill and Wates, *Provincial Congresses*, 24; "Journal of the Second Provincial Congress," November 3, 7–8, and 26, 1775, March 23, 1776, in Ibid., 87, 102–104, 152–153, 251–252.

25. Samuel Houston, FPA W7810; Bailey and Cooper, *Biographical Directory*, 96–97, 278–279, 410–411, 702–704, 777–778, 779–781; Moss, *South Carolina Patriots*, 109, 370, 920, 1005–1006; Maurice A. Moore, *The Life of General Edward Lacey* (Spartanburg, SC: Douglas, Evins & Company, 1859), 6, 12–14.

26. Edgar and Bailey, *Biographical Directory*, 374–377, 557–560; Bailey and Cooper, *Biographical Directory*, 541–542; Moss, *South Carolina Patriots*, 531, 758–759, 812.

27. The New Acquisition Electoral District also included the section of present-day Cherokee County lying east of the Broad River, and that portion of present-day Lancaster County bounded by Sugar Creek and the Catawba River on the west and the North Carolina-South Carolina state line on the east. "Journal of the House of Representatives," February 18, 1791, in Michael E. Stevens and Christine M. Allen, eds., *Journals of the House of Representatives, 1791* (Columbia: University of South Carolina Press, 1985), 280; Bailey and Cooper, *Biographical Directory*, 88–89, 324–325, 505–506, 523–524, 755–756; Moss, *South Carolina Patriots*, 96, 719, 971; William Hill, *Col. William Hill's Memoirs of the Revolution*, A. S. Salley Jr. ed. (Columbia: Historical Commission of South Carolina, 1921), 7, 11.

28. "Journal of the Second Provincial Congress," November 8, 20, 26, 1775, February 5, 7, 20, 1776, and March 23, 1776, in Hemphill and

Wates, *Provincial Congresses*, 102–103, 140–141, 152–153, 174, 177, 198–199, 251–253; Salley, *Orangeburg County*, 469.

29. Edgar and Bailey, *Biographical Directory*, 119, 559; Bailey and Cooper, *Biographical Directory*, 770; Hill, *Memoirs*, 6.

30. Joseph McJunkin, FPA S18118; Bailey and Cooper, *Biographical Directory*, 328–329, 693–695. For Sumter's actual commission, see John Rutledge to Thomas Sumter, October 6, 1780, in Thomas Sumter Papers, 1761–1838, Library of Congress.

31. Hill, *Memoirs*, 6–9. For an in-depth examination of this period, see Michael C. Scoggins, *The Day It Rained Militia: Huck's Defeat and the Revolution in the South Carolina Backcountry, May–July 1780* (Charleston: History Press, 2005), 41–131.

32. Bailey and Cooper, *Biographical Directory*, 477–480, 552–555; Salley, *Orangeburg County*, 470–471; McMaster, "Horse Troops," 48–49; Fitzhugh McMaster and Charles H. Cureton, "South Carolina Regiment of Militia Light Horse, 1781–1782," *Military Uniforms in America*, Plate No. 473, Company of Military Historians.

33. William R. Davie, *The Revolutionary War Sketches of William R. Davie*, Blackwell P. Robinson, ed. (Raleigh: North Carolina Department of Cultural Resources, 1976), 1–13; Blackwell P. Robinson, *William R. Davie* (Chapel Hill: University of North Carolina Press, 1957), 1–54.

34. Davie, *War Sketches*, 16–40; Robinson, *Davie*, 65–100.

35. Clyde R. Ferguson, "Functions of the Partisan-Militia in the South During the American Revolution: An Interpretation," in W. Robert Wiggin, ed., *The Revolutionary War in the South: Power, Conflict, and Leadership* (Durham, NC: Duke University Press, 1979), 241–242, 245–246, 255–256; "Journal of the First Provincial Congress," June 17, 1775, in Hemphill and Wates, *Provincial Congresses*, 55; "Journal of the Second Provincial Congress," November 10, 1775, and February 8 and 10, 1776, in Ibid., 114, 178, 182.

36. "Papers of the First Council of Safety, June 1775," in A. S. Salley, Jr., "Rebel Rolls of 1775," *Sunday News* (Charleston, SC), March 19, 1899, 12; William Tennent to Henry Laurens, August 20, 1775, in Robert W. Gibbes, ed., *Documentary History of the American Revolution*, 3 vols. (Spartanburg, SC: The Reprint Company, 1972), 1:145–146; Ferguson, "Partisan-Militia," in Wiggin, *Revolutionary War in the South*, 245, 248–249; James P. Collins, *Autobiography of a Revolutionary Soldier*, John M. Roberts, ed. (New York: Arno Press, 1979), 34; McMaster and Cureton, "Militia Light Horse," *Military Uniforms*, Plate No. 473; George C. Neumann and Frank J. Kravic, *Collectors Illustrated Encyclopedia of the American Revolution* (Texarkana, TX: Shurlock Publishing Company, 1975), 24–27, 65, 66–80, 125–127, 144–155, 156–159, 160–161, 171–174, 200–213, 219–224, 232–235, 249, 252–256.

37. "Journal of the First Provincial Congress," June 17, 1775, in Hemphill and Wates, *Provincial Congresses*, 54–55; "Journal of the Second

Provincial Congress," November 8, 21, 23, 24, 1775, and February 8, 18, 20, 1776, Ibid., 103–104, 142–144, 146–147, 149, 178, 195–196, 198–199, 206; William Carson, FPA S9305; James P. Collins, FPA R2173; John Darwin, FPA S21155; James Kincaid, FPA R5929; William Lewis, FPA R6335; John Mills, FPA W9194; Joseph Morrow, FPA S21892; Robert Wilson, FPA W2302; Ferguson, "Partisan-Militia," in Wiggin, *Revolutionary War in the South*, 245–246.

38. "Journal of the First Provincial Congress," June 17, 1775, in Hemphill and Wates, *Provincial Congresses*, 55; David R. Chesnutt, ed., *The Papers of Henry Laurens* 16 vols. (Columbia: University of South Carolina Press, 1985), 10:182–183, 236–237; Salley, "Rebel Rolls of 1775." For a captain's commission issued to an officer of the New Acquisition District by Gov. John Rutledge in December 1781, see John Henderson, FPA R4869, reprinted in Michael C. Scoggins, *Relentless Fury: The Revolutionary War in the Southern Piedmont* (Rock Hill, SC: Culture & Heritage Museums, 2006), 39; Rutledge to Sumter, March 8, 1781, in Edward McCrady, *The History of South Carolina in the Revolution, 1780–1783* (New York: Russell and Russell, 1969), 140; James Anderson, FPA W9699; James P. Collins, FPA R2173; Robert Cowden, FPA S1656; John Henderson, FPA R4869; William Hillhouse, FPA S7008; John Adair, FPA W2895 (quotation).

39. "Journal of the First Provincial Congress," June 17, 1775, in Hemphill and Wates, *Provincial Congresses*, 54; "Journal of the Second Provincial Congress," November 8, 10 1775, in Ibid., 102–104, 114; John Adair, FPA W2895; William Bishop, FPA S30275; John Carson, FPA S35819; William Gaston, FPA S32265; Hugh McClure, FPA W21789; John Miller, FPA S38950; Silas Sterling, FPA R101020; John Wallace, R11064; Samuel Watson, Jr., S17187; Robert Wilson, FPA W2302; Thomas Woods, FPA S32614; Alexander Brown, South Carolina Accounts Audited for Claims Growing out of Revolutionary War Service (hereafter AA) 792, Series No. 108092, South Carolina Department of Archives and History; James McClure, AA 4936; James Ramsey, AA 6233; William Kennedy, AA 4237; John Steel, AA 7342.

40. Davie, *War Sketches*, 10; Lt. Col. George Turnbull to Lt. Col. Francis, Lord Rawdon, July 12, 1780, in Cornwallis Papers, PRO 30/11/2/285–286, Public Record Office, United Kingdom; Banastre Tarleton, *A History of the Campaigns of 1780 and 1781 in the Southern Provinces of North America*, reprint edition (North Stratford, NH: Ayer Company, 1999), 94; John H. Logan, *A History of the Upper Country of South Carolina* (Spartanburg, SC: The Reprint Company, 1960), 7; Salley, *Orangeburg County*, 470–471; Bass, *Gamecock*, 166, 176–177, 234–235; Ferguson, "Partisan-Militia," in Wiggin, *Revolutionary War in the South*, 239–258; Scoggins, *The Day It Rained Militia*, 13–14, 30, 46, 68, 85, 96, 101, 122, 137.

41. McCrady, *South Carolina in the Revolution*, 511–512.

42. Philip Katcher, *Confederate Cavalryman, 1861–65* (Oxford, UK: Osprey Publishing Company, 2002), 4–5, 43–57; Simeon Miller Bright, "The McNeill Rangers: A Study in Confederate Guerrilla Warfare," *West Virginia History* 12, no. 4 (July 1951), 338–387.

43. Ferguson, "Partisan-Militia," in Wiggin, *Revolutionary War in the South*, 239–258; Russell F. Weigley, *The Partisan War: The South Carolina Campaign of 1780–1782* (Columbia: University of South Carolina Press, 1970), 1–24.

44. McMaster and Cureton, "Militia Light Horse," *Military Uniforms*, Plate No. 473; McMaster, "Horse Troops," 48–49.

45. Collins, *Autobiography*, 34–35; John R. Elting, ed., *Military Uniforms in America: The Era of the American Revolution, 1755–1795* (San Rafael, CA: Presidio Press, 1974), 110–111; Neumann and Kravic, *Illustrated Encyclopedia*, 84–85, 122–123, 136–138, 140, 142–143, 242–243, 271; Scoggins, *Relentless Fury*, 20–33.

46. Collins, *Autobiography*, 34.

47. Ibid., 34–35.

48. Joseph Graham, FPA S6937.

49. Collins, *Autobiography*, 38.

50. Ibid., 46.

51. Rawdon to Gen. Alexander Leslie, October 24, 1780, Cornwallis Papers, PRO 30/11/3/268.

52. William Bishop, FPA S30275; Robert Cowden, FPA S1656; Edward Doyle, FPA S32216; Hugh McClure, FPA W21789; John Mills, FPA W9194; Silas Sterling, FPA R101020.

53. Samuel Hammond, FPA S21807; Lawrence E. Babits, *A Devil of a Whipping: The Battle of Cowpens* (Chapel Hill: University of North Carolina Press, 1998), 41–42, 174–175 n 101, 177–178 n 28.

54. Rawdon to Gen. Charles, Earl Cornwallis, March 7, 1781, in Cornwallis Papers, PRO 30/11/69/9.

55. Ibid., PRO 30/11/69/10.

56. McCrady, *South Carolina in the Revolution*, 148, 513–514 n 1; Bass, *Gamecock*, 130–133.

57. Armstrong to Greene, July 10, 1781, in Dennis M. Conrad, ed., *The Papers of General Nathanael Greene* 13 vols. (Chapel Hill: University of North Carolina Press, 1995), 8:515.

58. Ferguson, "Partisan-Militia," in Wiggin, *Revolutionary War in the South*, 239–240.

59. "Journal of the House of Representatives," September 4, 1779, Feb. 4 and 11, 1780, in Hemphill, Wates, and Olsberg, *General Assembly*, 195, 273, 294–295.

60. "Journal of the House of Representatives," Aug. 31, 1779, in Hemphill, Wates and Olsberg, *General Assembly*, 181; McMaster, "Horse Troops," 48; Fitzhugh McMaster and Clyde A. Risley, "South Carolina

State Regiment of Light Dragoons, 1779–1780," *Military Uniforms in America*, Plate No. 593, Company of Military Historians.

61. Samuel Hammond, FPA S21807; Moss, *South Carolina Patriots*, 594; Babits, *Devil of a Whipping*, 41–42, 78, 174–175 n 98–101, 177–178 n 28.

62. Thomas Sumter to Francis Marion, March 28, 1781, in McCrady, *South Carolina in the Revolution*, 143; Colonel Richard Hampton to Major John Hampton, April 2, 1781, in Gibbes, *Documentary History*, 3:47–8; McCrady, *South Carolina in the Revolution*, 144–145; John Mills, FPA W9194; McMaster, "Horse Troops," 51; Fitzhugh McMaster and Charles H. Cureton, "South Carolina Light Dragoons, 1781–1782," *Military Uniforms in America*, Plate No. 558, Company of Military Historians.

63. Samuel Hammond, FPA S21807; McCrady, *South Carolina in the Revolution*, 143–145; McMaster, "Horse Troops," 51; McMaster and Cureton, "Light Dragoons, 1781–1782," *Military Uniforms*, Plate No. 558.

64. Richard Hampton to John Hampton, in Gibbes, *Documentary History*, 3:47–48; McCrady, *South Carolina in the Revolution*, 144–145; McMaster, "Horse Troops," 51; McMaster and Cureton, "Light Dragoons, 1781–1782," *Military Uniforms*, Plate No. 558.

65. Richard Hampton and Wade Hampton, AA 3287.

66. Robert W. Gibbes Collection of Revolutionary War Manuscripts, 1773–1820, Series no. S213089, South Carolina Department of Archives and History, Columbia.

67. McCrady, *South Carolina in the Revolution*, 145–147; Bass, *Gamecock*, 145–146, 154–155, 221–223.

68. McCrady, *South Carolina in the Revolution*, 322–323. Lee's Legion, also known as the Partizan Legion, included three troops of light dragoons and three troops of infantry from Virginia commanded by Lt. Col. Henry "Light-Horse Harry" Lee. Gen. George Washington sent Lee's Legion south in late 1780 to reinforce Maj. Gen. Nathanael Greene's Continental Army. Henry Lee, *The Revolutionary War Memoirs of General Henry Lee*, Robert E. Lee, ed. (New York: De Capo Press, 1998), 212.

69. Bailey and Cooper, *Biographical Directory*, 328; McCrady, *South Carolina in the Revolution*, 443; McMaster, "Horse Troops," 51.

70. General Greene's Orders, September 9, 1781, in Showman, et al., eds., *Papers of Greene*, 9:307; McCrady, *South Carolina in the Revolution*, 451–452.

71. Conrad, *Papers of Nathanael Greene*, 9:336 n 12.

72. Nathanael Greene to Thomas McKean, September 11, 1781, in Conrad, *Papers of Nathanael Greene*, 9:331.

73. Samuel Hammond, FPA S21807; McMaster, "Horse Troops," 52; McMaster and Cureton, "Light Dragoons, 1781–1782," *Military Uniforms*, Plate No. 558.

74. McCrady, *South Carolina in the Revolution*, 531, 533–534; McMaster, "Horse Troops," 51–52; McMaster and Cureton, "Light Dragoons, 1781–1782," *Military Uniforms*, Plate No. 558.

75. McMaster, "Horse Troops," 52; McMaster and Cureton, "Light Dragoons, 1781–1782," *Military Uniforms*, Plate No. 558.

76. Benson J. Lossing, *Field-Book of the American Revolution*, 2 vols. (New York: Harper, 1851–1852), 2:534; McCrady, *South Carolina in the Revolution*, 750–751; McMaster, "Horse Troops," 52; McMaster and Cureton, "Light Dragoons, 1781–1782," *Military Uniforms*, Plate No. 558.

77. Samuel Hammond, FPA S21807; Lee, *Memoirs*, 527–528; Lossing, *Field-Book*, 2:535; McMaster, "Horse Troops," 52; McMaster and Cureton, "Light Dragoons, 1781–1782," *Military Uniforms*, Plate No. 558.

78. McMaster, "Horse Troops," 52; McMaster and Cureton, "Light Dragoons, 1781–1782," *Military Uniforms*, Plate No. 558; Scoggins, *Relentless Fury*, 15, 32.

79. Ferguson, "Partisan-Militia," in Wiggin, *Revolutionary War in the South*, 239 n 1; "Journal of the House of Representatives," February 22, 1783, in Theodora J. Thompson and Rosa S. Lumpkin, eds., *Journals of the House of Representatives, 1783–1784* (Columbia: University of South Carolina Press, 1977), 183.

80. "Journal of the House of Representatives," March 4, 1783, in Ibid., 214; Salley, *Orangeburg County*, 471–475.

81. "Journal of the House of Representatives," March 4, 1783, in Thompson and Lumpkin, *House of Representatives*, 214.

82. Scoggins, *Relentless Fury*, 15.

83. "Journal of the House of Representatives," August 13, 1783, February 18, 20, and March 2, 1784, in Thompson and Lumpkin, *House of Representatives*, 360 (quotation), 462–463, 476, 514.

84. William Bratton to Benjamin Guerrard, February 13, 1784, in Legislative Papers, Series No. S165009 (Governors' Messages), South Carolina Department of Archives and History.

85. "Journal of the House of Representatives," March 2, 1784, in Thompson and Lumpkin, *House of Representatives*, 514.

86. "Journal of the House of Representatives," Mar. 17, 1785, in Lark E. Adams and Rosa S. Lumpkin, eds., *Journals of the House of Representatives, 1785–1786* (Columbia: University of South Carolina Press, 1979), 244n, 245, 248–249.

## Chapter Seven: Continentals in Tarleton's British Legion

1. Thomas Pynchon, *Gravity's Rainbow* (New York: Penguin Books, 1987), 251.

2. Alexander Chesney, *The Journal of Alexander Chesney, a South Carolina Loyalist in the Revolution and After*, ed. E. Alfred Jones. *Ohio State University Bulletin* 26 (October 30, 1921), 22.

3. Christopher L. Ward, *The Delaware Continentals* (Wilmington: Historical Society of Delaware, 1941), 537–538.

4. Alexander Garden, *Anecdotes of the American Revolution* (Charleston, SC; A. E. Miller, 1828), 207–208.

5. P. R. N. Katcher, *Encyclopedia of British, Provincial and German Army Units, 1775–1783* (Harrisburg, PA: Stackpole Books, 1973), 99; Henry Wells, Pension Application M804, January 29, 1834, National Archives, Washington, DC.

6. William Johnson, *Sketches of the Life and Correspondence of General Nathanael Greene*, 2 vols. (Charleston, SC: A. E. Miller, 1822), 2:220.

7. Katcher, *Encyclopedia*, 83–84.

8. Walter Edgar, *Partisans and Redcoats* (New York: William Morrow, 2001), 56–57, 81-82.

9. Lawrence E. Babits, *A Devil of a Whipping: The Battle of Cowpens* (Chapel Hill: University of North Carolina Press, 1998), 27–28; Mark A. Tacyn, "To the End: The First Maryland Regiment and the American Revolution," unpublished PhD dissertation, University of Maryland, 1999, 129–130, 213–215.

10. Ward, *Delaware Continentals*, 353.

11. Robert D. Bass, *Swamp Fox: The Life and Campaigns of Francis Marion* (Orangeburg, SC: Sandlapper Press, 1974), 44–46; Henry C. Peden Jr., *Revolutionary Patriots of Montgomery County, Maryland, 1775–1783* (Westminster, MD: Willow Bend Books, 2001), 1, 5, 38, 45, 110, 176.

12. Murtie June Clark, ed., *Loyalists in the Southern Campaign of the Revolutionary War*, 3 vols., (Baltimore, MD: Genealogical Publishing Co., 1981), 2:215.

13. Ibid., 197–251.

14. Babits, *Devil of a Whipping*, 150.

15. Bobby G. Moss, *South Carolina Patriots in the American Revolution* (Baltimore, MD: Genealogical Publishing Company, 1985), passim.

16. Thomas Young, "Memoir of Major Thomas Young," *Orion* 3, (1843), 100.

17. Babits, *Devil of a Whipping*, 20, 125.

18. Clark, *Loyalists in the Southern Campaign*, 2:227–228, 246–247; Richard Pindell, "A Militant Surgeon of the Revolution: Some Letters of Richard Pindell," *Maryland Historical Magazine* 18 (1923), 317–318.

19. George R. Stewart, *Pickett's Charge: A Microhistory of the Final Attack at Gettysburg, July 3, 1863* (Dayton, OH: Morningside Bookshop, 1980), 265.

20. Babits, *Devil of a Whipping*, 46.

21. Clark, *Loyalists in the Southern Campaign*, 2:201.

22. Roderick McKenzie, *Strictures on Lt. Col. Tarleton's History of the Campaigns of 1780 and 1781, in the Southern Provinces of North America* (London: privately printed, 1789), 99.

23. Robert McLeod, Pension Application, February 5, 1822, M804, Roll 412, Pension-Bounty-Land Warrant Files, National Archives.

24. Pindell, 317–318.

25. Peden, *Patriots of Prince George's County,* passim. See Table 5 for the pages referring to specific individuals.

26. Peden, *Patriots of Prince George's County,* 230; William H. Browne, ed., *Archives of Maryland—Muster Rolls and Other Records of Service of Maryland Troops in the American Revolution, 1775–1781,* reprint edition, 72 vols. (Baltimore, MD: Clearfield, 2000), 18:147, 286.

27. Browne, *Muster Rolls,* 18:578, 583–584.

28. Ryan Harris, personal communication to authors, December 12, 2001.

29. Record Group 81, "C" Series, Vol. 1884, 1779, Public Archives of Canada, Ottawa, Ontario; Clark, *Loyalists in the Southern Campaign,* 2:199.

CHAPTER EIGHT: CAVALRY OPERATIONS AT EUTAW SPRINGS

1. Robert K. Wright Jr., *The Continental Army* (Washington, DC: US Army Center of Military History, 2000), 160.

2. Richard Call to William Davies, August 28, 1781, transcript provided by Lee F. McGee; "Drill Manual for Colonial Horse," c. 1975, courtesy of C. F. William Maurer.

3. Robert Hinde, "The Discipline of the Light Cavalry, 1778," accessed June 8, 2011, www.replications.com/17LD/17hinde.htm; G Michell, "Dragoons Standing Orders, 1782," accessed June 8, 2011, www.south-frm.demon.co.uk/Manuscripts/Military.html; W. Pepper, *An Abridgement of the New Broad Sword Exercise* (London: privately printed, 1797), passim; Georges Guillet de St. Georges, *The Gentleman's Dictionary; I. The Art of Riding the Great Horse; II. The Military Art,* reprint edition (Los Angeles: Sherwin & Freutel, 1970), passim; Baron Friedrich von Steuben, *Regulations for the Order and Discipline of the Troops of the United States, Part Two, Manual, Exercise and Evolutions of the Cavalry,* (Bennington, VT: Anthony Haswell, 1794), passim; Jac Weller, "Irregular but Effective: Partizan Weapons Tactics in the American Revolution, Southern Theatre," *Military Affairs* 21 (1957), 118–131; Martin Read, "Cavalry Combat and the Sword: Sword Design, Provision and Use in the British Cavalry of the Napoleonic Era," accessed June 8, 2011, www.swordforum.com.

4. James Kirby Martin and Mark Edward Lender, *A Respectable Army: The Military Origins of the Republic, 1763–1789* (Wheeling, IL: Harlan Davidson, 2006), 114; Harold J. Peterson, *The Book of the Continental Soldier* (Harrisburg, PA: Stackpole Books, 1968), 19–20.

5. Mentges had been named to that post on November 5, 1782, upon the resignation of Colonel Jean Baptiste Ternant. Mentges had previously commanded a regiment of the Pennsylvania Line. When he became deputy inspector general, the 1st and 3rd Continental Light Dragoons had been officially consolidated into a single unit by Nathanael Greene;

the amalgamated unit was officially designated the 1st Continental Legionary Corps. See Dennis M. Conrad, ed., *The Papers of General Nathanael Greene*, 13 vols. (Chapel Hill: University of North Carolina Press, 2002), 12:147; Nathanael Greene to Benjamin Lincoln, November 12, 1782, in Ibid., 12:167; Francis Mentges to Baron von Steuben, January 9, 1783, Steuben Papers.

6. Lee F. McGee, "The Battle of Rugeley's Fort: A Spirit of Enterprize and Intrepidity Still Prevails," *Southern Campaigns of the American Revolution* 2, no. 8 (August 2005), 11–15; "The Better Order of Men: Hammond's Store and Fort Williams," Ibid., no 12 (December 2005), 14–21; "Most Astonishing Efforts: William Washington's Cavalry at the Battle of Eutaw Springs," Ibid., 3, no. 3 (March 2006), 15–33; "The Object Was Worthy of the Cast: The Patriot Cavalry Reexamined at the Battle of Hobkirk Hill," Ibid., 3, no. 4 (April 2006), 13–19; See also chapter 2 in this volume.

7. McGee, "Most Astonishing Efforts," 15.

8. Pension Application of Benjamin Fisher, Gaskins's First Virginia Battalion of 1781, accessed June 8, 2011, www.virginiacampaign.org/gaskins/tactics/html; C. F. William Maurer, *Dragoon Diary: The History of the Third Continental Light Dragoons* (Bloomington, IN: AuthorHouse, 2005), 328–329, 330, 331, 332–333, 335–336, 338–339.

9. Pension Applications of George Bussey and Thomas Brown, in John Frederick Dorman, *Virginia Revolutionary Pension Applications*, 51 vols. (Washington, DC: J. F. Dorman, 1958–1995), 11:69-71, 13:82–83; Wright, *Continental Army*, 128; "Drill Manual for Colonial Horse," 1. The dismounted troops were possibly trained at Ruffin's Ferry on the Pamunkey River per Brown's pension application.

10. Michell, *Dragoons Standing Orders*, 5; Guillet de St. Georges, *Gentleman's Dictionary: I*; Hinde, *Discipline of the Light Cavalry*, 11–35.

11. Michell, *Dragoons Standing Orders*, 14; Pepper, *Abridgment of the New Sword Exercise*, 1–34.

12. Steuben and General George Washington had designed the system adopted by Congress. See Steuben to Washington, October 23, 1780, in Maurer, *Dragoon Diary*, 271–272. Steuben favored the legionary system not only because it was customary in European armies but also to remedy the lack of camp security that had plagued the cavalry in the South during the 1780 campaign, when American dragoons unsupported by infantry were surprised and dispersed at Moncks Corner and Lenud's Ferry.

13. McGee, "Most Astonishing Efforts," 15. Such an adaptation by Greene would have been in line with his injunction to a council of war in Pennsylvania in December 1777 that "experience is the best of schools and the safest guide in human affairs—yet I am no advocate for blindly following all the maxims of European policy, but where reason

corresponds with what custom has long sanctified, we may safely copy their Example." Quoted in Wright, *Continental Army*, 139.

14. McGee, personal communication, August 16, 2007. Emphasis added.

15. McGee, "Most Astonishing Efforts," 20.

16. "Drill Manual for Colonial Horse," 16; Quoted in Maurer, *Dragoon Diary*, 18. This statement of Steuben's appears contrary to established Prussian doctrine; see McGee, "Most Astonishing Efforts," 18.

17. McGee, "Most Astonishing Efforts," 17, and personal communication to author, August 16, 2007.

18. McGee, "Most Astonishing Efforts," 19. For what it may be worth, nineteenth-century South Carolina author William Gilmore Simms, in his novel *Eutaw*, wrote that Washington made three separate charges on the blackjack thicket. Simms had a reputation for being scrupulous in adhering to established fact even in his fiction and was thought to have possessed many primary sources pertaining to the Revolutionary War in South Carolina, which were destroyed when his home was burned by stragglers from Gen. William T. Sherman's army during the Civil War. Simms may have consulted some now-lost source in ascribing the three charges to Washington's dragoons. Simms, *Eutaw: A Sequel to the Forayers, or The Raid of the Dog Days*, ed. David W. Newton, reprint edition (Fayetteville: University of Arkansas Press, 2006), 438, 514–518.

19. "Battle of Eutaw, Account Furnished by Colonel Otho Williams, with additions by Cols. W. Hampton, Polk, Howard and Watt," in R. W. Gibbes, ed., *Documentary History of the American Revolution*, 3 vols. (Columbia, SC: Banner Steam-Power Press, 1853), 3:149.

## Chapter Nine: The "Black Dragoons"

1. William Mathews to Gideon White, April 26, 1782, Gideon White Collection, Vol. 947, no. 130, microfilm, Harriet C. Irving Library, University of New Brunswick, St. John.

2. [Archibald?] Campbell to Lord George Germain, January 16, 1776, *George Sackville Germain Papers, 1683–1785*, Volume 4, William L. Clements Library, University of Michigan, Ann Arbor; Andrew Jackson O'Shaughnessy, *An Empire Divided: The American Revolution and the British Caribbean* (Philadelphia: University of Pennsylvania Press, 2000), 149.

3. Benjamin Quarles, *The Negro in the American Revolution* (Chapel Hill: University of North Carolina Press, 1961), 19–32. Pioneers performed engineering duties such as constructing fortifications and clearing obstacles.

4. Alexander A. Lawrence, *Storm over Savannah: The Story of Count d'Estaing and the Siege of the Town in 1779* (Athens: University of Georgia Press, 1951), 81–82.

5. One of the first historians to discuss the Black Dragoons was Benjamin Quarles, who suggested that the unit was formed in the spring

of 1782, numbered no more than a hundred men, and that one of its major functions was to capture British deserters. See Quarles, *The Negro in the American Revolution*, 149. Sylvia R. Frey also briefly discusses the Black Dragoons in *Water from the Rock: Black Resistance in a Revolutionary Age* (Princeton, NJ: Princeton University Press, 1991), 138–139.

6. Christopher Ward, *The Delaware Continentals, 1776–1783* (Wilmington: The Historical Society of Delaware, 1941), 476; Frey, *Water from the Rock*, 138.

7. C. Harrison Dwight, "Count Rumford: His Majesty's Colonel in Carolina," *South Carolina Historical Magazine* 57, no. 1 (January 1956), 23–24.

8. Benjamin Thompson to Germain, January 11, 1782, Germain Papers, Volume 15.

9. Thompson to Germain, January 24, 1782, Ibid.

10. Frey, *Water from the Rock*, 139.

11. For blacks' military service with the American land forces, see Quarles, *Negro in the Revolution*, 68–82. Congress's and Continental Army officers' efforts to convince state officials in Georgia and South Carolina to arm slaves are discussed in Jim Piecuch, *Three Peoples, One King: Loyalists, Indians, and Slaves in the Revolutionary South, 1775–1782* (Columbia: University of South Carolina Press, 2008), 121–123, 163–164, 214, 312–313, 324–325.

12. Frey, *Water from the Rock*, 139.

13. Lewis Morris to Ann Elliott, November 1, 1782; November 28, 1782, "Letters from Col. Lewis Morris to Miss Ann Elliott," *South Carolina Historical and Genealogical Magazine* 41, no. 1 (January 1940), 6, 10.

14. William Seymour, "A Journal of the Southern Expedition, 1780–1783," *Papers of the Delaware Historical Society* 15 (Wilmington: The Historical Society of Delaware, 1896), 35; Edward Rutledge to Arthur Middleton, April 23, 1782, in Joseph Barnwell, ed., "Correspondence of Arthur Middleton," *South Carolina Historical and Genealogical Magazine* 27, no. 1 (January 1926), 14; John Bell Tilden, "Extracts from the Journal of Lieutenant John Bell Tilden, Second Pennsylvania Line, 1781–1782," *Pennsylvania Magazine of History and Biography* 19 (1895), 225.

15. Rutledge to Middleton, April 23, 1782, in "Correspondence of Middleton," 14. Rutledge stated that March was once "the Governor's Man," apparently the slave of John Mathews. The encounter took place "near Mrs. Izard's Gate."

16. Seymour, "Journal," 35.

17. Rutledge to Middleton, April 23, 1782, in "Correspondence of Middleton," 14.

18. Joseph Lee Boyle, ed., "The Revolutionary War Diaries of Captain Walter Finney," *South Carolina Historical Magazine* 98, no. 2 (April 1997), 137.

19. Charles Cotesworth Pinckney to Middleton, August 13, 1782, in "Correspondence of Middleton," 65.

20. Francis Marion to John Mathews, August 30, 1782, "Genl. Marion's Report of the Affair at Wadboo," *South Carolina Historical and Genealogical Magazine* 17, no. 4 (October 1916), 176–177.

21. Entries for December 2 and December 3, 1782, "Diaries of Finney," 146.

22. Lt. General von Bose to Lt. Gen. von Lossberg, November 18, 1782, "Reports of the War under General von Lossberg, 1782–1784," Hessian Documents of the American Revolution, Band V, Lage 15.

23. Seymour, "Journal," 331.

24. Thomas Bee to John Mathews, December 9, 1782, Thomas Bee Papers, South Caroliniana Library, Columbia.

25. Thaddeus Kosciuszko to Nathanael Greene, November 29, 1780, in Metchie J. E. Budka, ed., *Autograph Letters of Thaddeus Kosciuszko* (Chicago: The Polish Museum of America, 1977), 130.

26. George F. Tyson Jr., "The Carolina Black Corps: Legacy of Revolution (1782–1798)," *Review Interamericana* 5, no. 4 (Winter 1975–76), 649–651; Leslie quoted in Frey, *Water from the Rock*, 139.

# Further Reading

The editor wishes to thank Samuel Fore of Dallas, Texas, for his efforts in compiling the majority of this material.

Adams, Charles Francis. "Cavalry in the War of Independence." *Proceedings of the Massachusetts Historical Society* 43 (1910), 547–593.

Arnold, James R. "A Northern Virginia Patriot: The Adventures of John Champe of Loudoun County." *Northern Virginia Heritage* 8 (February 1986), 11–14, 20.

Babits, Lawrence E. *A Devil of a Whipping: The Battle of Cowpens.* Chapel Hill: University of North Carolina Press, 1998.

Babits, Lawrence E., and Joshua B. Howard. *Long, Obstinate, and Bloody: The Battle of Guilford Courthouse.* Chapel Hill: University of North Carolina Press, 2009.

Bass, Robert D. *The Green Dragoon: The Lives of Banastre Tarleton and Mary Robinson.* New York: Henry Holt, 1957.

———. *Swamp Fox: The Life and Campaigns of General Francis Marion.* Orangeburg, SC: Sandlapper Publishing, 1974.

Bauer, Frederic Gilbert. "Notes on the Use of Cavalry in the American Revolution." *Cavalry Journal* 47 (1938), 136–143.

Bland, Theodorick. *The Bland Papers: Being a Selection from the Manuscripts of Colonel Theodorick Bland, Jr., of Prince George County, Virginia.* Ed. Charles Campbell. 2 Vols. Petersburg, VA: E. & J. C. Ruffin, 1840–1843.

Büttner, Johann Carl. *Narrative of Johann Carl Buettner in the American Revolution.* New York: C. F. Heartman, 1915.

Cashin, Edward J. *The King's Ranger: Thomas Brown and the American Revolution on the Southern Frontier.* Athens: University of Georgia Press, 1989.

Clinton, Sir Henry. Papers. William L. Clements Library, University of Michigan, Ann Arbor.

Copeland, Peter F., and Marko Zlatich. "1st Regiment of Continental Light Dragoons, 1777–1779." *Military Collector & Historian* 24 (Summer 1972), 51–52.

Cornwallis, Charles, Earl. *The Cornwallis Papers: The Campaigns of 1780 and 1781 in the Southern Theatre of the American Revolutionary War*. Edited by Ian Saberton. 6 Vols. Uckfield, East Sussex, England: Naval & Military Press, 2010.

Cureton, Charles H., and Marko Zlatich. "4th Regiment of Continental Light Dragoons, 1777–1778." *Military Collector & Historian* 37 (Fall 1985), 138.

Douwes, William F. "Logistical Support for the Continental Light Dragoons." *Military Collector & Historian* 24 (Winter 1972), 101–106.

Dwight, C. Harrison. "Count Rumford: His Majesty's Colonel in Carolina." *South Carolina Historical Magazine* 57 (1956), 23–27.

Ewald, Johann von. *Treatise on Partisan Warfare*. Edited by Robert A. Selig and translated by David Curtis Skaggs. New York: Greenwood Press, 1991.

Ewing, J. H. "Sergeant Major Champe." *Tyler's Quarterly Historical & Genealogical Magazine* 2 (1920), 331–334.

Graham, A. S., and M. W. Woodhull. "Anthony Walton White, Brigadier in the Continental Army." *Magazine of History* 1 (1905), 394–402.

Greene, Nathanael. *The Papers of General Nathanael Greene*. Eds. Richard K. Showman, Dennis M. Conrad, and Roger N. Parks. 13 Vols. Chapel Hill: University of North Carolina Press, 1976–2005.

Griffin, Martin I. J. *Stephen Moylan: Muster-Master General, Secretary and Aide-de-Camp to Washington, Quartermaster-General, Colonel of Fourth Pennsylvania Light Dragoons and Brigadier-General of the War for American Independence*. Philadelphia, PA: Privately Printed, 1909.

Haarman, Albert W. "General Armand and His Partisan Corps, 1777–1783." *Military Collector & Historian* 12 (Winter 1960), 97–102.

———. "Armand's Legion, 1781–1783." *Military Collector & Historian* 17 (Summer 1965), 62–63.

Hall, Charles S. *Benjamin Tallmadge: Revolutionary Soldier and American Businessman*. New York: Columbia University Press, 1943.

Hall, Wilbur C. "Sergeant John Champe and Certain of His Contemporaries." *William & Mary Quarterly* Second Series 17 (1937), 145–175.

Haller, Stephen E. *William Washington: Cavalryman of the Revolution.* Bowie, MD: Heritage Books, 2001.

Hartmann, John W. *The American Partisan: Henry Lee and the Struggle for Independence.* Shippensburg, PA: Burd Street Press, 2000.

Hayes, John T. *Connecticut's Revolutionary Cavalry: Sheldon's Horse.* Chester, CT: Pequot Press, 1975.

———. *Tomahawks and Sabres: Indians in Combat against Cavalry in the American Revolution, 1777–1778.* Fort Lauderdale, FL: Saddlebag Press, 1996.

———. *Prelude to Glory: Early Operations of Britain's Two Most Famed Cavalrymen of the American Revolution, 1775–1783, in Two Books.* Fort Lauderdale, FL: Saddlebag Press, 1996.

——— *Massacre: Tarleton vs. Buford, May 29, 1780, & Lee vs. Pyle, February 23, 1781.* Fort Lauderdale, FL: Saddlebag Press, 1997.

———. *Connecticut Yankees: Two Cavalrymen, One in Provincial Green, the Other in Continental Blue, in Two Books.* Fort Lauderdale, FL: Saddlebag Press, 1999.

Herr, John K., and Edward S. Wallace. *The Story of the U. S. Cavalry, 1775–1942.* New York: Bonanza Books, 1953.

Hill, Baylor. *A Gentleman of Fortune: The Diary of Baylor Hill, First Continental Light Dragoons, 1777–1781.* Edited by John T. Hayes. 3 Vols. Fort Lauderdale, FL: Saddlebag Press, 1995.

Holst, Donald W., and Marko Zlatich. "Dress and Equipment of Pulaski's Independent Legion." *Military Collector & Historian* 16 (Winter 1964), 97–103.

Kajencki, Francis C. *Casimir Pulaski, Cavalry Commander of the American Revolution.* El Paso, TX: Southwest Polonia Press, 2001.

———. *The Pulaski Legion in the American Revolution.* El Paso, TX: Southwest Polonia Press, 2004.

Kite, Elizabeth S. "Charles-Armand Tuffin, Marquis de la Rouerie." *Legion d'Honneur Magazine* 10 (1940), 451–462.

Lee, Henry. *The Revolutionary War Memoirs of General Henry Lee.* Edited by Robert E. Lee. New York: Da Capo Press, 1998.

Lockwood, James. B. "The Skirmish at Poundridge, Westchester, 1779." *Magazine of American History* 3 (1879), 685–687.

Loescher, Burt Garfield. *Washington's Eyes: The Continental Light Dragoons.* Fort Collins, CO: Old Army Press, 1977.

————. "Bland's Virginia Horse: The Story of the First Continental Light Dragoons." *Military Collector & Historian* 6 (Spring 1954), 1–6.

Maurer, William C. F. *Dragoon Diary: The History of the Third Continental Light Dragoons.* Bloomington, IN: AuthorHouse, 2005.

McBarron, H. Charles, Jr., and Frederick P. Todd. "2nd Continental Light Dragoons, Dismounted Service, 1780." *Military Collector & Historian* 2 (September 1950), 39.

McGroarty, William B. "Captain Cameron and Sergeant Champe." *William & Mary Quarterly* Second Series 19 (1939), 49–54.

Moylan, Stephen. "Selections from the Correspondence of Col. Stephen Moylan, of the Continental Line." *Pennsylvania Magazine of History & Biography* 37 (1913), 341–360.

Piecuch, Jim. *The Blood Be Upon Your Head: Tarleton and the Myth of Buford's Massacre.* Lugoff, SC: Southern Campaigns of the American Revolution Press, 2010.

Piecuch, Jim, and John Beakes. *Light Horse Harry Lee in the American Revolution.* Charleston, SC: Nautical & Aviation Publishing, 2012.

Raddall, Thomas H. "Tarleton's Legion." *Collections of the Nova Scotia Historical Society* 28 (1947), 1–50.

Rouerie, Charles Armand Tuffin, Marquis de la. *Collections of the New York Historical Society, Vol. XI: Letters of Col. Armand (Marquis de la Rouerie).* New York: New-York Historical Society, 1878.

Royster, Charles. *Light-Horse Harry Lee and the Legacy of the American Revolution.* New York: Alfred A. Knopf, 1981.

Rudulph, Marilou Alston. "Michael Rudulph, 'Lion of the Legion.'" *Georgia Historical Quarterly* 45 (1961), 201–222.

Scotti, Anthony J. Jr. *Brutal Virtue: The Myth and Reality of Banastre Tarleton.* Bowie, MD: Heritage Books, 2000.

Simcoe, John Graves. *Simcoe's Military Journal: A History of the Operations of a Partisan Corps, Called the Queen's Rangers, Commanded by Lieut. Col. J. G. Simcoe, During the War of the American Revolution.* New York: Bartlett & Welford, 1844.

Steffen, Randy. *The Horse Soldier, 1776–1943: The United States Cavalryman: His Uniforms, Arms, Accoutrements, and Equipments.* 4 Vols. Norman: University of Oklahoma Press, 1977–1979.

Steiner, Edward E. "Nicholas Ruxton Moore: Soldier, Farmer and Politician." *Maryland Historical Magazine* 73 (1978), 375–388.

Stutesman, John H. Jr. "Colonel Armand and Washington's Cavalry." *New-York Historical Society Quarterly* 45 (1961), 5–42.

Tallmadge, Benjamin. *Memoir of Col. Benjamin Tallmadge, Prepared by Himself, at the Request of His Children.* New York: Thomas Holman, 1858.

Tarleton, Banastre. *A History of the Campaigns of 1780 and 1781, in the Southern Provinces of North America.* London: T. Cadell, 1787.

———. "New War Letters of Banastre Tarleton." Ed. Richard Ketchum. *New York Historical Quarterly* 51 (1967), 61–81.

Urwin, Gregory J. W. *The United States Cavalry: An Illustrated History.* New York: Sterling Publishing, 1983.

Washington, George. *The Papers of George Washington: Revolutionary War Series.* Edited by Philander D. C, Frank E. Grizzard, and Edward G. Lengel. 20 Vols. to date. Charlottesville: University Press of Virginia, 1985–2010.

Weller, Jac. "Irregular but Effective: Partizan Weapons Tactics in the American Revolution, Southern Theater." *Military Affairs* 21 (1957), 118–131.

Whitridge, Arnold. "The Marquis de la Rouerie, Brigadier General in the Continental Army." *Proceedings of the Massachusetts Historical Society* 79 (1968), 47–63.

Wilson, Joseph Lapsley. *Book of the First Troop, Philadelphia City Cavalry, 1774–1914.* Philadelphia, PA: Hallowell Co., 1915.

Wright, Robert K., Jr. *The Continental Army.* Washington, DC: US Army Center of Military History, 2000.

Zlatich, Marko. "Uniforming the 1st Regiment of Continental Light Dragoons, 1776–1779." *Military Collector & Historian* 20 (Summer 1968), 35–39.

# Contributors

LAWRENCE E. BABITS received his PhD from Brown University. An acknowledged expert in the fields of history, battlefield archaeology, and nautical archaeology, Babits is the George Washington Professor of History at East Carolina University in Greenville, North Carolina, where he also serves as director of the Program in Maritime Studies. He is the author of numerous books on both history and archaeology, including *Long, Obstinate, and Bloody: The Battle of Guilford Courthouse* (2009), co-authored with Joshua B. Howard; *"Fortitude and Forbearance": The North Carolina Continental Line in the Revolutionary War, 1775–1783* (2004), also co-authored with Joshua B. Howard; and *A Devil of a Whipping: The Battle of Cowpens* (1998). In addition, Babits has written many book chapters and journal articles on a wide variety of historical and archaeological topics.

DONALD J. GARA has been researching the military aspects of the American Revolution for more than ten years. His goal is to tell the history of the war from the viewpoint of those Americans who chose to stay loyal to Great Britain and joined provincial military units to fight alongside the British Army. His research has focused on two loyalist corps that saw action in many of the major campaigns of the war: the Queen's American Rangers and the British Legion. He is preparing a history of the Queen's Rangers and has published an article in the *Journal of the Society for Army Historical Research* (2005). He has also contributed several essays on both the Queen's Rangers and the

British Legion to websites such as Southern Campaigns of the American Revolution (www.southerncampaign.org), The On-Line Institute for Advanced Loyalist Studies (www.royalprovincial.com) and "Oatmeal for the Foxhounds": Banastre Tarleton and the British Legion (http://home.golden.net/~marg/ bansite/_entry.html).

JOSHUA B. HOWARD is a research historian at the North Carolina Office of Archives and History in Raleigh. A specialist in the history of the Revolutionary War, he speaks frequently on the topic at conferences and other events. He has also coauthored two books with Lawrence E. Babits: *"Fortitude and Forbearance": The North Carolina Continental Line in the Revolutionary War, 1775–1783* (2004), and *Long, Obstinate, and Bloody: The Battle of Guilford Courthouse, March 15, 1781* (2009). The latter book received the 2010 Distinguished Book Award from the Army Historical Foundation.

JOHN M. HUTCHINS is a graduate of the University of Colorado and the University of Colorado School of Law. After serving as a captain in the US Army's 1st Cavalry Division, he went on to become an assistant attorney general for the state of Colorado and then worked as an attorney for the federal government. His historical interests span the globe and many centuries; he has published several award-winning articles on topics ranging from the American West to the 1655 Battle of the Severn in colonial Maryland. He is also the author of the book *Diggers, Constables, and Bushrangers: The New Zealand Gold Rushes as a Frontier Experience, 1852–1876* (2010). He is currently working on a biography of Judge Roy Bean.

LEE F. McGEE, an emergency medicine physician in Pittsburgh, Pennsylvania, earned his BA degree in psychology at Allegheny College in Meadville, Pennsylvania, and his medical degree at the Philadelphia College of

Osteopathic Medicine. As a historian by avocation, he has published five articles on cavalry in the American Revolution in *Southern Campaigns of the American Revolution,* including "The Battle of Rugeley's Fort" (2005), "Hammond's Store and Fort Williams" (2005), "William Washington's Cavalry at Eutaw Springs" (2006), and "Cavalry Actions at the Battle of Hobkirk's Hill—Remounted" (2008). In addition, he has given several lectures and conference presentations on cavalry in the War for Independence. He is currently continuing his research on the influences of eighteenth-century European cavalry practice on the American cavalry in the Revolution.

SCOTT A. MISKIMON is an attorney practicing in Raleigh, North Carolina, and a partner in the firm of Smith Anderson. He is the coauthor of the legal treatise *North Carolina Contract Law,* which he updates annually. Scott is currently researching and writing a book about the Battle of the Waxhaws and frequently writes and speaks on topics involving early American history, including the American Revolution. Scott earned his law degree in 1992 from the University of North Carolina–Chapel Hill and served on the Board of Editors of the *North Carolina Law Review.* Scott received his bachelor of journalism degree in 1982 from the University of Missouri–Columbia School of Journalism. He worked as a television photojournalist for seven years, winning an Emmy and was named North Carolina News Photographer of the Year.

JIM PIECUCH is an associate professor of history at Kennesaw State University in Georgia. He earned BA and MA degrees in history from the University of New Hampshire and a PhD in history from the College of William & Mary in Virginia. Piecuch is the author of numerous articles on colonial and Revolutionary history, as well as several books including *The Battle of Camden: A Documentary History* (2006); *Three Peoples, One King:*

*Loyalists, Indians, and Slaves in the Revolutionary South* (2008); *"Cool Deliberate Courage": John Eager Howard in the American Revolution*, co-authored with John Beakes (2009); and *"The Blood Be Upon Your Head": Tarleton and the Myth of Buford's Massacre* (2010). He has also been a contributor and assistant editor on several projects for reference publisher ABC-CLIO.

CHARLES F. PRICE is the author of *Nor the Battle to the Strong: A Novel of the American Revolution in the* South (2008), a fictionalized account of a crucial military campaign in South Carolina during the late summer of 1781. His chief characters are Maj. Gen. Nathanael Greene, commander of the Southern Continental Army, and an ordinary soldier, runaway indentured servant James Johnson. Price also wrote the Hiwassee series, four works of historical fiction set in his native Western North Carolina: *Hiwassee: A Novel of the Civil War* (1996); *Freedom's Altar* (1999); *The Cock's Spur* (2001); and *Where the Water-Dogs Laughed* (2003). Price is a native of Haywood County, North Carolina. He has been a Washington lobbyist, management consultant, urban planner, and journalist. He holds a master's in public administration from the University of North Carolina at Chapel Hill and an undergraduate degree in History and Political Science from High Point University.

MICHAEL C. SCOGGINS is the historian for the Culture & Heritage Museums and is research director of the Southern Revolutionary War Institute in York, South Carolina. He is the author of *Historic York County: An Illustrated History* (2009); *The Day It Rained Militia: Huck's Defeat and the Revolution in the South Carolina Backcountry, May–July 1780* (2005); and *Relentless Fury: The Revolutionary War in the Southern Piedmont* (2006). Scoggins also edited the republication of Benson Lossing's 1889 classic, *Reflections of Rebellion: Hours with the Living Men and*

*Women of the Revolution* (2005), and cowrote (with Dr. Bobby G. Moss) the acclaimed *African-American Patriots in the Southern Campaign of the American Revolution* (2004) and *African-American Loyalists in the Southern Campaign of the American Revolution* (2005). He has contributed articles to numerous historical publications and journals, and is a frequent lecturer on topics of local and regional history. Scoggins is president of the Confederation of South Carolina Local Historical Societies. He lives near McConnells, South Carolina.

GREGORY J. W. URWIN earned his PhD at the University of Notre Dame and is a professor of history at Temple University in Philadelphia, Pennsylvania. He is the author of many books including *Custer Victorious: The Civil War Battles of George Armstrong Custer; The United States Infantry: An Illustrated History, 1775–1918; The United States Cavalry: An Illustrated History, 1776–1944; Facing Fearful Odds: The Siege of Wake Island;* and *Black Flag over Dixie: Racial Atrocities and Reprisals in the Civil War.* His books and articles have won several prestigious awards, and he has been invited to lecture at venues such as the US Naval Academy, the US Army War College, the American Philosophical Society, and the David Library of the American Revolution. He has also made numerous appearances as an expert commentator on the History Channel, PBS, and the Arts and Entertainment (A&E) Network.

# Index

# Acknowledgments

The editor would like to thank everyone who made this volume possible. The idea for the book originated at the Revolutionary War Cavalry Conference held at Wofford College in Spartanburg, South Carolina, on November 9–10, 2007. Those who sponsored and managed the conference deserve special thanks: the South Carolina Historical Society and its executive director, Dr. Faye Jensen; *Southern Campaigns of the American Revolution* and its publisher, Charles B. Baxley, who also served as event coordinator; Charlie Gray, Dr. Doyle Boggs, and John Blair of Wofford College; Mike Coker and Gloria Beiter, who served respectively as event display manager and registrar at the conference; the staff of Cowpens National Battlefield Park, especially superintendent Tim Stone, chief ranger Kathy McCoy, and ranger Ginny Fowler; David P. Reuwer, co-editor of *Southern Campaigns*; Steve Rauch, deputy event director; John Allison, who handled tours and logistics; Daniel Murphy and Ron Crowley for the cavalry demonstrations; Judy D. Baxley, finance; Dave McKissack, Sandra Allison, Dale and Janet Williams; tour guides Mike Burgess and Brian Robeson; Eric Williams, chief ranger at Ninety Six National Historic Site; and Chris Revels, chief ranger at Kings Mountain National Military Park. The contributions of all these individuals made both the conference and book possible.

Also deserving gratitude are the contributors to the volume, who labored long and hard on their essays; Bruce H. Franklin of Westholme Publishing; copyeditor Rachelle Mandik; cover designer Trudi Gershenov; artist Werner

Willis, who in addition to his role at the conference made his painting *The Assault* available for use in this volume; Barry Grant, who also contributed illustrations; and the South Caroliniana Library at the University of South Carolina in Columbia for providing additional artwork.